3:7,

Politics and Modernization
In South and Southeast Asia

STATES AND SOCIETIES OF THE THIRD WORLD

A Schenkman Series Edited by Richard Harris

LATIN AMERICA: THE STRUGGLE WITH DEPENDENCY
AND BEYOND

Edited by Ronald H. Chilcote and Joel C. Edelstein

THE POLITICAL ECONOMY OF AFRICA

Edited by Richard Harris

POLITICS AND MODERNIZATION IN SOUTH
AND SOUTHEAST ASIA

Edited by Robert N. Kearney

POLITICAL ELITES AND POLITICAL DEVELOPMENT
IN THE MIDDLE EAST

Edited by Frank Tachau

Politics and Modernization In South and Southeast Asia

Edited by Robert N. Kearney

Schenkman Publishing Company

Halsted Press Division

JOHN WILEY AND SONS

New York   London   Sydney   Toronto

Copyright © 1975
Schenkman Publishing Company, Inc.
Cambridge, Mass. 02138

Distributed solely by Halsted Press, a Division
of John Wiley & Sons, Inc., New York

Library of Congress Cataloging in Publication Data

Kearney, Robert N
   Politics and modernization in South and Southeast Asia.
   (States and societies of the Third World)
   "A Halsted Press book."
   1. Asia, Southeastern—Politics. 2. South Asia—Politics and government. 3.
Asia, Southeastern—Social conditions. 4. South Asia—Social conditions.
I. Title.
JQ96.A3K4 1975   320.9'59   74-13637
ISBN 0-470-46232-9
ISBN 0-470-46233-7 (pbk.)

Contents

SOUTH AND SOUTHEAST ASIA

vi

Contributors

ROBERT N. KEARNEY is a Professor of Political Science at Syracuse University. He holds a Ph.D. from the University of California, Los Angeles, and previously taught at Duke University and the University of California, Santa Barbara. He is the author of *Communalism and Language in the Politics of Ceylon* (1967), *Trade Unions and Politics in Ceylon* (1971), and *The Politics of Ceylon (Sri Lanka)* (1973), and more than twenty published papers and articles.

STANLEY A. KOCHANEK is an Associate Professor of Political Science at the Pennsylvania State University. He holds a Ph.D. from the University of Pennsylvania and has extensive field experience in India. He was a Fulbright Scholar in India from 1959 to 1961, a faculty research fellow of the American Institute of Indian Studies in 1967-68, and spent several months in India in 1973. He is the author of *The Congress Party of India* (1968), *Business and Politics in India* (1973) and numerous articles on Indian affairs.

ROBERT LAPORTE, JR. is an Associate Professor of Public Administration and Assistant Director of the Institute of Public Administration at the Pennsylvania State University. He holds a Ph.D. from Syracuse University. He is the coauthor of *Cultivating Revolution: The United States and Agrarian Reform in Latin America* (1971), *Peru: Revolutionary Transformation or Modernization* (1971), and the author of more than a dozen published articles on South Asia and Latin America.

GORDON P. MEANS obtained his Ph.D. from the University of Washington in Seattle. He has lived in Malaya and Singapore for over ten years, has taught at the University of Malaya and the University of Singapore, and was affiliated with the Himalayan Border Countries Project of the University of California (Berkeley) for a year of research relating to social change and modernization among hill tribal peoples in South Asia. He is the author of *Malaysian Politics*, a contributor to three other books, and has written extensively on South and Southeast Asian politics. Currently he holds the position of Associate Professor of Political Science at McMaster University in Canada.

CLARK D. NEHER is an Associate Professor of Political Science at Northern Illinois University. He holds a Ph.D. from the University of California, Los Angeles, and has previously taught at Chulalongnom and Chiang Mai Universities in Thailand. He is the author of numerous articles and monographs on rural and national politics in Thailand.

ALLAN A. SAMSON is a lecturer in Political Science at the University of California-Berkeley. He holds a Ph.D. from the University of California-Berkeley. He has published several articles on Indonesian politics and Islam in Indonesia. He is currently working on a study of organizational aspects of Javanese mystical groups.

Preface

This is one of a series of volumes dealing with the states and societies of the "Third World." Initiated by Richard L. Harris, the series editor, the series is intended to provide a fresh look at the panorama of nations of Asia, Africa, the Middle East, and Latin America. Each volume in the series id devoted to one of the major Third World regions. Each includes an anlytic survey of the entire region, followed by in-depth case studies of a selection of nations within the region. The intent is to provide a broad comparative perspective, necessarily stressing sharp contrasts as well as common experiences and circumstances, while at the same time preserving and conveying the distinctiveness of the unique social, economic, cultural, and political contexts of the individual nations.

This volume covers the largest in population of the Third World regions, in which live approximately one billion persons. Although within regions contrasts and contradictions abound, each region tends to be typified by certain widely shared experiences, conditions, or developments. South and Southeast Asia cradled very ancient cultures producing sophisticated religions, complex social structures, and extensive literatures. Within the last three decades, most nations of the region emerged from extended periods of Western colonial rule, an experience that continues to exert an influence on social and political attitudes and activities. Overwhelmingly agricultural and rural societies, dense populations, cruel poverty, and growing tensions between expanding hopes, wants, and needs and painfully slow economic and social advancement are characteristics widely shared across the region. The societies and peoples of South and Southeast Asia are undergoing extensive and relatively profound social, economic, political, and psychological changes which are swiftly or almost imperceptibly transforming the societies and altering the character of life of vast numbers of persons in the region, giving rise to the use of the term "modernization" in the title of the volume and the concern through these pages with the processes of change and adaptation.

Each of the case studies was prepared for this volume by a scholar specializing in the study of the country on which he has written, each of whom has had recent research experience in the country and has authored earlier works dealing with the country.

I wish to express my thanks to Richard L. Harris, with whom I have enjoyed a professional association of more than a decade, for the idea that launched this project and the encouragement that kept it alive. I am also grateful to the authors of the essays in this volume, who by contributing from their considerable knowledge of the region and the countries within it made the volume possible. Furthermore, I would like to note my appreciation to Alfred S. Schenkman, Mandira Sen, and Virginia Savage of the Schenkman Publishing Company for a very cordial association and for their patience and concern in seeing this volume through the successive and sometimes tedious stages of publication.

Syracuse, N.Y.   Robert N. Kearney

1   South and Southeast Asia: A Regional Survey

Robert N. Kearney

Along the southern and southeastern rim of the great Eurasian land mass, in a broad arc extending from Kabul to Manila, live about one billion people, nearly 30 percent of the world's population. The region is bounded on the north by the towering ranges of the Himalaya mountains and on the south and east by the Indian and Pacific Oceans, with the narrow Timor and Arafura Seas separating the Indonesian island chain from the northern coast of Australia at the region's southeastern corner. In the west, it shades into the Middle East. The region is customarily divided into two great geographic and, to some degree, cultural areas, separated by the Bay of Bengal and the hills and jungles of the Indian-Burmese border. South Asia includes the nations of India, Pakistan, Bangladesh, Ceylon (redesignated the Republic of Sri Lanka in 1972),[1] Nepal, and Afghanistan. The tiny Himalayan territories of Sikkim and Bhutan are linked by treaty with India. Bhutan in 1971 was admitted to the United Nations and exchanged diplomatic representation with India, implying a bid for independent status, although India has continued to supervise the small kingdom's external affairs. Southeast Asia is divided by the South China Sea and the Straits of Malacca into island and peninsular segments. In Southeast Asia are the island nations of Indonesia and the Philippines, the city-state of Singapore, Malaysia straddling the South China Sea, and the mainland countries of Burma, Thailand, Cambodia (renamed the

---

1. The former, more familiar names for Cambodia (now the Khmer Republic) and Ceylon (now the Republic of Sri Lanka) have been retained in this work.

Khmer Republic in 1970), Laos, and the two states of Viet Nam. In addition, the small sultanate of Brunei remains under British protection and Portugal continues to rule a part of the island of Timor.

Prior to the breakup of Pakistan in 1971, three of the six largest countries in the world were situated in South and Southeast Asia. More than half the combined population of the two areas, however, is contained within the single country of India (see Table I.1). Although including the landlocked mountainous countries of Afghanistan and Nepal, peninsulas and islands predominate. The climate varies from the high, cold, arid plateaus of the Himalayan kingdoms to the rain-swept tropical islands of Ceylon, Indonesia, and the Philippines. Despite tremendous variations within the region—and indeed within in-

Table I.1

Estimated Population, Midyear 1971

	Population (in thousands)
Afghanistan	17,480
Bangladesh	60,675[a]
Bhutan	854
Brunei	135
Burma	27,584[a]
Cambodia (Khmer Republic)	6,701[b]
Ceylon (Sri Lanka)	12,669
India	551,827
Indonesia	125,810
Laos	3,033
Malaysia	10,674
Nepal	11,290
Pakistan	53,514[a]
Philippines	37,919
Portuguese Timor	614
Sikkim	198
Singapore	2,110
Thailand	35,335
Viet Nam, Democratic Republic (North)	21,595
Viet Nam, Republic (South)	18,809
Total	998,826

a. Estimate for 1970.
b. Estimate for 1969.

Source: United Nations, Statistical Office, *Population and Vital Statistics Report: Data Available as of 1 April 1973*. Statistical Papers, Series A, Vol. XXV, No. 2 (New York: United Nations, 1973), pp. 16-21.

dividual countries—the majority of the region's peoples live within tropical, monsoon Asia.

South and Southeast Asia are characterized by diversity in culture, religion, language, and racial stock, as well as in climate and topography. Few generalizations beyond the most obvious or superficial can be made for the sprawling and heterogeneous nations included in the region. Nonetheless, certain characteristics, perhaps appearing commonplace and certainly admitting of a host of qualifications, are broadly shared by most of these countries and tend to typify the region as a whole. Economically, they are very poor, with low productivity, economies dominated by agriculture, and low per capita incomes and living standards. Social patterns associated with subsistence agriculture and village life—rigid stratification, low social and territorial mobility, and tight bonds of family and possibly caste or sect—are generally evident. Many nations are internally divided by ethnic, linguistic, or religious cleavages.

Relatively rapid, frequently disturbing and disorienting change is an additional characteristic widely shared by these societies. Processes of social, economic, political, and ideological change have commenced which have already produced important alterations in the patterns of life and work of vast numbers of persons in the region and bode further, far-reaching transformations, creating what are often described as "modernizing" or "transitional" societies. A few nations, and certain sections of other nations, seem relatively impervious to the transformations, and some traditional customs and attitudes have proved to be astonishingly persistent. Yet, if one looks from the perspective of the last 50 or 100 years at the impact of technology—the radio, printing press, railroads, motor transport, electricity, and medical science, or at the gradual spread of education and literacy, the growth of urbanization, the modifications of economic activities, and other agents and·concomitants of modernization, wide-ranging and relatively profound change can scarcely be denied. The transformations have been rapid both in comparison with rates of change in these societies over previous centuries and relative to the speed with which comparable changes came about in the industrialized nations of the West. There presumably are areas and peoples that have remained virtually untouched by the twentieth century, but they are the exception rather than the rule.

Modernization and Political Development

"Modernization" is a term that has come into use to refer to the complex processes of change that are producing significant social, economic, political, and psychological transformations in Asia and many other parts of the globe. The cluster of interrelated transformations labelled "modernization" includes changing forms of economic and social activity as production for the market and wage labor make inroads into subsistence agriculture and non-monetary exchange of goods and services, growing urbanization and non-agricultural employment, broadening application of technology, and increasing specialization and division of labor. In the modernization process, old social relationships, customary patterns of social and economic activity, and former attitudes and values are being eroded and gradually replaced or joined by new and different social and psychological patterns. Accompanying these changes have come wider exposure to mass communications media, new and broader identifications and loyalties, and an expansion of political awareness and participation. The disruption of familiar relationships and patterns of activity and the undermining of old values and attitudes is a stressful and deeply disturbing experience. The transformations not only create new freedoms and opportunities, but also produce new uncertainties, stresses, and conflicts.

Modernization need not be confused with "progress," nor should it involve teleological assumptions. That roughly similar patterns of change are occurring throughout the globe is not to say that any nation is presently at the end point of modernization, or indeed that there is a final end point at which modernization will be complete. The contemporary transformations are not inexorably bound to terminate in presently definable societies, economies, and political systems. The possibility exists that some nations may never attain such assumed indicators of modernity as a technologically advanced, industrialized economy, high per capita income and mass affluence, or relatively egalitarian and universalistic social and political relationships. Similarly, modernization is not identical with Westernization. The nations of South and Southeast Asia have moved and generally are striving to move toward positions similar to those reached in the West in such fields as industrial production, the application of science and technology, the wide diffusion of education, and to some degree economic and political practices and organizational forms, which may reasonably be considered as aspects of the modernization process. Of a different nature is the adoption of Western language, religion, dietary habits, mode of dress, and similar cultural attributes not necessarily relevant to modernization. Contemporary Western society is not the inevitable model of the modernized Asian society of the future.

Central to many contemporary views of modernization and political change is the concept of "social mobilization."[2] Social mobilization is

2. The concept was developed in Karl W. Deutsch, "Social Mobilization and

an aspect of the broader processes of modernization. It is a consequence of modernization, and in turn becomes a stimulant toward further modernization. Economic, technological, and social changes involved in the modernization process lead gradually to the growth of literacy, increasing exposure to mass communications media, heightened territorial mobility, the appearance of new occupations, and the spread of wage labor and production for the market. These changes cause a dislocation of traditional patterns and relationships and an erosion of old values and attitudes, leaving those persons affected "socially mobilized," ready for new patterns of commitment and behavior. Among the consequences of social mobilization are transformations of political attitudes and behavior. The changes in productive activities and conditions of life create new needs and stimulate new aspirations. New patterns of association and more broadly inclusive loyalties emerge. The rate at which social mobilization is occurring is assumed to be more significant politically than the absolute level of social mobilization that has been reached. The political impact of swiftly growing social mobilization, thus, may be profound, although the absolute level of mobilization attained may not be great.

The concept of "political development" remains surrounded by a number of ambiguities and disagreements.[3] Political development implies systemic change, that is, alterations of a relatively fundamental nature in the functioning of the political system. Frequently, the term is used to refer to a cluster of changes including: (1) the development of differentiated, functionally specific political structures; (2) changes in values and attitudes from the sacred, ascriptive, and particularistic toward the scientific and secular, egalitarian, and universalistic; (3) the penetration of society by governmental agencies and activities; and (4) a broadening of participation in politics. The first includes the emergence of such differentiated political structures as political parties, legislatures, associational interest groups, and specialized bureaucratic agencies. The second refers to attitudinal shifts such as declining confidence in magic and increasing reliance on rational and scientific techniques, and the replacement of commitments to narrow and unalterable statuses by broader and more flexible commitments. The third

Political Development," *American Political Science Review* 55 (September 1961): 493-514.

3. Ten different definitions of political development are cited in Lucian W. Pye, *Aspects of Political Development* (Boston: Little, Brown and Co., 1966), pp. 33-45. A critique of efforts to build theories of political development appears in Lawrence C. Mayer, *Comparative Political Inquiry: A Methodological Survey* (Homewood, Ill.: Dorsey Press, 1972), pp. 248-272.

involves the effective extension of government authority through the territory and population of a country. The fourth specifies the mobilization of increasing numbers of persons from a wider range of social strata and groups to the performance of political acts, including not only voting or political party membership, but participation in a demonstration or riot, possibly membership in a trade union or other organized associational group, and a variety of other forms of behavior with political consequences. Political development has also been viewed in terms of the capacity of the political system to define and implement collective goals, resolve the issues by which it is confronted, or respond and adapt to a series of "crises" or challenges involved in the emergence of a modern polity.[4]

Concern over political instability and disorder, which often has accompanied rapid modernization, has led to the notion of "negative" development or political "decay." From this perspective, political development is distinguished from the processes of modernization, which are seen as politically disruptive. Swift social mobilization followed by rising popular demands and mounting political participation may widen the gap between aspirations and satisfactions, producing social frustration, which in turn may lead to political unrest or upheaval. Political development is viewed as the growth of political institutions characterized by adaptability, complexity, autonomy, and organizational coherence. If the institutionalization of political organizations has not progressed sufficiently to allow the political system to withstand the stresses of rapidly rising participation and to respond to the growing demands, the result is likely to be turbulence, instability, and resort to repressive regimes. Hence, for political order without repression, a balance must be maintained between the rate of growth of

4. Gabriel A. Almond and G. Bingham Powell, Jr., *Comparative Politics: A Developmental Approach* (Boston: Little, Brown and Co., 1966), pp. 299-332; James A. Bill and Robert L. Hardgrave, Jr., *Comparative Politics: The Quest for Theory* (Columbus, Ohio: Charles E. Merrill Publishing Co., 1973), pp. 43-83; Leonard Binder et al. *Crises and Sequences in Political Development* (Princeton, N. J.: Princeton University Press, 1971); Alfred Diamant, "Political Development: Approaches to Theory and Strategy," in *Approaches to Development: Politics, Administration and Change*, eds. John D. Montgomery and William J. Siffin (New York: McGraw-Hill Book Co., 1966), pp. 15-47; S. N. Eisenstadt, *Modernization: Protest and Change* (Englewood Cliffs, N.J.: Prentice-Hall, Inc., 1966); Samuel P. Huntington, "The Change to Change: Modernization, Development, and Politics," *Comparative Politics* 3 (April 1971): 283-322; Pye, *Aspects of Political Development;* and Fred W. Riggs, "The Theory of Political Development," in *Contemporary Political Analysis*, ed. James C. Charlesworth (New York: Free Press, 1967), pp. 317-349.

participation and the rate of institutionalization within the political system.[5]

In most nations of South and Southeast Asia over recent decades, rapid change has been particularly marked in the spread of education and mass communications and the related growth of social mobilization and political participation. In some cases, traditional structures, or transformed representations of traditional structures, have been adapted to the performance of such functions as mobilizing and channeling the growing political participation.[6] Increasingly, the alleviation of discontents and the satisfaction of demands have been sought through political action. Most political systems of these areas are involved in an attempt to contain mounting participation and to cope with swiftly rising aspirations and demands generated by the processes of modernization and social mobilization.

The Colonial Experience

The deep imprint of Western colonial rule is evident in contemporary South and Southeast Asia. Three decades ago, there were few peoples in the entire region who were not governed directly or indirectly by Western colonial officials. Of sixteen states, only three did not experience colonial rule, and two of these were the relatively inaccessible landlocked mountain kingdoms of Nepal and Afghanistan. In peninsular and island South and Southeast Asia, Thailand alone did not share the colonial experience, and it did not entirely escape the manifold Western influences and pressures.

Britain was the dominant colonial power through the region, controlling seven of the presently independent states (see Table I.2). British rule stretched from the Khyber Pass on the Afghan border to the northern coast of Borneo. French possessions and protectorates were grouped at the eastern edge of peninsular Southeast Asia, while the Netherlands and the United States governed the southeastern islands. British colonial rule has left a commonality of experience and similarity of institutions throughout the culturally and historically diverse lands it ruled. Marked similarities in civil and military organization, educational systems, courts and legal systems, and associational

5. Samuel P. Huntington, "Political Development and Political Decay," *World Politics* 17 (April 1965): 386-430; Samuel P. Huntington, *Political Order in Changing Societies* (New Haven, Conn.: Yale University Press, 1968), esp. pp. 1-92.
6. A prominent example is provided by the caste association in India. See Lloyd I. Rudolph and Susanne Hoeber Rudolph, *The Modernity of Tradition: Political Development in India* (Bombay: Orient Longmans, 1969), pp. 17-154.

Table I.2
Colonial Background

No colonial rule	Year of independence
Afghanistan	
Nepal	
Thailand	

British rule	Year of independence
Bangladesh	1947[a]
Burma	1948
Ceylon	1948
India	1947
Malaysia	1957[b]
Pakistan	1947
Singapore	1963[c]

French rule	
Cambodia	1949[d]
Laos	1949[e]
Viet Nam, North	1949[f]
Viet Nam, South	1949[f]

Netherlands rule	
Indonesia	1949[g]

U. S. rule	
Philippines	1946

a. Became independent of Britain as a part of Pakistan in 1947; separated from West Pakistan in 1971.

b. The Federation of Malaya became independent in 1957. Malaysia was created in 1963 with the federation of eleven peninsula Malay States and Sarawak, Sabah, and Singapore. Singapore left the federation and became a separate independent state in 1965.

c. Became independent of Britain in 1963 with the creation of Malaysia; separated from Malaysia in 1965.

d. Obtained autonomy within the French Union in 1949; left the French Union in 1955.

e. Obtained autonomy within the French Union in 1949; left the French Union in 1956.

f. The Democratic Republic of Viet Nam was proclaimed in 1945, a French-sponsored state of Viet Nam was formed in 1949, and the de facto division of Viet Nam was recognized in the 1954 Geneva accords.

g. Recognized as independent by the Netherlands in 1949, following an Indonesian proclamation of independence in 1945 and several years of warfare.

groups such as trade unions and business associations remain as evidence of the expanse of British rule. Among the elites, common education at British universities or in local colleges modeled on British lines encouraged some similarities in values, outlooks, and experiences. Furthermore, Britain, along with the United States, withdrew in a more graceful and orderly manner than did France and the Netherlands, largely sparing their ex-colonies the trauma of the protracted armed conflict in Indonesia or the devastation of the interminable wars of Indo-China.

The impact of colonial rule merged with socio-economic changes of wider dimensions as repercussions of the industrial revolution spread through the world. The nineteenth and twentieth centuries saw the spread of technology, the growth of commerce, gradual urbanization, the expansion of education, and subtle or abrupt alterations of social and economic patterns which touched Japan, China, Latin America, and the Middle East, as well as the Asian colonies of the West. Colonial rule often facilitated and encouraged the socio-economic changes by administrative consolidation, activities in public health and education, advances in transportation and communications, and the stimulation of new forms of production for the metropolitan or world market by large-scale capitalist companies, which were often extractive or agricultural but were organized on new lines and produced subsidiary light industry and supporting service trades. In the mid-nineteenth century, Karl Marx wrote, perhaps more prophetically than descriptively, of British rule in India:

> England has broken down the entire framework of Indian society, without any symptoms of reconstitution yet appearing. This loss of his old world, with no gain of a new one, imparts a particular kind of melancholy to the present misery of the Hindu, and separates Hindustan, ruled by Britain, from all its ancient traditions, and from the whole of its past history.[7]

The impact of socio-economic change fell unevenly on countries, on regions within the countries, and on ethnic, religious, and other groups within the societies. The changes commonly were more evident in the cities than in the rural areas, on the coast than in the hinterland, and among communities that—because of territorial location, traditional skills and habits useful to the new activities, or a capacity for

7. Karl Marx, "The British Rule in India," *Tribune* (New York), June 25, 1853, contained in Karl Marx and Friedrich Engels, *Basic Writings on Politics and Philosophy,* ed. Lewis S. Feuer (Garden City, N.Y.: Anchor Books, 1959), p. 476.

adaptation—were more able to adjust to new social and economic roles. Indian Brahmins were more readily able to step into administrative and professional roles as a result of traditions of education and favorable socio-economic status. Indian Muslims lagged behind Hindus in secular education and non-traditional employment, exacerbating communal suspicions and rivalry. The Chinese in Southeast Asia followed the spread of commerce to Singapore, Malaya, and Burma, establishing themselves in trade in the cities and towns, while the Malay and Burmese cultivators responded more slowly and weakly to the forces of modernization. The Tamils of Ceylon early took to Western education and began to enter the public services in disproportionate numbers. Many contemporary social and communal tensions are traceable to the uneven impact of nineteenth and early twentieth century changes.

Colonial rule was not a uniform and undifferentiated experience. The duration and intensity of Western rule and concomitant cultural, social, ideological, and economic influences varied markedly across South and Southeast Asia. The Portuguese were established at Colombo, Goa, and Malacca early in the sixteenth century and the Spanish in the Philippines a century later. Bengal came under British control in the mid-eighteenth century. Upper Burma, however, was not annexed until 1886, and British control of peninsular Malaya was not consolidated until the last years of the nineteenth century. Cambodia became a French protectorate in 1863 and Laos in 1893. In some places, particularly the seaboard and urbanized areas, foreign rule was direct, immediate, and pervasive. In other locations, it was distant and inconspicuous. Certain territories were ruled directly by the imperial power, while others remained until independence under indirect rule through intermediaries drawn from the indigenous aristocracy. By independence, which followed rapidly after the Second World War, some areas had undergone more than four centuries of sustained European penetration and control, while other areas had experienced less than a century of indirect colonial rule. With independence came the need to establish and develop new political institutions and processes. The experiences with limited self-government under colonial rule and the extent to which political organizations emerged prior to independence varied considerably. But even in the colonies with the most "advanced" tutelage, independence required major political alterations, adaptations, and innovations.

The Economic Dimension

The economies of South and Southeast Asia are heavily dependent on primary production, with their work forces concentrated in agriculture (Table I.3). In many countries of the region, a small "modern" economic sphere based on large-scale production units utilizing technology fairly extensively exists alongside a "traditional" sphere of small-scale, predominantly subsistence agriculture marked by little use of technology and low productivity. The two spheres generally interact very little and development in one has slight impact on the other.

Table I.3

Percentage of Economically Active Population in Agriculture, 1965

	Percentage
Afghanistan	87
Burma	62
Cambodia	80
Ceylon	50
India	70
Indonesia[a]	66
Laos	81
Malaysia	55
Nepal	92
Pakistan	74
Philippines	57
Singapore	7
Thailand	78
Viet Nam (North)	80
Viet Nam (South)	85

a. Excludes West Irian.

Source: "Social Development in Asia," *Economic Bulletin for Asia and the Far East* 20 (December 1969), p. 23.

Contributions to Gross Domestic Produce (GDP) by industrial sector are indicated in Table I.4[8] With the exception of the unique city-state of Singapore and of South Viet Nam, with a large share of GDP attributed to public administration and defense, agriculture and related activities constituted the largest sector by a substantial margin, contributing more than 40 percent of GDP in five countries, despite extremely low productivity in agriculture. Structural economic changes have been very slow, but a small and gradual shift from agriculture to manufacturing can be detected, as indicated in Table I.5. In each of the countries for which data were available for about 1950 and 1968, agriculture declined and manufacturing rose as a proportion of GDP.

8. Although UN, ECAFE, and country data are used here on the assumption of general reliability and rough comparability, many uncertainties exist in cross-national comparisons of data.

Table I.4

Industrial Origin of Gross Domestic Product, 1968 [a]

	Percentage originating in each sector							
	Agriculture, forestry, hunting, fishing	Manufacturing	Mining and quarrying	Transportation, storage, communication	Wholesale and retail trade	Public administration and defense	Services	Other
Burma	34.3	9.1	0.7	6.6	29.0	8.2	8.2	5.0
Cambodia	40.8	10.3	—	2.2	22.7	12.1	5.0	6.8
Ceylon	38.8	10.9	0.7	9.4	12.1	4.8	12.7	10.7
India	50.4	13.2	1.1	4.6	10.8	4.7	6.4	8.5
Indonesia	51.7	8.9	3.8	2.0	17.9	4.4	6.7	4.6
Malaysia (West)	28.4	10.9	7.7	3.5	15.6	7.5	10.0	12.5
Nepal	65.7	10.7	0.4	1.8	4.8	1.4	2.5	12.7
Pakistan	46.0	11.4	0.3	6.7	12.2	5.7	5.7	12.0
Philippines	35.4	17.4	1.7	3.5	10.6	8.2	15.7	7.5
Singapore	3.5	16.6	0.2	—	30.7	7.1	31.2	10.7
Thailand	31.5	15.0	1.8	6.2	17.3	4.3	10.3	13.7
Viet Nam (South)	28.6	9.2	0.2	4.3	14.4	24.4	6.9	10.6

a. Data for 1968 except for Burma (1967), Cambodia (1966), Malaysia (1966), Nepal (1965), and South Viet Nam (1966). Data for Burma, Cambodia, Indonesia, and Thailand are for GDP at market prices and for India and the Philippines for Net Domestic Product at factor cost. Data for all other countries are for GDP at factor cost.

Source: United Nations, Economic Commission for Asia and the Far East, Economic Survey of Asia and the Far East, 1970 (Bangkok: United Nations, 1971), p. 106.

Table I.5
**Percentages of Gross Domestic Product
Originating in Agriculture and
Related Pursuits and in Manufacturing,
ca. 1950 and 1968 [a]**

	Agriculture, forestry, hunting, and fishing		Manufacturing	
	1950	1968	1950	1968
Burma	40.3	34.3 [b]	7.1	9.1 [b]
Ceylon	54.8	38.8	4.0	10.9
India	51.2	50.4	. . . [c]	13.2
Malaysia (West)	46.5 [d]	28.4	5.3 [e]	10.9
Pakistan	58.0	46.0	7.6	11.4
Philippines	39.4	35.4	12.3	17.4
Thailand	50.1 [f]	31.5	10.3 [f]	15.0

a. Figures for Burma and Thailand are percentages of GDP at market prices;
for Ceylon, Malaysia (West), and Pakistan, of GDP at factor cost; and for India
and the Philippines, of Net Domestic Product at factor cost.
b. Figure for 1967.
c. Not available.
d. Figure for 1955.
e. Figure for 1955 and including construction.
f. Figure for 1951.
Source: UN, ECAFE, *Economic Survey of Asia and the Far East, 1970,* p. 106.

Living standards and per capita income are distressingly low
throughout the region. Estimated per capita GDP is presented in Table I.6. Again excluding the uniquely situated Singapore, in only two
countries was per capita GDP above $200, the highest being a modest
$322. In six of 14 countries, including the two most populous nations,
per capita GDP was under $100. Although consistently low relative to
the industrialized nations of the world, the levels of per capita GDP
differ significantly among the countries of the region. The levels found
in India, Burma, and Nepal are one-fourth or less of the levels of the
region's wealthier nations, the Philippines and Malaysia, and about
half those of Thailand, Ceylon, and South Viet Nam.

Economic Growth

Through most of South and Southeast Asia, economic growth has
been painfully slow and unsteady. The annual rate of growth of total
production in the "development decade" 1961-1970, compared to
growth rates of "developing" countries in other regions of the world,
exceeded only that of Africa and was below the world average for developing countries (Table I.7). Modest expansion of production, com-

Table I.6

Estimated Per Capita Gross Domestic Product

Country	Year	Per capita GDP (in U.S. dollars)
Above $200:		
Singapore	1969	779
Philippines	1969	322
Malaysia	1966	280
$100 to $200:		
Thailand	1969	162
Ceylon	1969	148
South Viet Nam	1967	148
Pakistan	1969	141
Cambodia	1966	127
Less than $100:		
Indonesia	1968	93
India	1968	78
Burma	1968	70
Nepal	1968	69
Laos	1963	59
Afghanistan	1963	55

Source: United Nations, Statistical Office, *Statistical Yearbook, 1970* (New York: United Nations, 1971), pp. 599-600.

Table I.7

Average Annual Rate of Growth of Total Production in Developing Countries, By Region, 1961-1970

Developing countries in	Average annual rate of growth, 1961-1970 (percentage)
West Asia	7.6
Western Hemisphere	5.2
South and Southeast Asia	4.9
Africa	4.4
Developing countries in all regions	5.1

Source: United Nations, Department of Economic and Social Affairs, *World Economic Survey, 1971: Current Economic Developments* (New York: United Nations, 1972), p. 83.

bined with rapid population growth, has in most countries of the region resulted in very low rates of per capita growth (Table I.8). Furthermore, performance has been markedly uneven. Of the countries included in the table, Pakistan achieved the second highest rate of growth in per capita GDP in 1960-1968, but had the poorest rate of growth in 1950-1960. The political turmoil culminating in civil war, a brief international war, and the declaration of independence by Bangladesh, previously East Pakistan, seems certain to have dealt a severe economic blow to both former wings of Pakistan. Burma, which according to these data had achieved the highest rate of per capita growth in 1950-1960, had negative growth in 1960-1967. Of the five countries with 1950-1960 per capita growth rates above 1.0 percent, all but Thailand suffered a decline in the rate of growth during the 1960-1968 period. Only Ceylon, Malaysia, and Thailand registered higher growth rates in the more recent period.

Table I.8

Annual Growth Rates of Real Gross Domestic Product and Per Capita Gross Domestic Product, 1950-1968 [a]

	1950-1960		1960-1968	
	GDP	Per capita GDP	GDP	Per capita GDP
Burma	6.3	4.3	1.3[b]	-0.7[b]
Ceylon	3.0	0.5	4.8	2.4
India[c]	3.5	1.6	3.3	0.8
Indonesia	3.3[d]	1.2[d]	2.6	0.2
Malaysia (West)	4.0[e]	0.9[e]	5.9[f]	2.7[f]
Pakistan	2.5	0.4	5.6	3.4
Philippines	6.9	3.7	4.6	1.1
Thailand	6.4[b]	2.5[d]	7.8	4.6
Developing ECAFE countries[g]	4.0	1.9	4.4	1.9

a. At market prices, except for India and Pakistan, which are at factor cost.
b. 1960-1967.
c. Net Domestic Product.
d. 1951-1960.
e. 1955-1960.
f. 1960-1966.
g. Includes, in addition to the countries listed in the table, Afghanistan, Brunei, Cambodia, China (Taiwan), Fiji, Hong Kong, Iran, Republic of Korea, Laos, Nepal, Papua and New Guinea, Singapore, Republic of Viet Nam, and Western Samoa.
Source: UN, ECAFE, *Economic Survey of Asia and the Far East, 1970,* p. 95.

In most nations of the region, governments have assumed the major responsibility for economic development and have become deeply enmeshed in economic decision-making and resource allocation. Centralized economic planning, intended to rationalize and direct investment and maximize its long-range economic gains, is common. There is virtual consensus on the desirability of improving the material circumstances of the masses of the people and particularly of the more disadvantaged sections of society. The Indian Planning Commission, in defining the objective of the Fourth Five Year Plan, thus explained: "The basic goal is a rapid increase in the standard of living of the people, through measures which also promote equality and social justice. Emphasis is placed on the common man, the weaker sections and the less privileged."[9] Socialist and egalitarian goals have been particularly prevalent in India, Ceylon, and Burma, and less emphatically endorsed in Malaysia, Thailand, and the Philippines.

Despite the commitments to economic advancement and egalitarian distribution of the benefits, however, the rate of economic expansion has frequently fallen below expectations (or, at least, hopes). Furthermore, it was Gunnar Myrdal's conclusion that, except possibly in Ceylon, economic inequality has actually been growing in the region over recent years.[10] The Economic Commission for Asia and the Far East somberly observed after 1971: "It is increasingly apparent that large groups of people experienced no improvement in the standard of living in the First Development Decade [1961-1970] and may even have become worse off, despite the regional rate of growth of GNP [Gross National Product] at 5 per cent or more per annum."[11] The disappointing economic performances have been attributed to a variety of factors. Rapid population growth generally retarded improvement in per capita income and living standards. Primary products, the principal exports of countries in the region, have suffered steadily declining prices on world markets, resulting in increasingly unfavorable terms of trade and reducing foreign exchange available for the purchase of capital equipment. In addition, political and social institutions, administrative and entrepreneurial practices, psychological and cultural characteristics, and technological and distribution bottlenecks have been among the restraints blamed for impeding economic growth.

9. Government of India, Planning Commission, *Fourth Five Year Plan, 1969-74* (Delhi: Manager, Publication Branch, n.d.), p. 4.
10. Gunnar Myrdal, *The Challenge of World Poverty* (New York: Vintage Books, 1970), p. 49.
11. United Nations, Economic Commission for Asia and the Far East, *Economic Survey of Asia and the Far East, 1971* (Bangkok: United Nations, 1972), p. 23.

Unemployment

By the early 1970s, massive and apparently growing unemployment and underemployment had loomed as major economic and social problems. Figures on unemployment are of dubious accuracy in most developing countries. Nonetheless, in Indonesia, unemployment appears to have climbed from 5.4 percent of the labor force in 1961 to an estimated 10-11 percent in 1970. In the Philippines, the totally unemployed reportedly constituted 8.2 percent of the labor force in 1965, and the full incidence of unemployment may have been much greater. Comparable conditions are thought to exist in several other countries of the region. Despite the fragmentary and uncertain nature of statistical indications, it seems clear that unemployment is extensive and increasing, with particularly high unemployment rates found among young persons seeking their first employment and among the relatively educated. The mounting problem of insufficient employment has been attributed to a rapid growth of the labor force as a result of swift population growth, which is adding large numbers of new entrants to the labor force each year; the inability of the modern sector of the economy, especially manufacturing, to absorb more than a small proportion of the labor force; and social changes that have enhanced the mobility of workers and have allowed more women to enter the labor force.[12] The growth of unemployment not only leads to human distress, retards the improvement of living conditions, and increases economic inequalities, but contains grim social and political implications. Massive unemployment of youths, particularly educated youths, appeared to lie at the root of an insurrection in Ceylon in 1971.[13]

The Social Dimension

The peoples inhabiting South and Southeast Asia are primarily rural, mostly engaged in agriculture, and generally have very low incomes and living standards. Sharp divisions of culture and living style often separate the urban from the rural populations and the more affluent from the poorer classes. Ties of kinship remain strong. Despite the inroads of other forms of association, vertical patron-client linkages, and the imprint of the patron-client model on other, newer linkages, are evident. Astrology and magic persist as significant influences in many persons' lives.

A suggestion of the varying social circumstances existing within the region may be obtained from Table I.9. (Singapore—which might

12. *Ibid.*, pp. 25-28.
13. This is argued at length in Robert N. Kearney, "The 1971 Ceylonese Uprising: An Ecological Interpretation" (Paper presented at the Research Conference on Communist Revolutions, St. Croix, V.I., Jan. 24-28, 1973).

Table I.9
Selected Indicators of Social Conditions[a]

	Per capita GDP (in U.S. dollars)[b]	Percentage of population in urban areas[c]	Percentage of population 15 years of age and over literate[d]	Percentage of population 5-14 years of age enrolled in primary schools[e]	Hospital beds per 100,000 population[f]	Miles of road per 1,000 sq. miles of area[g]	Miles of railroad per 1,000 sq. miles of area[g]
Afghanistan	55	...	...	9	14	43	—
Burma	70	...	58	34	73	59	7
Cambodia	127	10	41	45	...	134	5
Ceylon	148	19	75	64	302	991	38
India	78	20	28	38	49	490	30
Indonesia	93	12	39	44	73	67	5
Laos	59	15	...	27	61	45	...
Malaysia	280	38	43	54	300	102	11
Nepal	69	4	9	14	19	...	...
Pakistan	141	13	19	25	30	38	21
Philippines	322	30	72	60	105	340	6
Thailand	162	12	68	60	81	63	12
Viet Nam, Republic	148	...	...	61	152	192	12

18

a. Elipsis (. . .) indicates data were unavailable. A dash (—) indicates nil or negligible.

b. For the years of the data, see Table I.6.

c. Local definitions of urban areas, which vary considerably, are used. Figures are for the following years: Cambodia, 1962; Ceylon, 1963; India, 1970; Indonesia, 1965; Laos, 1969; East Malaysia, 1960; West Malaysia, 1957; Nepal, 1961; Pakistan, 1970; and the Philippines, 1960.

d. Figures are for the following years: Burma, 1954; Cambodia, 1962; Ceylon, 1963; India, 1961; Indonesia, 1961; East Malaysia, 1960; West Malaysia, 1957; Nepal, 1961; Pakistan, 1961; Philippines, 1960; and Thailand, 1960.

e. Figures are for 1963 except for Burma and Nepal, both 1964; India, 1962; and Indonesia, 1967-1968.

f. Figures are for 1968 except for Nepal, Pakistan, and Thailand, all 1967; and Afghanistan, 1969.

g. Figures are for 1968 except for Afghanistan, Burma, and Ceylon, all 1969.

Source: United Nations, Economic Commission for Asia and the Far East, *Statistical Yearbook for Asia and the Far East, 1970* (Bangkok: United Nations, 1970); United Nations, Statistical Office, *Demographic Yearbook, 1970* (New York: United Nations, 1971); United Nations, Statistical Office, *Statistical Yearbook, 1970;* and UN, ECAFE, *Economic Survey of Asia and the Far East, 1970.*

19

more appropriately be compared with Bombay, Jakarta, or Manila—has not been included in the table.) It is notable that the poorer countries rank near the bottom and the richer countries near the top on nearly all indicators. Ceylon ranks highest on all indicators except per capita GDP and urbanization, reflecting the nation's high level of social services and developed social infrastructure. Ceylon, Malaysia, and the Philippines are among the top five nations on all except the two transportation indicators, and Thailand ranks among the highest five on all except urbanization and road mileage. Afghanistan, Nepal, and Laos are consistently near the bottom. Hidden in the aggregate figures are, of course, major variations within individual countries.

Population Growth

Among the most stark, and in the long run perhaps most significant, developments in contemporary South and Southeast Asia is the rate and magnitude of population growth. Between 1950 and 1970, the population of the region rose by almost 55 percent, an increase of more than 350 million persons.[14] Annual rates of population growth in 1950-1960 and in 1960-1968 for selected countries are shown in Table I.10. Comparison of growth rates for the two periods indicates that for half the countries included in the table, and for the region as a whole, an increased rate of growth was recorded in the second of the two periods. The sharp increases in population were largely a product of declining mortality rates resulting from improved public health measures and the near-eradication of certain diseases such as malaria. The population increases were recently described by Gunnar Myrdal as "the most important social and economic change that has taken place in the under-developed world in the postwar era" and, if present growth rates continue, an insuperable barrier to the countries' hopes for economic development.[15]

The "Plural Society"

South and Southeast Asian societies are commonly composed of clusters of solidary communal groups that live in close proximity to each other but remain clearly demarcated by distinctive language, religion, race, or sense of historical experience. Membership in the community is ascriptive. The individual is born into the group and membership in the group remains with him throughout his life. The notion of the "plural society" composed of diverse cultural groups as the typical pattern in Southern Asia was described several decades ago by J.S. Furnivall:

14. Calculated from United Nations, Statistical Office, *Demographic Yearbook, 1970* (New York: United Nations, 1971), pp. 128-130.
15. Myrdal, *The Challenge of World Poverty*, pp. 35 and 142-143.

Table I.10

**Annual Rates of Population Growth,
1950-1960 and 1960-1968**

	1950-1960	1960-1968
Burma	1.9	2.1[a]
Ceylon	2.5	2.4
India	1.9	2.5
Indonesia	2.1[b]	2.4
Malaysia (West)	3.1[c]	3.1[d]
Pakistan	2.1	2.1
Philippines	3.1	3.5
Thailand	3.8[b]	3.1
Developing ECAFE countries	2.1	2.5

a. 1960-1967.
b. 1951-1960.
c. 1955-1960.
d. 1960-1966.
Source: UN, ECAFE, *Economic Survey of Asia and the Far East, 1970*, p. 95.

> Each group holds by its own religion, its own culture and language, its own ideas and ways. As individuals they meet, but only in the market-place, in buying and selling. There is a plural society, with different sections of the community living side by side, but separately, within the same political unit.[16]

The deep cleavages of "cultural pluralism" create persistent and powerful lines of self-identification and solidarity within communal groups and differentiation from other groups, which may seriously threaten the cohesion of the larger society. Furnivall characterized plural societies as lacking "a common will except, possibly, in matters of supreme importance, such as resistance to aggression from outside."[17]

A variety of communal configurations can be identified. In Thailand, an overwhelming Thai-speaking, Buddhist majority exists, with very small ethnic and religious minorities at the periphery. Elsewhere, a large and dominant majority is confronted by several smaller minorities, as in Burma, where a dominant Burman ethnic majority exists along with considerably smaller Karen, Shan, Mon, and other minor-

16. J. S. Furnivall, *Colonial Policy and Practice* (Cambridge: Cambridge University Press, 1948), p. 304.
17. J. S. Furnivall, *Netherlands India* (Cambridge: Cambridge University Press, 1944), p. 447.

ities. The Javanese confront the Sumatrans and other outer islanders in a roughly similar pattern in Indonesia. The predominantly Buddhist Sinhalese comprise 71 percent of the Ceylonese population, with largely Hindu Ceylon Tamil and Indian Tamil minorities each forming approximately a tenth of the population and a few smaller minorities. Malaysia is characterized by a very close balance between the Malays, about 47 percent of the population, and the Chinese, about 34 percent, with a smaller Indian community constituting 9 percent of the population. In the Philippines, a number of ethnic-linguistic groups of various sizes exist, no one of which is of dominating size. In religious terms, a huge Christian majority, nearly 90 percent of the Philippine population, confronts a small Muslim minority on the southern island of Mindanao.

India contains extraordinarily complex patterns of religious and linguistic groupings. Following the creation of Pakistan as an independent state for Indian Muslims, the Indian population has been about 85 percent Hindu, with a Muslim minority of about 10 percent and considerably smaller Christian, Sikh, Jain, Parsi, Buddhist, and other religious minorities. In linguistic terms, India is strikingly diverse. The language spoken by the largest number of persons, Hindi, is the language of nearly 135 million people, but they constitute only about 30 percent of the total Indian population. Bengali, Marathi, Tamil, and Telugu are each spoken by more than 30 million persons, between 7 and 9 percent of the population. Each of 14 languages are spoken by 5 million or more persons, and 24 languages each have at least 1 million speakers.[18]

Although the cultural diversity underlying the "plural society" is of venerable origin, the social and political changes of modern times have had a major impact on the character and significance of the communal cleavages. The spread of a market economy, growing urbanization, the appearance of new occupations and activities, and political reforms and reorganizations tended to bring diverse communal groups into a single relatively integrated political system and network of trade and commerce. The social and economic changes involved in the modernization process often proceeded unevenly, leaving some communal groups lagging behind others, and generating communal grievances and tensions. Advancing social mobilization brought new aspirations and demands, which frequently exacerbated communal frictions. The twentieth century expansion of the activities of government increased considerably the benefits obtainable through political action. Follow-

18. Government of India, Ministry of Information and Broadcasting, Research and Reference Division, *India: A Reference Annual, 1970* (Delhi: Publications Division, Ministry of Information and Broadcasting, 1970), pp. 14-15.

ing the removal of colonial rule and the socio-economic changes that widened concern with educational opportunities, non-agricultural employment, and governmental services, political rivalries between communal groups intensified.[19] New groups were brought into politics or became more active politically, increasing the opportunities for conflict, and new arenas for competition appeared with the creation of national legislative and executive organs and the proliferation of local authorities. A British Colonial Office commission, reporting on Ceylon shortly before independence, noted: "When political issues arise, the populace as a whole tends to divide, not according to the economic and social issues which in the West would ordinarily unite individuals belonging to a particular class, but on communal lines."[20] Divisions within the community, based on locality or socio-economic stratification, were often reduced by the force of growing group self-consciousness and unity in political action, while cleavages between groups frequently were accentuated and widened.

Questions of special status for an ethnic group or its language or religion have agitated the politics of many nations of the region. Special provisions for Malays and the Islamic faith embedded in the Malaysian constitution have been a source of recurring Malay-Chinese tensions. Bitter communal riots between Malays and Chinese were touched off by election campaigning in 1969. The position of Buddhism troubled Burmese politics prior to the military coup of 1962. A special status for Buddhism was recognized in the Ceylonese constitution adopted in 1972. Under the 1973 Pakistani constitution, Islam became the state religion of Pakistan.

The official language of government, affecting access to coveted public service careers and opportunities for improved life circumstances as well as containing symbolic and emotional implications, has been the subject of particularly intense controversy in South Asia. The declaration in 1952 that Urdu was to be the national language of Pakistan led to riots in the Bengali-speaking East and was eventually modified, but language differences remained among the grievances driving East from West Pakistan. In Ceylon, the Sinhalese-speaking majority in

19. Clifford Geertz, "The Integrative Revolution: Primordial Sentiments and Civil Politics in the New States," *Old Societies and New States*, ed. Clifford Geertz (New York: Free Press of Glencoe, 1962), pp. 105-157; Alvin Rabushka and Kenneth A. Shepsle, *Politics in Plural Societies: A Theory of Democratic Instability* (Columbus, Ohio: Charles E. Merrill Publishing Co., 1972), esp. pp. 20-21.

20. Great Britain, Colonial Office, *Ceylon: Report of the Commission on Constitutional Reform*, Cmd. 6677 (London: His Majesty's Stationery Office, 1945), p. 40.

1956 secured the designation of Sinhalese as the sole official language over the empassioned protests of the Tamil-speaking minority. Efforts to establish Hindi as the official language of India collided with the emotions and aspirations of those Indians who spoke other languages, particularly the speakers of Tamil in the south and Bengali in the east. Language riots in the southern city of Madras in 1965 stalled plans for the use of Hindi for governmental purposes outside the Hindi-speaking areas. Mounting agitation in the 1950s drove a reluctant central government in New Delhi to undertake a sweeping reorganization of state boundaries, seeking to create linguistically homogeneous states within the Indian Union. Ironically, the first Indian state to be created as a result of the linguistic-states movement, Telugu-speaking Andhra Pradesh, in the early 1970s was beset by demands for sub-division and the formation of an additional state based on the regional grievances of the interior Telengana area.

The Political Dimension

The political processes and governmental forms of the countries of South and Southeast Asia reflect the diversity of the region, as well as the stresses of change and the disruption of international conflict. Authoritarian and coercive regimes of one type or another predominate. In mid-1973, following the overthrow of the traditional monarchy of Afghanistan by military coup, the military dominated six governments; four were transitional or emergency regimes, the eventual character of which was difficult to predict; three were traditional monarchies; four could be classified as constitutional democratic systems based on competitive popular elections; and one, North Viet Nam, was a revolutionary communist regime (see Table I.11).

Since 1971, both the truncated Pakistan and the new nation of Bangladesh have been struggling to establish stable civilian governments. An election held in Bangladesh in 1973 resulted in an overwhelming triumph for the governing Awami League, presumably strengthening prospects for a viable political order based on competitive elections and representative institutions. In 1972, the Philippine president imposed martial law and assumed sweeping powers, claiming the state was threatened by insurgency and separatism. Promised drastic restructuring of the nation's political institutions left the political future of the Philippines in doubt. By 1973, only four states in the region— Ceylon, India, Malaysia, and Singapore—had preserved civilian constitutional government and meaningful competitive elections since independence. With the conspicuous exception of India, all are relatively small and, along with the Philippines, enjoy some of the highest levels of per capita income, education, and social services in the region.

Few nations in the region have been free of major internal or inter-

Table I.11
Types of Political Regimes, 1973

Competitive democracy	Traditional monarchy
Ceylon (Sri Lanka)	Bhutan
India	Nepal
Malaysia	Sikkim
Singapore	

	Revolutionary regime
Military dominance	Viet Nam, People's
Afghanistan	Republic (North)
Burma	
Cambodia (Khmer Republic)	Transitional/emergency regime
Indonesia	Bangladesh
Thailand	Pakistan
Viet Nam, Republic (South)	Laos
	Philippines

national violence, with profound ramifications for their political in-stitutions and processes. Southeast Asia has been battered by more than three decades of international and domestic wars, commencing with the Japanese invasion during the Second World War. The effort to reimpose colonial rule after the defeat of Japan led to fighting in Viet Nam and Indonesia. The protracted warfare in Viet Nam not only embroiled the major world powers but repeatedly spilled over into neighboring Laos and Cambodia. The nations of South Asia have seen less organized warfare, although three short wars were fought by India and Pakistan between 1947 and 1971, and India was involved in a bor-der conflict with China in 1962.

Major insurrections or armed uprisings have occurred during the past 25 years in Burma, Indonesia, the Philippines, Malaya (now Malaysia), Ceylon, and Pakistan, in addition to Viet Nam, Laos, and Cambodia. Insurgencies erupted soon after the Second World War in Indonesia, the Philippines, Malaya, and Viet Nam. A multi-sided in-ternal war has continued to smolder in Burma for a quarter of a cen-tury. In 1965, an attempted communist uprising in Indonesia was crushed with a heavy loss of life. Communal riots in 1969 produced nearly two years of emergency rule in Malaysia. In 1971, Ceylon was jolted by an unsuccessful insurrection. In the same year, East Pakistan suffered through eight months of civil war before becoming, with the assistance of Indian intervention, the independent nation of Bangla-desh. Sporadic insurrectionary violence has flickered at the northern and southern fringes of Thailand in recent years. The eruptions of political violence have reflected sharp ethnic and regional tensions, the erosion of deference and customary values by modernizing social and ideological trends, fundamental disagreements over the character of the polity and the direction and purposes of public policies, and frustration and despair produced by the failure of opportunities and circumstances to keep pace with rising aspirations. The basic problems of preserving order and preventing the violent overthrow of the regime or disintegration of the nation are among the most pressing of the monumental challenges facing the governments of South and Southeast Asia.

Regionalism and Separatism

A frequent source of political tensions and contributor to the level of political violence has been the force of regional or separatist pressures. Where ethnic, linguistic, or religious groups are concentrated territorially, their grievances and aspirations have often taken the form of agitation for regional autonomy or even secession. Because of the power of particularistic communal loyalties, minorities frequently have anticipated discrimination or domination by the majority and have demanded autonomous or separate political units. The Muslim leader, Mohammad Ali Jinnah, in demanding the partition of India into separate Muslim and Hindu states, argued in 1940: "Muslim India cannot accept any constitution which must necessarily result in a Hindu majority government. Hindus and Muslims brought together under a democratic system forced upon the minorities can only mean Hindu rāj [rule]."[21] The Dravida Munnetra Kazhagam (DMK) originally advocated an independent Dravidian- or Tamil-speaking nation-state in South India, modified its demand to one of enhanced state powers within the Indian federal system, and after coming to power in Tamil Nadu state (formerly Madras state, renamed the "Tamil Land" by the DMK) in 1967 appeared to accommodate itself to the national political system, although still suspicious of central government powers. In 1970, the DMK sent tremors through New Delhi by proposing to adopt a distinctive Tamil Nadu state flag.[22] In the hill country on the eastern fringes of India, Naga and Mizo separatist demands appeared for a time, but apparently have abated. Similarly, an independent state was sought by the Pushtu-speaking people of the Pakistani-Afghan border region. Sumatra in Indonesia and Mindanao in the Philippines have produced comparable pressures for secession or regional autonomy. The Karen, Shan, and Kachin minorities in Burma have been engaged in sporadic armed rebellion for years in support of autonomy or separatist demands. Regional and separatist tensions

21. Quoted in William T. de Bary, ed., *Sources of Indian Tradition,* comp. by Stephen Hay and I. H. Qureshi (New York: Columbia University Press, 1958), Vol. 2, p. 285.
22. *Sunday Statesman* (New Delhi), Aug. 23, 1970, p. 11.

were cited to justify the seizure of power by General Ne Win in Burma in 1962 and the assumption of extraordinary powers by Philippine President Ferdinand Marcos in 1972.

The most dramatic example of regional grievances and antagonisms was provided by the 1971 bifurcation of Pakistan. Pakistan had been created in 1947 as a result of the demand by Indian Muslims for an independent nation-state, separate from predominantly Hindu India. The two wings of Pakistan were separated by 1,000 miles of Indian territory and the peoples of the East and West were divided by language, ethnic background, and sense of historical experience. The Bengali-speaking people of East Pakistan, who outnumbered the West Pakistanis, had long felt themselves dominated and exploited by West Pakistan. Mounting Bengali grievances were channeled into demands of East Pakistani autonomy. When, in 1971, the West-dominated government of Pakistan sought to assert control in the East by military force, the independent nation of Bangladesh was proclaimed and the East was plunged into civil war. The provisional prime minister of Bangladesh called for "a national liberation struggle against the colonial oppression of West Pakistan," and declared "Pakistan is now dead and buried under a mountain of corpses."[23]

In 1947, the Bengali-speaking Muslims in the East had joined in the formation of Pakistan, separating themselves from the Bengali-speaking Hindus of India and joining with the Muslims of the West on the basis of the common bond of Islam. By 1971, the Muslim identification had apparently been submerged and replaced by a Bengali linguistic and cultural identification, which distinguished and divided the Muslim Bengalis from their co-religionists in the West. A subtle shift of identity had transformed the 1947 Muslims (who lived in Bengal) into the 1971 Bengalis (who were Muslims). The resurgence of the sense of Bengali identity in Bangladesh was accompanied by murmurs of latent greater-Bengal sentiment among Hindu Bengali intellectuals in India. Apparently essentially cultural, the heightened Bengali consciousness on both sides of the India-Bangladesh border, nonetheless, raised intriguing speculation on future political trends among the Bengali-speaking population of the two countries.

The Military

In the fifteen years between 1958 and 1973, successful military coups occurred in Pakistan, Burma, Thailand, South Viet Nam, Indonesia,

23. Statement by Tajuddin Ahmed, April 17, 1971, reprinted in *Seminar* (New Delhi), No. 142 (June 1971), quotations from pp. 46 and 49. The circumstances leading to the creation of Bangladesh are discussed further in Chapter 3.

Cambodia, and Afghanistan. Constitutional civilian government was never firmly established in many of the countries in which the military came to power. The Thai military held political predominance long before the most recent coup d'etat in 1971 eliminated a veneer of constitutionalism. In South Viet Nam and Cambodia, the military coups reflected the stresses of the Viet Nam War. The 1963 coup in South Viet Nam followed an erosion of the strength of President Ngo Dinh Diem, caught between the Viet Cong insurgents and growing protest by Buddhist and other groups. The Cambodian coup led by General Lon Nol ousted President Norodom Sihanouk in 1970 as the incursions of the Viet Nam War mounted. The military seized power from Indonesian President Sukarno in 1965 after an abortive communist uprising, which climaxed years of communist-army maneuvering and rivalry for influence in the Sukarno regime. Military coups in Burma and Pakistan were prompted by the civilian government's instability and real or imagined lack of capacity to deal with the problems facing the countries.

Military officers, by training and experience habituated to issuing and receiving orders, often have appeared impatient with argument, persuasion, and the need to obtain consent or to reconcile divergent outlooks and interests. Military intervention in politics frequently has been encouraged by the apparent instability, venality, or incapacity of civilian government. The Pakistan president, ex-General Iskander Mirza, in overturning the Pakistani constitution and bringing the military to power in 1958, claimed that civilian politicians had allowed corruption to skyrocket and had stimulated divisive regional and particularistic tendencies that endangered the integrity of Pakistan. It is ironic that a decade later Field Marshal Mohammad Ayub Khan, who had succeeded Mirza as head of the military government, left office on the eve of the dismemberment of Pakistan, amid a torrent of accusations of corruption among his own supporters and relatives.

Governmental power may be held by the military in order to keep rivals from power or to protect the specific interests of the military as an organization or of the officer corps as a social group, as has appeared to be the case in Thailand and Indonesia. The military figures dominating a regime often must rely on the civil bureaucracy to gather taxes, manage the economy, and perform numerous other governmental functions for which the military is neither organized nor trained. Hence, some military regimes have in practice resembled alliances between the military and the civil bureaucracy, usually with the military as the senior partner but with the civil bureaucracy possessing influence and veto power over major policies.

The regime in power in Burma since 1962 has exhibited some characteristics significantly different from those of the more conventional military regimes of Thailand or Indonesia. Although clearly dominated by the military, the Burmese regime displays some of the trappings, at least, of the "revolutionary regime," including the promulgation of an official and self-consciously revolutionary ideology, the sweeping replacement or abolition of governmental institutions, and the establishment of a single legal political party intimately linked with the regime. The regime headed by General Ne Win came into existence as a result of a military seizure of power from the constitutionally selected premier, U Nu, in 1962 and for a decade military officers held virtually all leading posts in the government.[24] In 1972, after a decade in power, Ne Win and a number of his top associates formally resigned their military ranks and continued in their governmental roles as nominal civilians. The formal discarding of military titles did not appear to mark a return to effective civilian government or any significant change in the dominant position of the military in the governance of the nation. However, in contrast with the military regimes of Thailand, Indonesia, and pre-1971 Pakistan, the Ne Win regime professed dedication to socialism and the revolutionary transformation of Burmese government and society. After coming to power in 1962, Ne Win and his fellow military officers demolished the existing parliamentary institutions and exercised power through a Revolutionary Council. A program, labeled the "Burmese Way to Socialism," was formulated and propounded at the commencement of the regime as an ideological formula for radical social reconstruction. Over the next decade, the regime nationalized industries and extended governmental control of the economy. An "official" political party, the Burma Socialist Program Party, was created in 1962 and has functioned for more than a decade as the only party legally permitted to exist. In 1971, efforts commenced to transform it into a mass party. A fundamental reorganization of the administrative apparatus of the state was launched in 1972. Although apparently as repressive and harsh with political opposition as other governments dominated by the military, the Ne Win regime's perspective, purpose, and style have differentiated it from the military-dominated regimes of neighboring countries.

Bureaucracies

Most public bureaucracies of South and Southeast Asia developed under colonial rule and their organization and outlook largely re-

24. The following information on the Ne Win regime is largely based on Richard Butwell, "Ne Win's Burma: At the End of the First Decade," *Asian Survey* 12 (October 1972): 901-912.

flected the imperial requirements of upholding law and order and gathering taxes. The colonial bureaucracies commonly were among their nations' most "modern" social structures, organized on rational, secular lines and utilizing relatively universalistic criteria in recruitment and the implementation of public policy. Generally, they were at least as capable and free of corruption and favoritism as past governing agencies those societies had known. Some colonial bureaucratic structures, notably the famous Indian Civil Service, developed wide reputations for competence and integrity. The colonial bureaucracies, however, tended to remain elite bodies, insensitive to public desires, interests, or convenience. Controlled at the top by European officials and responsible to a Western capital, they provided little scope for discretion, initiative, or the delegation of authority. Consequently, they tended to become formalistic, inflexible, and prone to rigid adherence to rules, regulations, and established routine.

Bureaucratic formalism and inertia became a subject of major concern in many countries after independence, when the public services were called upon to shoulder vastly expanded functions and responsibilities. Despite innumerable efforts at administrative reform, the bureaucracies have been slow to give up the practices and perspectives of a passive, regulatory colonial administration or the elite status of the past. A description of the Burmese civil service, written prior to the 1962 military coup, might well apply to many other bureaucratic structures in the region:

> It [the Burmese civil service] is peculiarly attached to the past and to conserving established practices, and yet it is also commonly identified as the principal agent for modernizing the country. . . . It seems to be designed to fulfill modern functions of government; its standards of performance and its ideals of action are all taken from the modern world. Yet in spite of this apparent attachment to change and progress, it is in fact in the grip of tradition, and a tradition that reaches back not only to British colonial rule but also in some respects to the old East India Company and to the ethos of government of the Burmese kings.[25]

A vital role in the struggle for economic and social advancement has been thrust upon the bureaucracies. In addition to duties connected with enlarged social-welfare activities, they have been assigned responsibility for executing the economic planning and development programs of government. Subjected to the stresses of a changing and turbulent social and political environment and clinging tenaciously to

25. Lucian W. Pye, *Politics, Personality, and Nation Building: Burma's Search for Identity* (New Haven, Conn.: Yale University Press, 1962), p. 213.

the practices of the past, they have commonly appeared to be uncertain instruments for achieving swift socio-economic development. A survey of the ECAFE region noted

> an impressive consensus that the performance of public administration in most Asian countries has not measured up to the governments' proclaimed intentions of rapidly accelerating economic and social progress; shortcomings in this area have probably been more directly responsible than anything else for the serious shortfalls in development plan implementation experienced by the majority of countries in the region.[26]

The hopes for improved material circumstances for the peoples of South and Southeast Asia, and perhaps for their nations' stability and viability, depend to a major extent on bureaucratic adaptation to its new tasks and the skill, determination, and dedication displayed by the public services.

Political Parties and Party Systems

The diversity of political institutions and styles of ordering power is reflected in the widely differing character and significance of political parties and party competition in the various political systems of South and Southeast Asia. In a number of nations, parties are, or for significant periods have been, totally banned. In others, parties have existed but have been generally ineffectual or marginal to the operation of the political system. North Viet Nam provides the only unambiguous example in the region of a "movement-regime" type of party, in which a single mass revolutionary party provides the official ideology and leadership for the state and tends to merge with the formal agencies of the state.[27] Differing in function and character are the "official" or regime-sponsored parties created by persons holding power, often without benefit of elections or other form of popular mandate, in an effort to legitimize their rule and mobilize a broad base of support. Thus, Field Marshal Mohammad Ayub Khan, as president of Pakistan, encouraged the resuscitation of the Pakistan Muslim League, and General Ne Win of Burma directed the formation of the Burma Socialist Program Party.

Where relatively autonomous parties are allowed to function free of

26. "Social Development in Asia," *Economic Bulletin for Asia and the Far East* 20 (December 1969): 39.
27. The notion of the "movement-regime" is from Robert C. Tucker, "Towards a Comparative Politics of Movement-Regimes," *American Political Science Review* 55 (June 1961): 281-289.

regime manipulation and control, a variety of types of parties can be identified. Many are the personal following of an individual, bound together by personal loyalty or veneration for the leader. Others are oriented to the winning of power for the patronage and other benefits it can provide for the party faithful. Several major parties in the region can be described as "front" or "umbrella" parties. Generally a product of the independence movement, the "front" attempts to embrace a broad spectrum of class, regional, and other interests and outlooks, frequently relying on patronage and generalized appeals to broadly held aspirations and sentiments, rather than rigorously defined programs or doctrine. The Indian National Congress is the most prominent and venerable of the "umbrella" parties, although the Alliance Party of Malaysia and possibly the People's Action Party of Singapore display similar characteristics. In the early years of independence, the Muslim League in Pakistan and the Anti-Fascist People's Freedom League in Burma apparently sought to function as broad "front" parties, but both split and eventually crumbled.

Ideological and regional or communal parties are common. The ideological parties, distinguished by strong commitment to a relatively precise political doctrine and program for the reordering of society, are usually based on Marxism or a related radical ideology transferred from the West during the colonial period. The Sino-Soviet division in international communism has been reflected in splits in the communist parties of the region. The Ceylon Communist Party split into pro-Moscow and pro-Peking sections in 1963. The Communist Party of India (CPI) underwent a schism in 1964 which produced a second party, the Communist Party of India-Marxist (CPM), which in turn split in 1969 with the creation of the Communist Party of India-Marxist-Leninist (CPML). The Indonesian Communist Party was the largest and, outside of Viet Nam, probably the most powerful of the communist parties in the region until it was annihilated in the aftermath of its attempted uprising in 1965. Radical parties have been of some significance in election contests and legislatures in India and Ceylon. CPM-led United Fronts for a time governed the Indian states of West Bengal and Kerala. In Ceylon since 1970, both the Ceylon Communist Party (pro-Moscow) and the Lanka Sama Samaja Party, a Trotskyist party (which was expelled from the Fourth International in 1964), have formed a part of a governing United Front and have been represented in the nation's cabinet.

Many parties, including ideological parties, obtain their principal support from one ethnic, linguistic, or religious community. The Malayan Communist Party, although espousing a universalistic ideology of class protest, was overwhelmingly and conspicuously Chinese in membership. Some parties, however, are avowedly based on a particular community or region and are almost exclusively concerned with articulating the grievances and aspirations of that section of the polity. The Awami League became the principal spokesman of rising Bengali discontent in Pakistan prior to the 1971 rupture. The Dravida Munnetra Kazhagam has championed the claims of the Tamil-speaking population in South India. In Ceylon, the Federal Party and the Tamil Congress vie with each other for the right to speak politically for the Ceylon Tamil minority. The Alliance Party of Malaysia functions as a "front" party, but is itself composed of three organizations—the United Malays National Organization, the Malayan Chinese Association, and the Malayan Indian Congress—each representing one of the country's ethnic groups.

In India, Malaysia, and Singapore, "one-party dominant" competition has existed for many years. Until 1967, the Indian National Congress regularly captured nearly three-fourths of the seats in the Lok Sabha, the lower house of the national Parliament, where it faced a badly divided opposition. The Congress also controlled most governments of the Indian states until 1967. In the 1967 elections, the Congress appeared to falter. Its proportion of the popular vote cast for parliamentary candidates slipped from 45 percent in 1962 to 41 percent, while its proportion of the seats plummeted from 73 to 55 percent, due principally to the increased unity of the opposition parties. In the state legislative assemblies, the proportion of seats captured by Congress candidates fell from 58 percent in 1962 to 49 percent and the Congress lost control of half the state governments.[28] Less than three years later, the Congress split, momentarily requiring the central cabinet to depend on the votes in Parliament of the CPI and the DMK for its continuation in office. In an election in early 1971, however, Prime Minister Indira Gandhi was able to lead her wing of the Congress to an impressive triumph, capturing more than two-thirds of the seats in Parliament.[29] State elections in the following year reestablished Congress dominance in most of the Indian states.[30] Predictions of the decay of the Congress and grave political instability in India appeared betrayed by the reassertion of Congress strength, at least for the present.

In Malaysia, the Alliance Party became established firmly in power before independence. Faced by small and mutually antagonistic opposition parties, the Alliance has been able to win overwhelming predominance in Parliament by bargaining and balancing among its con-

28. Indian National Congress, *The Fourth General Elections: A Statistical Analysis* (New Delhi: Indian National Congress, 1967).
29. *Times of India* (New Delhi), March 31, 1971, p. 19.
30. *Ibid.*, March 16, 1972; *Hindustan Times* (New Delhi), March 17, 1972. For further discussion of the Indian party system, see Chapter 2.

stituent ethnic organizations and by conceding preferences for the Malay people and the Islamic religion. The position of the Alliance has depended, however, on the maintenance of a precarious and delicate communal balance, which was shaken by growing communal tensions during the 1969 election and subsequent communal riots. Although the Alliance secured nearly two-thirds of the seats in Parliament in 1969, its proportion of the popular vote for the first time dipped below 50 percent.[31]

Singapore's People's Action Party (PAP) in 1968 and 1972 performed the unusual feat of winning every seat in the city-state's legislative assembly. The PAP has held secure control of the Singapore government since 1959, when it captured 43 of 51 legislative assembly seats. In 1966, the legislators of the Barisan Socialist Party, the only opposition party represented in the assembly, resigned from office, and in subsequent by-elections PAP candidates won all the vacated seats. The 1968 assembly election was boycotted by the Barisan Socialists and two smaller organizations. As a result of the boycott, 51 PAP candidates were returned unopposed. Seven others easily defeated their independent and minor-party opponents, giving the PAP all 58 legislative assembly seats.[32] The performance was repeated in 1972, when the PAP again captured every legislative assembly seat. The overwhelming PAP dominance has been facilitated by curbs on activities by leftists and communal groups, as well as by the city-state's economic dynamism and the prestige of the party's leader, Prime Minister Lee Kuan Yew.

In Ceylon, competition between coherent and durable parties has flourished without the presence of one dominant party, and elections have resulted in repeated transfers of power between opposing parties. In 1970, for the fifth time since independence, a governing party or coalition was defeated in a parliamentary election and handed control of the government to its opponents. Seats in Parliament were won by six parties in 1970 and nine in 1965. However, three of the parties have been linked in a United Front for almost a decade and parliamentary elections have tended to develop into direct contests between the United Front and its principal opponent, the United National Party, although two additional parties contest the areas inhabited by the Ceylon Tamil minority. In the last two elections, the United Front parties and the

---

31. Stuart Drummond and David Hawkins, "The Malaysian Elections of 1969: An Analysis of the Campaign and the Results," *Asian Survey* 10 (April 1970): 329-331. The character and situation of the Alliance is described more fully in Chapter 4.

32. Tae Yul Nam, "Singapore's One-Party System: Its Relationship to Democracy and Political Stability," *Pacific Affairs* 62 (Winter 1969-1970): 465-480.

United National Party together obtained 80 percent or more of all popular votes and seats in Parliament.[33]

In the Philippines prior to the 1972 imposition of emergency rule, two large parties, the Nacionalista Party and the Liberal Party, had contended for and alternated in office. In 1969, Ferdinand Marcos became the first Philippine president to be returned to office. The Philipine parties, however, exhibited a marked absence of cohesion, discipline, or enduring commitment. They basically resembled unstable and shifting coalitions of office-seekers and local notables with their personal followers. Switches between parties by politicians as well as voters occurred frequently. Even in the nomination of presidential candidates, party commitment apparently was not essential. Ramon Magsaysay was chosen as the Nacionalista presidential candidate in 1953 although he was a member of the Liberal Party and held a cabinet post under a Liberal president until shortly before his nomination. Similarly, in 1965, Marcos was given the Nacionalista presidential nomination although he had recently been a Liberal.[34] The events of 1972 clouded the future of the nation's party system.

Following are studies of politics in six countries: India, Indonesia, Malaysia, Thailand, and the recently parted nations of Pakistan and Bangladesh. The six collectively contain four-fifths of the one billion people of South and Southeast Asia and include the four largest nations in the region. They display a wide variety of institutions, problems, and achievements and failures. India, Pakistan, Bangladesh, and Malaysia share a heritage of British colonial rule which has left a clear imprint on their political and other institutions, and contrasts with the Dutch colonial heritage of Indonesia. India, Pakistan, and Indonesia became independent about a quarter of a century ago, Malaysia about a decade later. Only Thailand did not experience colonial rule. India, gigantic and complex, seems to be institutionalizing party and parliamentary government and to be containing its regional and social diversities, but is still struggling with abysmal economic and social conditions for staggering numbers of its people. Bangladesh and Pakistan are commencing efforts to evolve stable constitutional systems after the failure to bridge the divisions between East and West, which left a devastated East—Bangladesh—and a defeated and humiliated West—the truncated Pakistan—to search separately for political order and social and economic progress. Malaysia reveals the delicate

33. Robert N. Kearney, *The Politics of Ceylon (Sri Lanka)* (Ithaca, N.Y.: Cornell University Press, 1973), pp. 90-124.
34. Carl H. Landé, "Parties and Politics in the Philippines," *Asian Survey* 8 (September 1968): 725-747.

balancing of ethnic interests and aspirations. Indonesia in the aftermath of the Sukarno era faces a host of neglected economic, social, and political problems. Adaptation and continuity are major themes of the politics of Thailand, as traditional structures are molded to the altered circumstances of the contemporary world. Spared the jolts of decolonization and the strains of marked cultural pluralism, Thailand presents an intriguing contrast to the other nations examined. Together, these nations offer a broad survey of the social, economic, and political circumstances of the nations of South and Southeast Asia.

Selected Readings

Braibanti, Ralph. ed. *Asian Bureaucratic Systems Emergent from the British Imperial Tradition*. Durham, N.C.: Duke University Press, 1966.

Brass, Paul R., and Franda, Marcus F. eds. *Radical Politics in South Asia*. Cambridge, Mass.: M.I.T. Press, 1973.

Brecher, Michael. *The New States of Asia: A Political Analysis*. New York: Oxford University Press, 1966.

Brown, W. Norman. *The United States and India, Pakistan, Bangladesh*. Cambridge, Mass.: Harvard University Press, 1972.

DuBois, Cora. *Social Forces in Southeast Asia*. Cambridge, Mass.: Harvard University Press, 1959.

Furnivall, J.S. *Colonial Policy and Practice*. Cambridge: Cambridge University Press, 1948.

Geertz, Clifford ed. *Old Societies and New States*. New York: Free Press of Glencoe, 1962.

Lambert, Richard D., and Hoselitz Bert F., eds. *The Role of Savings and Wealth in Southern Asia and the West*. Paris: UNESCO, 1963.

Myrdal, Gunnar. *Asian Drama: An Inquiry into the Poverty of Nations*. New York: Pantheon, 1968. 3 vols.

Onslow, Cranley. ed. *Asian Economic Development*. New York: Frederick A. Praeger, 1965.

Purcell, Victor. *The Chinese in Southeast Asia*. 2nd ed. London: Oxford University Press, 1965.

Pye, Lucian W. "Party Systems and National Development in Asia." In *Political Parties and Political Development*, edited by Joseph LaPalombara and Myron Weiner. Princeton, N.J.: Princeton University Press, 1966, pp. 369-398.

Scalapino, Robert A. ed. *The Communist Revolution in Asia*. 2nd. ed. Englewood Cliffs, N.J.: Prentice-Hall, Inc., 1969.

Scott, James C. "The Erosion of Patron-Client Bonds and Social Change in Rural Southeast Asia." *Journal of Asian Studies* 32 (November 1972): 5-37.

Smith, Donald E. ed. *South Asian Politics and Religion*. Princeton, N.J.: Princeton University Press, 1966.

"Social Development in Asia." *Economic Bulletin for Asia and the Far East* 20 (December 1969): 19-42.

Tilman, Robert O. ed. *Man, State, and Society in Contemporary Southeast Asia*. New York: Frederick A. Praeger, 1969.

United Nations. Economic Commission for Asia and the Far East. *Economic Survey of Asia and the Far East*. Bangkok: United Nations, annual.

——— *Statistical Yearbook for Asia and the Far East.* Bangkok: United Nations, annual.

Von der Mehden, Fred R. *Religion and Nationalism in Southeast Asia.* Madison: University of Wisconsin Press, 1963.

Weidner, Edward W. ed. *Development Administration in Asia.* Durham, N.C.: Duke University Press, 1970.

2   The Indian Political System

Stanley A. Kochanek

A study of the Indian political system is important not only as an attempt to understand one of the twentieth century's most complex societies but also as an attempt to sharpen theories of modernization, development and change. Empirical studies of change in India have called into question a great deal of theorizing about the process of political development.

Applied to the Indian context the tradition-modernity typology, for example, has been shown to be asymmetrical and ambiguous. While theorists have been reasonably precise in defining modernity, they have tended to treat tradition as a convenient but static residual category. Such a conceptualization, however, obscured the fact that traditions are too complex and heterogeneous to be analytically useful at the level of generalization required for the predication of a simple dichotomy. This failure of analysis could not help but impede efforts to establish the precise relationship between the two concepts and thus there has been a tendency to accede to the assumption that social change is a unidirectional process in which some homogeneous "modernity" will automatically supplant "tradition." As a result of empirical studies of the process of change in India, however, such simplistic models of development have begun to give way to the search for a more dynamic model which will reflect more accurately a heterogeneous world and its enormous variations in the scope, nature, method and rate of social change.[1]

1. See Samuel P. Huntington "The Change to Change: Modernization, Development, and Politics," *Comparative Politics* 3 (April 1971): 283-322;

Similar problems have been encountered in taking the social process approach to the study of political development with its stress on the importance of quantitative changes as the key to understanding the modernizing process.[2] At first glance the quantitative indices of level of development in India suggest that India conforms to most Third World stereotypes. Indeed, India appears to epitomize the model of an underdeveloped society. It is basically rural with 73 percent of its population in 1967 dependant upon the land. Its per capita income of $84 in 1967 was among the lowest in the world. Its major foreign exchange earners are raw materials, for cotton, jute and tea still provide the bulk of the exports that help make up for the massive trade deficits arising from the import of materials needed for industrial development. India has been heavily dependent upon foreign aid both from the West and the Soviet block. India is the second most populous nation in the world with 548 million people in 1971, a birth rate of 41 per 1,000, a population growth rate of 2.5 percent per year, and a literacy rate of 25 percent. The population is extraordinarily heterogenous. Although 83 percent of its population is Hindu, India contains a substantial Muslim minority of 11 percent as well as relatively small but significant groups of Christians, Sikhs, Buddhists and Jains. Hinduism itself is characterized by a myriad of caste groups, and within the country exist some 15 major language groups. This concert of obstacles to harmonious social and economic development helps to explain why a study in the late 1950s showed that India ranked 19th in a ranking of 46 Asian and African states according to eleven indices of economic development.[3]

In qualitative terms, however, the picture of India is quite different. India has held five successful national elections, has enjoyed remarkable political stability, and has been undergoing a program of massive change under a democratically oriented political leadership. Thus, so far from being the stereotype of an underdeveloped society, India has turned out to be the Third World's most conspicuous deviant case. The index devised by Almond and Coleman revealed no correlation

Joseph R. Gusfield, "Tradition and Modernity: Misplaced Polarities in the Study of Social Change," *American Journal of Sociology*, 72 (Jan. 1967): 351-362; Lloyd and Susanne Rudolph, *The Modernity of Tradition: Political Development in India* (Chicago, Illinois: University of Chicago Press, 1967).

2. For a general survey of the social process approach see Richard L. Merritt, *Systematic Approaches to Comparative Politics* (Chicago, Illinois: Rand McNally, 1971) pp. 24-64.

3. Gabriel A. Almond and James S. Coleman (ed) *The Politics of the Developing Areas* (Princeton, N.J.: Princeton University Press, 1960), p. 542.

between the state of Indian economic development and the nature of the Indian political system. Similarly in a study of political development, Huntington concluded that "in terms of political institutionalization, India was far from backward. Indeed, it ranked high not only in comparison with other modernizing countries in Asia, Africa and Latin America, but also in comparison with many much more modern European countries."[4]

In order to understand this peculiarly Indian pattern of development, therefore, one cannot rely on quantitative analysis and high level generalization; one must examine the nature of India's traditional heritage, the timing, scope and duration of external stimuli for change and the result of this collision between tradition and change on the multifarious elements of the Indian political system. A political system can be thought of as a pattern of interacting elements each changing at a different rate. For analytical purposes four major elements require attention: the political culture, elites and groups, structures of decision making, and political performance. Political culture involves the values, attitudes, orientations and myths relevant to politics. These beliefs and attitudes have evolved with the history of the nation and shape both the social order and the ideologies that have emerged over time in a particular society. The study of elites and groups involves a delineation of the major social and economic formations and how they participate in politics by controlling or making demands on political structures. The study of structures of decision-making includes not only tracing the formal organization through which society makes authoritative decisions but a determination of the groups and individuals who play the dominant leadership role within these structures. Policy and performance are the outcomes of governmental decisions. They reveal the distribution of benefits and penalties in society which in turn have an important impact on the maintenance or change of values and expectations of the population at large. These four elements of the modern Indian political system will be examined against the background of the nature of India's traditional heritage and the timing and scope of external stimuli for change.

Traditional Heritage

Because of the sheer size and diversity of its population and the long continuity of its civilization, in all of which it is comparable only to China, India is one of the twentieth century's most complex societies. It is not the mere endurance but the characteristic adaptability of this

4. Samuel P. Huntington, *Political Order in Changing Societies* (New Haven, Conn.: Yale University Press, 1968), p. 84.

dynamic, complex past that has shaped and continues to shape both the attitudes and values of the society as well as the nature of its constituent groups and their leaders. Three such forces have played an especially critical role in creating the contemporary situation: the traditional Hindu social order, the timing and scope of the colonial heritage, and the special characteristics of Indian nationalism. At least some knowledge of the accumulation and interplay of these historical forces is essential to an understanding of modern Indian government and politics.

Despite the ostensible protection offered by ranges of lofty mountains in the north and equally formidable expanses of ocean to the south, the Indian subcontinent has fallen prey to a large number of invasions which have successively and profoundly altered its racial distribution and culture, conditioned the development of its political structure, and contributed to the heterogeneity of the population today. Before improved maritime design and steamships made possible the European incursions by sea, India was particularly susceptible to invasions through the mountain passes of the north-west. Century after century hordes of invaders from Central Asia and the Middle East swept through these gateways to the Indus and the plains of Punjab. Often these invaders retired after plundering the plain, but there have been numerous instances in which invaders became conquerors, founded kingdoms, and remained as rulers.

Although our knowledge of India's past prior to the fourth century B.C. is scanty, what can be established shows that many of the basic outlines of Hindu civilization were formed during this pre-historical period. India like China is one of the oldest civilizations in the world. Its earliest traces go back to several centers which flourished during the third millennium B.C. in the Indus Valley. The two most important archeological remains of early Indian civilization are found at Harappa in south-western Punjab and Mohenjo-Daro in Sind. Archaeological evidence, including the ruins of its planned towns, the remains of its sophisticated metallurgy, and the excellence of its art forms, indicate that Harappa culture was a highly developed civilization for its time. The Harappa people are believed to have been at least partly Dravidian and related to the present day population of southern India whose various interrelated Dravidian languages contrast strikingly with the Sanskrit derived languages of the north. From the state of its remains, archaeologists have concluded that Harappa culture came to an end by some sudden devastation, and scholars have speculated that it was destroyed by the Aryans, a central Asian, nomadic people who invaded the sub-continent from the north during the second millinium B.C.

The Aryan invasion of the Indian subcontinent turned out to be the most significant cultural intrusion the subcontinent was ever to experience. The Aryans gave the subcontinent its classical language Sanskrit, from which most of the northern Indian regional languages developed; a set of sacred texts known as the *Vedas* from which stem the many later schools of Indian philosophy and theology; and a system of social organization which, combined with certain Dravidian elements, formed the basis of Hinduism which thereafter could not be supplanted as the dominant religious system of the subcontinent. This unique social system which developed shortly after the Aryan invasions stratified the society into a fourfold structure of varnas with the Brahmins (priestly and learned class) at the top. Next in status stand the Kshatriya (warrior-ruler) class and then the Vaisya (merchant). The bulk of the society, however fell into the lowly ranks of the Sudra (worker) class. The Vedic theory and practice of varna became the basis of the infinitely more complex modern Indian caste system. Thus the primary legacy of the Aryan invasion was not merely the imposition of an alien rule but the creation of a cultural and social pattern that laid the basis for all subsequent Hindu thought and civilization.

The ensuing history of Hindu civilization is complex, but it is generally agreed that Hindu culture was particularly flourishing during the political ascendency of India's two great Hindu empires: the Mauryan Empire (321 B.C. to 184 B.C.) and the Gupta Empire (A.D. 320 to A.D. 540). While both these empires made substantial contributions to the development of Indian civilization, only the Mauryan Empire succeeded in unifying the subcontinent under a single political control. The Gupta Empire was confined predominantly to North India. But even that degree of consolidation was a major accomplishment, for between these periods of political unity and stability India was congenitally divided into a congeries of warring kingdoms. This endemic lack of political unity was to have several significant consequences for India. In the first place, the Hindu social order evolved as a strong localistic tradition based on clearly delineated responsibilities to family, kin, caste, and village. This localism was reinforced by the lack of commercialization of village agriculture and the relative self-sufficiency of the rural economy. This localized and segmented social order became increasingly rigidified as a result of continuous alien occupation during the period of Muslim ascendency and culminated in the highly ossified Hindu social system found by the European traders in the seventeenth and eighteenth centuries. By this time the protective impulse had led to cultural and intellectual stagnation. Yet this very system of localism, however, also enabled the classical Hindu heritage to survive long periods of foreign rule and occupation. Thus, the Hindu renaissance of the nineteenth century was a fertile mixture of the old and the new.

A second aspect of the political fragmentation of the subcontinent is geographical, for many of the peculiarities of Indian political history correspond to the physicographic characteristics of the subcontinent itself. The Indian subcontinent falls roughly into three geographic regions: the north, the Deccan and the south. North India is composed of the great Gangetic plain and its dependencies. It is bounded by the Himalayas in the north, and its southern reaches are defined by the Vindhya mountains in the center of the subcontinent. Because the Gupta Empire was predominently confined to this north Indian region, the peoples of the Gangetic heartland tend to feel they are still close to the font of Indian civilization. Despite the relative geographic unity of north India in which the only barrier to communication was distance, separate regional identities coincident with mutually unintelligible languages developed from the original Sanskrit base.

The Deccan tableland, though seemingly no less geographically integrated than the north and the south, breaks down into four separate political and linguistic entities with little sense of a mutual history. Because of its location in central India the Deccan acted as the agent of cultural transfer between north and south. Maharashtra and Orissa, the two northern areas of the Deccan, therefore became more oriented toward the north. Their languages have a Sanskritic base. The languages of Karnataka and Andhra, the two southern regions, on the other hand, have a Dravidian base.

South India, which covers the area of the present Tamil Nadu and Kerala, represents a second great and almost independent focus of Indian civilization. For long periods of its history totally autonomous from the north, South India developed its own political and cultural orientations within the larger though amorphous possibilities of Hindu civilization. It is not surprising therefore that the Tamils of South India have, of all ethnic-linguistic groups on the subcontinent, been the most conscious of their own special identity.

A third thrust toward endemic lack of political unity on the Indian subcontinent was the vulnerability of the area to foreign invasion and foreign rule. While the omnivorous Hinduism found little difficulty over time in absorbing a considerable variety of tribal peoples who successively invaded India from the Middle East and Central Asia, it proved incapable of assimilating the invaders representing highly organized rival systems of Islam and the West once they had established themselves as a dominant political force on the subcontinent.

The Muslim invasions which began as early as 712 A.D. culminated in the founding of the Moghul Empire in the Sixteenth Century.

While the Moghuls thus succeeded in unifying the subcontinent for the first time since the days of the Mauryan Empire, the major effect of their political achievement was to drive Hinduism into a protective shell and to leave behind on their eventual dissolution a huge unassimilated Muslim minority throughout north India. This group fearful of the resurgent Hindu majority developed its own nationalism, which led to the partition of the subcontinent and in post independence India to problems of communal rivalry and violence between Hindus and the Muslims who either could not or would not join Pakistan.

Some centuries after the last of the Islamic incursions India was in the direct path of the expansion of the western colonial powers into Asia. The vacuum created by collapse of the Moghul Empire was filled almost immediately by the rise of the British Empire, for the British East India Company had already, bit by bit, succeeded in gaining control of the chips from the fragmenting Moghul Empire and its successor or tributary states. Soon Britain was able to establish direct control over most of the Indian subcontinent, and the scope and intensity of the British presence made its impact on the political, economic and social system of modern India to be more far reaching and of greater endurance than that of the Moghuls.

The chief political contribution of British rule was to strengthen a traditionally weak central political authority. In the process of unifying almost all of India under one power for the first time in 2000 years peace and stability were restored to a subcontinent suffering from the gradual decline and collapse of the Moghul Empire. For the first time, moreover, a uniform legal order, one applicable to all sectors of the diverse Indian society, was established. In addition, the English surpassed all other welders of an Indian Empire in the creation of a unified central administration based on the emerging principles of a modern bureaucracy recruited on the basis of open competition and merit. Gradually under British rule a model of government evolved which was ultimately to be accepted as the structure of government for independent India.

With the development of railroads and the beginning of industrialization the actions of the English in the mid-nineteenth century resulted in a significant economic legacy. While the railroads united the subcontinent physically as never before, the beginnings of industrialization led to the emergence of both foreign and indigenous entrepreneurial elites. Thus, as sectors of India's traditional, trading communities, especially the Parsis, Gujaratis, Marwaris and Chettiars, moved from trade to lay the foundation of Indian industrialization, indigenous Indian capital, unlike that in many former colonial areas, became a force in its own right. This Indian entrepreneurial elite came into sharp conflict with the British colonial regime over economic and trade policies which were perceived by Indian capital as discriminating in favor of foreign capital in India while it placed Indian industry in an unfavorable trading position with the British home islands. As a result of competition between foreign and indigenous capital and resentment toward British economic policy, the Indian entrepreneurial elite became strongly committed to the cause of political and economic nationalism. They joined the educated middle class to oppose continued British domination of India, and Indian business became the chief source of funds for the nationalist movement.

Of all the changes brought about by British colonial policy the most profound, however, was the change in the pattern of education introduced in the nineteenth century. The introduction of western education in 1835 determined the pattern of Indian modernization more than any other policy decision. It brought into being a new Indian elite. This new largely urban elite, superimposed on the larger segmented society, was to play a dominant role in the future development of the country.

The introduction of western education in 1835 drew its most enthusiastic response not from princes, big landholders, traders, merchants, or even from the artisans or peasants who were not so well established but from the moderately well-to-do middle classes including the members of old literati, composed in large part of the Brahmanic and other highly placed castes. Finding but limited opportunity in the colonial bureaucracy and the military and discouraged from entering business because of caste attitudes, these products of the new English education were the first to enter the modern professions of law, medicine, and journalism. They were also the founders of modern voluntary associations based on patterns of interaction resulting from their common experience and education and reflecting new sets of values in the society. These associations, which marked the beginning of modern politics in India, were designed to bring about the social, religious, educational, and political revitalization of the society. Finally, the expanded social consciousness of this new professional elite led to the organization of provincial political associations, which in 1885 banded together at the all-Indian level to create the Indian National Congress.

The Indian National Congress became the primary instrument for pressing the demands of the new elite on the colonial regime. At first their demands were moderate indeed. They focused on the need to secure for Indians positions in the colonial bureaucracy and to gain them representation in the government councils which had been established at the provincial and national levels as advisory bodies to the colonial administration. Since the British government moved too slowly to meet these demands, the pace of nationalism quickened and spread to a larger segment of Indian society. Ultimately, discouraged by the former and inspired by the latter, the newly emerged political elite would settle for nothing less than the end of the British Raj in India.

The Congress movement passed through three stages of development from 1885 to 1947. Each stage was marked by an increasing differentiation of the Congress elite and by an ever more clearly articulated set of nationalist demands. During the first twenty years of its existence the Congress was dominated by a moderate leadership drawn largely from the new western educated, upper middle class and supported by large landowners or zamindars and princes. It behaved more like a pressure group than a nationalist movement with demands centering not upon calls for independence but for administrative reform. Through peaceful constitutional processes by means of an annual petition of grievances to the British government, the Congress pressed these demands for greater Indianization of the civil service at the higher levels, for broadening of the electoral base of the Viceroy's Legislative Council, and for greater assistance to the development of indigenous capital.

By 1905 the moderate upper middle class professional leadership of the Congress was being challenged by an emergent urban lower middle class, who unlike the earlier westernized group had not achieved status or position under the British. Not only was this new group convinced that desirable Hindu values were being threatened by British rule, but many of its members once educated were either unable to find employment or, more often, were confined to uninspiring lower income jobs as clerks. These religious and economic resentments gave rise to a radical expression of nationalism closely linked to Hindu revivalism. To press their demands for self-government the proponents of this new variety of nationalism rejected gradualist and constitutional approaches for a reliance on various forms of direct action including violence and economic boycott.

One of the most influential leaders of the militant new nationalism was Bal Gangadhar Tilak, a Maharashtrian Brahmin who drew his inspiration from the Hindu past. Tilak, deeply committed to the traditions of Hinduism, opposed any attempt to reform its ancient ways. He violently denounced the Age of Consent Bill which was designed to prevent infant marriage; he organized anti-cow killing societies; and he considered Hindu spirituatism to be the ultimate salvation of mankind.

Paralleling Tilak's militancy in the west of India was the development of terrorist and anarchist movements in the eastern presidency of Bengal, where British policy had given the Bengali militants an issue which could be used for purposes of mass mobilization. In the interest of administrative efficiency, Lord Curzon in 1905 decided to partition the province of Bengal into two smaller, more manageable units. Ironically, the partition approximated the lines that would be traced in 1947 to create East Pakistan, now Bangladesh. Curzon's action was welcomed by the Muslims of Bengal, but Bengali nationalists saw the move as a blatant attempt to reduce their influence. They responded with mass demonstrations and a boycott of British goods. The communal overtones of this issue frightened the Muslims and led to the founding of the Muslim League in 1906 as an instrument to protect Muslim rights.

Meanwhile the militant nationalists led by Tilak, who had been fighting a protracted battle with the old moderates in the Congress, succeeded in 1906 in committing the Congress to a policy of *swadeshi* (economic boycott) and to the demand for self-government within the British Empire. As the Congress became more radicalized, it lost the support of sections of the upper class, among them the princes and zamindars and segments of the old Parsi and Gujarati industrial elite. The Congress was, however, compensated for this loss by the gaining of a wider base in the urban centers of India.

From 1905 to the end of World War I the moderates and the extremists fought a running battle within the Congress which on several occasions threatened to split the movement. This situation prevailed when Gandhi appeared on the scene to completely re-orient the leadership, organization, goals, tactics, and appeal of the Congress movement. Because of his complex background and training, Gandhi appealed to more segments of the fragmented Indian society than any of his predecessors. As a non-Brahmin, Gujarati Bania, Gandhi was attractive to the Gujarati and Marwari industrialists who had begun to move from trade into industry during World War I and who were to become the chief financial backers of the movement. As a British trained lawyer, Gandhi gained the confidence of the educated middle class, especially those in the smaller centers outside of Bombay, Calcutta and Madras. As a result of his campaign to support the indigo plantation workers in 1919 and the agrarian struggles in his home state of Gujarat, he found a following among the peasantry. Finally, Gandhi appealed to Hindu traditionalists through his emphasis on personal asceticism, his championing of the simple life, his advocacy of the use of homespun and handwoven cloth, and his founding of ashrams. Moreover, Gandhi's use of traditional symbols and leadership style gave nationalism a compelling indigenous flavor and content.

Gandhi succeeded in re-uniting and reorganizing the entire Congress movement which thereupon accepted his program of achieving *swaraj* (freedom) through a process of *satyagraha* (non-violent passive resistance). This goal and this strategy were to transform the Congress from an urban middle class movement into a true mass movement which Gandhi was able to organize and imbue with the discipline needed to carry out the objective. The loosely organized Congress was restructured into what Gandhi called a parallel government designed to win the loyalty of the Indian people. The directing of the movement was placed in the hands of the Congress President and a small Working Committee charged with seeing to the implementation of the policies laid down by the more broadly based All-India Congress Committee (AICC) and Annual Sessions. The actual carrying out of these policies was the function of the various provincial congress committees which departed from the administrative organization of the British Raj in being based on linguistic geographic units to facilitate communications with the masses.

For a brief period Gandhi even succeeded in gaining the support of India's Muslims, who had become temporarily alienated from the British because of their decision to dismember the Ottoman Empire and to allow the dissolution of the office of caliph, the highest office in the Islamic world. Unfortunately for Indian national unity, this anti-British alliance lasted only until 1924 when the Muslims of the subcontinent went their own way. Eventually, they succeeded in wresting an Islamic state from the integument of the British Raj.

Despite attempts at constitutional reform which gradually transferred elements of power to Indian hands, British efforts to meet the rising tide of nationalist demands were generally too little and too late. From 1920 onward, Gandhi's non-cooperation movement became the major stream of political activity and the British were ill equipped to counter it effectively. Three great civil disobedience campaigns took place. Each succeeded in mobilizing a wider segment of the Indian population for political action. In no case, however, did new entrants inundate the old; instead, these diverse elements of the population came to coexist in the mosaic of the nationalist movement, which became broadly representative of the bulk of Indian society. The first civil disobedience campaign of 1921-22 succeeded in recruiting the lawyers of the smaller cities and district towns; the salt satyagraha of 1930-33 brought in the rural landlords and lower non-Brahmin castes of the Deccan and the south, and with the Quit India movement the Congress extended its base to include most sections of Indian society. Overall the trend in recruitment was from urban to rural, from high caste to middle and low caste, from the professions to the peasantry. In short, unlike a large number of nationalist movements of Asia and Africa, the Congress under Gandhi succeeded in transcending its origins as an urban middle-class intellectual movement. It acquired a reasonably heterogeneous mass base which was to play a major role in the politics of mass franchise after 1947.

Although there was some attrition in the support base of the Congress immediately after independence, the party retained most of its appeal to a variety of caste, language, regional, ethnic and modern interests. The leadership continued to be provided by the educated intellectuals who, ironically perhaps, were able to play the traditional Hindu role of a learned elite. In addition, the long history of the movement had enabled it to develop into a well-institutionalized party which possessed both the skills and the mechanisms for the management of men and ideas in a political arena. The very heterogeneity of the Congress had forced Congress leaders to deal with a wide variety of interests and tensions generated by a pluralistic society. The leadership had learned how to persuade, pressure, cajole and compromise and thus, through a process including various combinations of conflict, mediation, bargaining, and consensus building, reach workable decisions. In short, the party had developed an integrative style which actually prevented the disintegration repeatedly predicted for it. The programmatic implications of this integrative style enabled the Congress to pre-empt the middle ground of the Indian political spectrum and to force the opposition to the fringes, thereby strengthening the appeal of the party.

The end of the British colonial rule which had replaced the Moghul Empire brought self government to India in the guise of a federal republic with a parliamentary system of government based on a mass franchise. At first, the legacy of the colonial vice regal tradition and the character of the nationalist movement and its leadership permitted the continued primacy of the educated elite who worked through highly centralized structures of decision-making. However, under the sustained impact of the politics of mass franchise and the pattern of mobilization which translated constitutional right into a political reality, a shift of power away from the urban educated elite to new consciously rural and regional elites took place. This shift in leadership was accompanied by an expansion, dispersion and democratization of political power which resulted in a fragmentation and dissolution of power within the political system and the strengthening of the federal base of the Indian polity.

Political Culture

Although British rule and the development of Indian nationalism had a profound impact on India's tradition of segmented localism, independence still found India with a dual political culture corresponding roughly to the urban-rural distribution of its population. A national, elite political culture existed among the urban middle class political leadership, bureaucracy, military leaders, and industrialists. The political culture of the vast peasant rural sector, however, tended to be segmented along caste, community, language and regional lines. Yet, despite the existence of this dual political culture, the values, norms and attitudes of both cultures have never been as dichotomized as the necessity to distinguish the two implies. Most groups in Indian society share in varying but significant degrees the attitudes and orientations of the larger political culture despite their tendency simultaneously to exhibit contrasting sets of common orientations and shared values that set them apart as separate sub-cultures. While the elite political culture has been influenced to a greater degree by nineteenth century British intellectual history, by nationalism, and to a lesser degree by secularism, both the elite and the segmented cultures of India are proud of their shared historical and cultural tradition, including the synthesis of values reflected in Gandhian thought, and they undergo in the course of maturation a not wholly dissimilar pattern of socialization. The result has been a considerable sharing of certain underlying values and orientations toward authority, decision-making and modes of thought. Reinforcing these common traditional values in the decades since independence, the constricted pattern of identities in the segmented rural sectors has begun to open up to wider loyalties under the impact of mass franchise, the devolution of political power, and other forces of modernization.

The strength of India's long, continuous cultural tradition and the equal persistence and relative uniformity of its patterns of socialization have enabled the society to share a series of basic values which influence the conduct of government, the shape of popular attitudes toward government and the determination of patterns of development. Though these themes have not been systematically studied in all their ramifications, they are pervasive enough to have been singled out both by foreign and Indian commentators. A number of orientations have been stressed as particularly fundamental: a tolerance of ambiguity, a low level of trust in interpersonal relations, a strong desire to maintain harmony because of a belief in the undesirability of conflict and competition, a hyper-rationality in the approach to problem solving, a belief in the efficacy of norms and law, a tendency to judge by motive rather than action, and a concern with the distribution rather than the creation of wealth. These orientations, therefore, affect both the behavior and impact even of interest groups in the modern sector of Indian society.

Numerous commentators have observed that Indians have a high tolerance for ambiguity which is often defined as a facility for the absorption and synthesis of diverse and even contradictory ideas or interests. Historically and culturally, India's response to successive inundation by a variety of groups and ideas has been to graft them onto a system which enabled each to exist, encapsulated, but truly secure. Traditional India thus became the quintessence of a stable "plural society." As Hutton has observed, "the caste system has afforded a place in society into which any community, be it racial, social, occupational or religious, can be fitted as a cooperating part of the social whole, while retaining its own distinctive character and its separate individual life."[5]

If one considers the matter from the point of view of the Muslims or the untouchables, one might, however, say that the integrative stress here is a bit naive, for this intersection of these myria of components of Indian society was determined by a functional necessity that was rigidly enforced by tradition, habit, ritual and law. The caste mechanism may have kept society running but not without deep seated resentments and an inclination to litigiousness whenever expressions of latent conflict were legitimized in village society. Those who attempted to cross caste and defy community boundaries were punished both by superiors and peers, as case studies of those who allowed their affections to settle on exogamous objects have abundantly shown.

Still, groups survived in India as they could not have survived without such strict enforcement of conformity and orthodoxy. The pragmatic elasticity of the social fabric that encouraged culturally diverse groups to preserve their distinctive features was enhanced by a philosophic system which placed major emphasis on self-identity or salvation through self-realization. It is characteristic of Indian philosophy to contend that there are many paths to truth, not one of them worthy to claim unquestioned supremacy. If each social group has its own internally consistent mores, and each path to truth its own rationale, then "both group values and individual morality" must be seen as "transient and situation-specific." Hence, Indian society is known for its legitimizing "of ethical relativism and tolerance of dissent."[6] Ramified in the political sphere, this lack of a sense of a singular objective reality enables the "leadership to accept and live with contradictions in policies without submitting them to an analysis and test of workability."[7] While such an intellectual predisposition may inhibit the

5. J. H. Hutton, *Caste in India: Its Nature, Function and Origins* (London: Oxford University Press, 1963), p. 115.

6. Rajni Kothari, *Politics in India* (Boston: Little, Brown and Company, 1970), p. 258.

7. Van Dusen Kennedy, *Unions, Employers and Government: Essays on Indian Labour Questions* (Bombay: Manaktalas, 1966), p. 20 .

ability to establish and implement priorities, it does permit the articulation of policies which create the widest possible following. In ambiguity lies consensus. The notion is not unheard of elsewhere, but in India, perhaps, the motives for an ambiguous statement may be given a more charitable, not wholly opportunistic interpretation.

A second peculiarly Indian orientation stressed by commentators is the strong sense of mutual distrust which appears to underlie interpersonal relationships in India.[8] Carstairs attributes this sense of distrust to patterns of socialization and child rearing,[9] which he finds to be characterized by a constant suspicion of favoritism, by partiality in the distribution of rewards and punishments, and by unfairness or lack of candor in interpersonal relationships. It is, then, as if each member of the family were treated like a separate caste to be governed only by its own rules and yet could not help feeling that family membership should imply a uniformity of status and responsibility, in the absence of which jealousy, suspicion and latent hostility arise. A similar sense of mistrust seems not only to influence the government's attitude toward groups but to affect the internal relations of the groups themselves. For example, bureaucrats feel that business groups cannot be trusted. "Our businessmen have no self-restraints".[10] Yet, even within relatively homogeneous groups there is no mutual confidence. As one observer put it, "it is not that Indian businessmen do not want to cooperate, but they feel that they cannot trust the other guy." Businessmen may get together and, so long as they are actually together, agree on a particular course of action, as, for instance, to refrain from purchasing an agricultural raw material like jute or cotton to prevent touching off a rapid price increase of a commodity in short supply. Yet as soon as the meeting is over it is quite likely that the participants will hurry to buy all they can through intermediaries. When such apparent inconsistencies or treacherous actions are questioned, each disavows personal responsibility. It had to be done, the argument goes, because the others could be counted on to violate the agreement. In a fragmented and compartmentalized society it is not perhaps surprising that members of different groups should regard one another with hostility or suspicion, but it is startling that such attitudes should also dominate the way in which members of the same group regard one another.

8. G. Morris Carstairs, *The Twice-Born* (Bloomington: Indiana University Press, 1961), pp. 40, 45, 47 and 158.
9. *Ibid.*, p. 58.
10. Richard P. Taub, *Bureaucrats Under Stress: Administrators and Administration in an Indian State* (Berkeley, California: University of California Press, 1969), p. 169.

Where there is such a climate of apprehension at every point of human contact, the third orientation, the Indian passion for harmony and consensus, stands out almost as a form of wish fulfillment mechanism. Distaste for conflict and commitment to harmony are fundamental to the epic literature from which the masses draw everyday inspiration and to the philosophical, intellectual and (to a lesser extent) historical norms of the Indian culture. These are the social norms stressed in development of character and the organization of life, whether in village decision-making or in the management of coalitions in the national movement.[11] Just as law and other values in other societies have been exploited as a means by which dominant groups might preserve the existing patterns of privilege and subordination, the traditional Indian values of harmony and consensus have been put to similar use. In recent years, the pressure of modern technology, economic change, and the ideas which have accompanied them have made it more difficult to justify the old ways, yet they are still reflected in the decision-making styles of some Indian leaders. Lal Bahadur Shastri relied on a consensual decision-making style during his brief tenure as prime minister.[12] Mrs. Gandhi's refusal to pay lip service to the ideal of consensus which even Jawaharlal Nehru at the height of his power and influence might manipulate but never impugn, contributed more than a little to the circumstances that led to a rupture in the Congress. Inherent in the concern with harmony is a reluctance to use power openly or for obvious personal gain.[13] This customary tacit agreement to subordinate or at least ignore differences so as to create a harmonious united front also results in a tendency to view interest groups which flaunt their differences and pursue particularistic demands as potentially disruptive and thus lacking in legitimacy.

The fragmentation of Indian society into suspicious isolates together with its regard for the avoidance of open conflict explains much of the emphasis Indians place on the role of the arbitrator and the peacemaker. The role of the peacemaker is to intervene in disputes and to urge self-control and compromise. "So constantly is the intervention of a third party associated with quarrels," says Carstairs, "that it occurs also in dreams."[14] One of the factors which played an important

---

11. Susanne Hoeber Rudolph, "Consensus and Conflict in Indian Politics," *World Politics* 13 (April 1961): 385-399.

12. Michael Brecher, *Nehru's Mantle: The Politics of Succession in India* (New York: Frederick A. Praeger, 1966), pp. 92-137.

13. For a discussion of the anti-power orientation of Indian politics see Myron Weiner, *Party Politics in India* (Princeton: Princeton University Press, 1957), pp. 254-258; and Myron Weiner "Struggle Against Power" *World Politics* 8, 3 (April, 1956): 392-403; Kennedy, pp. 16-18.

14. Carstairs, p. 47.

role in maintaining Congress party cohesion despite its incorporation of such a diversity of interests was the ability of the party to develop arbitrators who could help keep factional quarrels within the party under control. The loss, by death of some of the more highly regarded, most trustworthy of these arbitrators, was a key factor in the Congress party split.[15] Since to rise above suspicion and to gain the esteem of members of opposing groups is no easy matter in India, these pivotal individuals are difficult to replace. With the increasing tendency to accept a clash of ideas as a legitimate mode of resolving differences, moreover, few individuals are likely to aspire to such status.

A fourth orientation underlying characteristic Indian behavior is a hyper-rationality which leads to a form of optimism based on logical sequences. Decision-makers believe decisions should be based on rational calculation and public interest and turn a deaf ear to the groups directly concerned. They become so unresponsive that groups resort to direct action and violence to press their claims. This hyper-rationality also leads to a focus on ideological discourse and to a concern with form rather than substance of the sort that has been noticed in the Indian five year plans. "No one reading the plans can fail to be impressed by the frequent unrealism of these assumptions," observes Hanson. "So much appears to be contingent upon the realization of the unrealizable. . . ." Admitting that "the sources of this unrealism are complex" he finds it significant "that many of the plan formulators are ideologues in whose minds a variety of Western-derived theories, all too often divorced from Indian reality, jostle for predominance."[16]

Among the ideologies which have made the greatest impact on the modern day descendants of the great Indian system-rulers, or the politicians, are socialism, communism and Gandhianism. The appeal of socialism is particularly strong among the urban educated elites responsible for drawing up and administering the plans. As John Kenneth Galbraith once remarked when discussing the problems of the public sector in India, "above all it is the Socialists who are responsible for the paralyzing belief that success is a matter of faith, not works."[17] The predisposition for drawing up but not bringing to fruition these elaborate schemes for economic salvation, when combined with the pervasive sense of distrust and the emphasis on motives, leads to charges that failures or malfunctions spring not from deficiencies in

15. Stanley A. Kochanek, *The Congress Party of India: The Dynamics of One-Party Democracy* (Princeton, N.J.: Princeton University Press, 1968), pp. 251-259, 275, 286; Myron Weiner, *Party Building in a New Nation* (Chicago, Illinois: University of Chicago Press, 1967), pp. 476-480.
16. A. H. Hanson, *The Process of Planning: A Study of India's Five-Year Plans,* 1950-1964 (London: Oxford University Press, 1966), p. 258.
17. Quoted in Kennedy, p. 15.

the planning process but from public sellouts by bribed officialdom. No group is more frequently charged with such peccancies than organized business interests.

A fifth value is the strong faith in the efficacy of norms embodied in codes of conduct and law. As one cynical former Indian Civil Service official put it, "In India, if you cannot solve a problem, then you pass a law. There is a belief that legislation can do more than it really can."[18] The result is that legislators keep adding to the fund of legislation even when the existing legislation has not been implemented. Merely passing laws, as a substitute for grappling with the problems has, in turn, reinforced the feeling that there is a gap between expectation and reality which can only be explained by the unreliability or chicanery of others. This gap, Kothari argues, is "filled by pious declarations, a continuous flow of new ideas which were never implemented, and a snobbish attitude on the part of the planners and the administrators who shifted the blame to low motivation of farmers and the rural people."[19] And yet, the faith in law and codification may also be seen as the desire to embody the rational, to eliminate the differential and the arbitrary to which the uncodified is susceptible and so to achieve a system that operates openly and fair-handedly for all who must live by it, no matter who administers it. The rule of law is the orchestration of social harmony, the contract that cannot be broken.

A sixth tendency among Indians is the disposition to judge people's achievements by their motives rather than by their actions. Similarly, the good society must be built by "a spirit of self-sacrifice" and not as a result of motives like enlightened self-interest. Organizations are judged by the character of their members and leaders and by their personal motives more than by their program, which after all may be a masterpiece of deception. Ever since Gandhi, politicians have become a new priesthood. It is expected that the politician must be above all a moral man.[20] Together, according to Weiner, "these prejudices strengthen the elite's distaste for the profit motive and the private sector and attract it to socialist ideals."[21] When political leaders apply for party tickets they tend to stress the sacrifices they have made, their exemplary character, and their previous service to the nation rather than

18. This same point is made in Kennedy, pp. 14-15.
19. Kothari, p. 149.
20. Joseph R. Gusfield, "Political Community and Group Interests in Modern India," *Pacific Affairs* 38 (Summer, 1965): 137, 139-141; W. H. Morris-Jones, *The Government and Politics of India* (London: Hutchinson University Library, 1964), pp. 52-61.
21. Myron Weiner, "India's Two Political Cultures" in *Political Change in South Asia* (Calcutta: Firma K. L. Mukhopadhyay, 1963), p. 142.

the experience, education, and position on current issues that would be a factor in other systems.[22]

If the politician like the arbitrator is the disinterested, even-handed father one never had and is always searching for, the socialist ideal seems to promise an end to the conflict, hierarchical privilege, and mistrust that socioeconomic systems based on competition and self-interest can only intensify. Thus, there is a tendency in India to be concerned with the distribution rather than the creation of wealth. Factional struggles within the Congress party, for instance, have been oriented more toward controlling the administration so as to distribute rewards in a slightly different way than toward disputes over means of providing policy initiatives to step up the pace of growth. "Equality," says Weiner, "has also been a cardinal principle of the national leadership and where this principle has run into conflict with the goal of maximizing the nation's wealth, the latter has often been submerged."[23] Yet, their predisposition would seem to make sense in a society which is not habituated to an annual increase in the gross national product. At this point the reality principle seems to be operating; while there may be no more to distribute, the proper plan and the proper motives may redistribute what already exists, thus providing the just economic basis of the ideal society.

To the extent that these closely interrelated orientations are shared by the political leadership and the masses of the Indian society, they have an important effect on both the form and content of decisions and the behavior of groups in the society.

Groups and Interest Articulation

Groups, like all structures in society, are multi-functional. They affect the nature of the political culture in a variety of ways. Patterns of group identity, mobilization and politicization tend to raise levels of political consciousness and participation. They also have a critical impact on the patterning of group cleavages and conflict within the society and they serve as critical agents of social integration and channels of communication between the individual and the state. Perhaps the primary function of groups, however, is to serve as mechanisms for the articulation of demands and the pressing of group claims on the political system.

The role and effectiveness of groups in the process of articulating group demands is dependnt upon the limits set by the larger political system on group activity and to a lesser extent by the attributes and

22. Kochanek, *The Congress Party*, pp. 272-273.
23. Weiner, *Two Cultures*, pp. 144-145.

capabilities of the particular group itself. Despite the rapid increase in the number of groups in India since 1947, the articulation of demands by organized groups is still in its early phase of development and vast sectors of Indian society remain unorganized. Organized groups have thus been slow to develop, are characterized by low levels of group mobilization, are organizationally weak and poorly institutionalized, and with few exceptions are closely linked to political parties and thus lack functional autonomy. Most mass organizations in India, including the trade unions, student organizations, women's organizations, and peasants, were first mobilized by the leaders of the nationalist movement and continue to be closely allied with political parties. They serve, therefore, more as agents of mobilization than as articulators of group demands.

The difficulties faced by groups in maximizing their capabilities are reinforced by the limitations of the environment within which groups in India must function. The articulation of group demands is still viewed with suspicion and distrust by the society at large as well as by Indian decision-makers. The political culture has tended to find interest-group activity lacking in legitimacy. The nationalist leadership consciously resisted pressures from primordial groups as threats to Indian unity, and pressures from groups in the modern sector were considered to be equally devisive demands from small but highly organized vested interests. The bureaucracy, fresh from a colonial tradition built on the role of the rational and efficient but paternalistic administrator, was not supposed to be influenced by the extraneous political pressures of the society. Since decision-making in India has tended to be highly concentrated in precisely these hands, the nationalist elite and the higher echelons of the bureaucracy where these views are strongest, groups have had a difficult time gaining acceptance in policy-making circles. Altogether then, the patterns of interest articulation and the nature of the groups performing the interest articulation function in India have been heavily conditioned by the resiliency of the traditional social order, the patterns of modernization, the structure of colonial rule and the special character of the nationalist movement. The result has been a highly diverse system of structures of interest articulation exhibiting varying degrees of organizational capabilities.

Since the course of modernization in India has so far resulted in only a partial differentiation of society, India exhibits two basic patterns of interest articulation. The first pattern is represented by the variety of modern voluntary associations which have emerged among the small but important sectors of the urban middle class and industrial proletariat. The urban middle class represents about 6.5 million households or ten percent of the total population and consists of leading businessmen, bureaucrats, intellectuals, clerks, minor government officials, school teachers, journalists, professionals, and petty shopkeepers organized into a variety of associations. The urban proletariat consists of about 15 million workers of whom about one-third are organized. While both the urban middle class and the industrial proletariat still manifest dimensions of caste, communal, family, and other primordial loyalties in the operations of their associations, they are among the most highly organized groups in the society.[24]

The seventy percent of the rural population which constitute the mass of the Indian peasantry remain socially fragmented along caste lines within which, as the previous section indicates, class differences are only slowly beginning to emerge. By and large, social change and the politics of mass franchise have tended to strengthen rather than diminish the role of community interests by encouraging a proliferation of community associations and ethnic interest groups since independence. The result has been that the most potent interest articulators have not been the social and economic forces in the modern sector but the particularisms of their still pervasive community, caste, language, and regional antecedents functioning through a variety of loosely organized non-associational groups.

In addition to groups representing basic economic and social formations in Indian society, the colonial heritage with its centralized system of decision-making has given rise to the institutionalizing of interests among the most influential interest articulators in the country who are situated within the structure of the government of India. Most major decisions in India involve a complex interaction of institutional interests consisting of the actions of agencies within the government of India. Thus, there is a balancing of interests among the Planning Commission, the Reserve Bank, the Finance Ministry, the Commerce Ministry, and other ministries of the government of India, each reacting to imperatives emanating from mission-biased perceptions as well as to party pressures generated both in and out of Parliament.

Supplementing and at times supplanting relatively organized demands of associational, non-associational and institutional interests are the demands which emanate from the variety of anomic disturbances in the agitational politics of protest which have become an established characteristic of the Indian scene, partly reflecting the low level of organized demands and partly reflecting a style of action inherited from the nationalist movement. The techniques of civil disobedience developed by Gandhi and the nationalist movement have become an established part of the Indian political scene: processions,

24. See Myron Weiner, *The Politics of Scarcity* (Chicago, Illinois: University of Chicago Press, 1962).

protest meetings, hartals, strikes, political fasts, non-violent obstruction, the courting of arrest, and rioting. Individuals, groups and parties feel that the judicious use of agitation, including selective defiance
of the law, is an essential element in backing almost any group demand on the political system. Though many agitations begin as almost ritualistic exhibitions of strength, they turn into violent confrontations leading to loss of life and damage to both private and especially
public property. Moreover, the level of public protest in India is at
times so high that it is difficult for decision-makers to distinguish between expressions of timely, important demands and outburts of peripheral or ephemeral demands.[25] In either case, moreover, the aura of
martyrdom resulting from offering satyagraha still provides status to
those who engage in it on behalf of nearly any group cause.

Among the major organized modern associational interests in India
which must be taken into account are business, labor, and the kisans or
peasants.

Business

Just as British educational policy led to the emergence of a new urban
middle class professional and political elite, the impact of British trade
and commerce and the beginnings of industrialization in the mid-
nineteenth century led to the development of both a foreign and indigenous entrepreneurial elite. It was the new entrepreneurial elite,
both British and Indian, which was responsible for the creation of
modern trade and industry associations in the nineteenth century.

The historical development, diversity, and heterogeneity of the business community in India have so shaped the patterns of mobilization,
leadership and institutionalization of modern business associations in
India that their present configurations and their orientation toward
government can only be explained in terms of these origins. Business
associations in India exhibit a number of distinctive characteristics.[26]

In the first place, two parallel systems of apex business associations
grew up in India: The Federation of Indian Chambers of Commerce
and Industry (F.I.C.C.I.) and the Associated Chambers of Commerce
and Industry (Assocham) which traditionally, though no longer, reflected the conflicting interests of indigenous and foreign capital respectively. Modern business associations developed first among the
European merchants of the port cities of Calcutta, Bombay, and Madras in the early nineteenth century. By the end of the century parallel

25. David H. Bayley, *The Police and Political Development in India* (Princeton, N.J.: Princeton University Press, 1969), pp. 248-279.
26. See Stanley A. Kochanek, *Business and Politics in India* (Berkeley, California: University of California Press, 1974).

associations of Indian businessmen had emerged. Each of these loose networks or regional associations federated after World War I. A second point to bear in mind is that although the pattern of organization of both resulting apex structures was federal, reflecting years of uneven economic development in India leading early to the founding of the original regional organizations in Calcutta and Bombay, the representation within each of Calcutta and Bombay interests continues to overshadow in ability, experience, numbers, and financial backing the representation of all other areas. As a result, the larger regional associations in Bombay and Calcutta have come to play a disproportionate role in the control and decision-making of the apex associations.

Thirdly, unlike the business associations in most countries, the major apex organizations in India combine both industrial and trade interests within a single organization. Because business associations in India antedate the introduction of industry, they retain elements of their origins as chambers of commerce. Just as it was the distinctive nature of the managing agency system in India for the various managing agency houses to provide common administrative and financial service to the firms it controlled, the existing chambers tended to provide common services to newly formed industrial associations. As a result, the old chambers of commerce were transformed into chambers of commerce and industry, creating a unitary system in dramatic contrast to the separate structures existing in most other countries. The combination of these interests under the same roof, though a potential source of great strength, has rather more often raised serious problems of maintaining cohesion, especially in the larger and more diverse F.I.C.C.I.

Fourthly, even in any one major commercial and industrial center of India a multiplicity of chambers exist where in other countries one would suffice. This fragmentation reflects the historic split between indigenous and foreign capital, the partial differentiation of the Indian business community and the survival among those with common economic interests of traditional social divisions of caste, community, family, language and regional loyalties. By weakening group solidarity, these loyalties tend to prevent the emergence of a united business class. They also play an important role in the internal politics and organization of Indian chambers where they are a major cause of factional conflict. As a result, Indian business lacks the degree of unity exhibited by British business associations.

Another distinctive aspect of Indian business associations arises from the fact that the dominant leadership role in both the F.I.C.C.I. and Assocham is performed by the executives, officers, and directors of the older managing agency houses. These houses also contribute the bulk of the resources. Those who provide leadership and funds are likely to control the organization.

Finally, compared to those in many other countries, business associations in India developed a more intense political orientation and tended to be less concerned with performing other functions. Indian business associations came to put primary stress on the political element for several reasons. During the early colonial period they were one of the few non-official bodies in existence and thus, they were uniquely able to express independent views. Later, furthermore, business organizations were given functional representation in the colonial legislatures. The termination after independence of functional representation, the lack of a business party to fill the gap, and the under-representation of business and businessmen in Parliament made business associations the only viable means for business interests to formulate positions on public policy and articulate its demands. Finally, the difference in origins and in original orientation toward government of the F.I.C.C.I. and Assocham has had a major effect on their style. Though often critical of the British colonial government, the leaders of Assocham preferred to work through a system of quiet diplomacy in close contact with their countrymen. The preference for quiet diplomacy survives. By contrast, the chambers of indigenous businessmen, like the nationalist movement itself, developed a highly vocal and critical style which is employed to this day. While the importance of caste and community may be declining, its effect on the organizational behavior of the business community still cannot be ignored. Not only do divisions between indigenous and foreign capital persist in post independence India, but family, caste, region, and language continue to play a role in business politics. In addition, the more managerially oriented British, Parsi and Gujarati firms disagree fundamentally with the family dominated Marwari groups over such critical issues as business ethics, strategies of dealing with government and political philosophy.

In many ways, however, the character of business associations in India underwent considerable alteration under the impact of changes in the Indian political system after independence. The emergence of Congress dominance, the centralization of decision-making in the hands of the cabinet and bureaucracy, and the development of a government policy emphasizing planning, rapid industrialization, a mixed economy, protectionism, regulation and control and restrictions in regional disparities resulted in major changes in patterns of interest articulation in India which affected business as well as other interest groups in the society.

Though the bulk of the business community remains unorganized, business has made major strides in the last twenty years in mobilizing its potential resources for sustained collective action. Interest articulation is moving from a highly personal system of elite representation to the use of more specialized structures like chambers of commerce, trade and industry associations and employers' associations. The difficulties of mobilization arising from the diversity and heterogeneity of the business community itself have had a significant impact on the nature of business organizations, their leadership and the pattern of cohesion and conflict within the organized sector. Many of the peculiar features of the pre-independence period which were a product of unique Indian conditions therefore continue to play an important role in the developing and functioning of the major business associations.

Although the distinctions between Assocham and the F.I.C.C.I. are beginning to blur as a result of Indianization of Assocham membership and increasing overlapping membership between the two, and although foreign and indigenous capital are drawing closer and closer together in other ways, the separate organizational structures persist and the two associations differ from each other in several ways. In the first place, Assocham through its constituent chambers represents 2,500 large public companies staffed by professional managers and employing about 2 million workers. The F.I.C.C.I., by contrast, is both larger and more varied in the type of interests it represents. Through its many member bodies the F.I.C.C.I. represents 100,000 business firms employing over 5 million workers, including both medium and large scale industry as well as retail trade. The politics of the F.I.C.C.I., moreover, is dominated by large family firms which, though they may employ professional managers, retain the final decision-making power within the family. Secondly, the organization of Assocham is much simpler and in theory more federal in character than that of the F.I.C.C.I. Thirdly, Assocham's style is one of "quiet diplomacy" which focuses attention on the higher echelons of the bureaucracy and the ministries. Publicity is shunned and generally there is no attempt to lobby in Parliament. Unlike Assocham, with its defensive, unobtrusive, non-agitational approach, the F.I.C.C.I. is at times publicly critical of government. It also functions at all levels of access, including lobbying in Parliament and financing political parties. The F.I.C.C.I. also has a vigorous public relations program. Finally, Assocham tends to focus on issues which are of particular interest to foreign business, whereas the F.I.C.C.I. takes a stand on almost all issues.

Trade Unions

The trade unions representing the working class in India are small, weak, and highly politicized.[27] Modern industry in India developed in the 1850s and 1860s, but for the first 60 years industry was confined to

27. See Harold Crouch, *Trade Unions and Politics in India* (Bombay: Manaktalas, 1966).

railroads, jute and cotton textiles, mining and plantations. By World War I, there were about 600,000 railway workers, 200,000 jute mill workers, 260,000 cotton textile workers, 150,000 workers in mining, and 700,000 in plantations, but real diversification of the industrial work force did not take place until World War II. As might be expected the first trade unions were organized in the cotton, jute, and railway industries. Mining and plantation workers were much harder to organize.

By 1961, the industrial work force in India was still relatively small. In a national population of 439 million the industrial work force in India in 1961 totaled about 15 million of whom about 9 to 10 million were employed in the large scale modern sector. Yet though the industrial proletariat of India is small, it occupies an extremely strategic position in the economy. These workers produce a significant proportion of the gross national produce, they play a key role in heavy industry, and they dominate the export industry. Thus, they are a force that cannot be ignored despite their relatively small size compared to the rest of the work force.

Many characteristics of the Indian working class have made it difficult to organize. The working class in India is still unstable and somewhat uncommitted. Not only is there a lack of discipline, with employee absenteeism and turnover at high levels, but many workers are illiterate. They also belong to communities which are quite different from management. Though desperately poor by world standards, the economic conditions of Indian labor are still superior to that of the rest of the masses, especially the rural poor. This relative prosperity tends to weaken labor's ability to gain widespread public sympathy. Finally, as a result of sustained mass unemployment, there exists a vast reservoir of potential labor which not only makes it difficult to organize the still unorganized segments of labor but acts to weaken the negotiating position of the already organized sector of the working class.

As a result of these weaknesses, the proportion of the working class that is organized is still relatively small. In 1960-61 it was estimated that only 4 to 5 million workers were organized. The level of organization, in addition, continues to vary from industry to industry. The most highly organized industries are iron and steel, cotton textiles, railways, and manufacturing industries. Yet even the small proportion of the working class which is organized are not united so much as divided into 6,040 unions of which 4,913 have a membership of less than 500. The remaining 1000 unions have 82 percent of the total membership. One major result of this fragmentation is a high level of inter-union conflict among the multiplicity of unions in each factory. While this competition tends to increase worker mobilization, it also works to reduce the quality of trade union effort because of fragmentation and competition.

In addition, though trade unions in India are extremely vocal, they are badly financed and poorly organized. They have very small office staffs and little internal cohesion. The working class in India is still characterized by a low level of proletarianization of membership who continue to identify with village structures, caste, and linguistic or religious community, all of which combine to reduce working-class solidarity. Whatever cohesion does exist is heavily dependent upon leadership. If there exists a strong bond of trust and loyalty between the leadership and the membership, then cohesion is maintained. However, it is maintained at the price of strong oligarchical control with the result that when dissatisfaction with leadership does develop it takes the form of a split and the resulting creation of a new union. Thus, the trade union movement in India has been organizationally weak, fragmented and lacking in cohesion and economic strength.

Trade unions and trade union leadership in India are highly politicized. Almost from the very beginning, the working class was not mobilized by its own leaders but by the professional urban middle class, which sought to enlist labor as part of the nationalist movement's effort to weaken the British hold on India and gain political independence. As a result, the working class was unable to develop the autonomous structures that would permit them to work independently of the parent political organization which was the Indian National Congress. The tradition of mobilization by outsiders which results in political unionism has continued into the post-independence period as labor continues to be mobilized by the leadership of political parties for purposes of electoral support rather than by working class leaders themselves as mechanisms for the articulation of specialized demands of the urban proletariat. The continued political role of trade unions also reflects the fact that union demands for better working conditions and higher wages are less frequently determined by management than by government which plays a major role in labor-management relations. Thus awards by government arbitration tribunals play a much greater role than the almost non-existent system of collective bargaining.

Most of the trade unions in India today started out under the umbrella of the All-India Trade Union Congress (AITUC), which was founded in 1920. The AITUC was subsequently captured by the communists, but by the time of independence it had splintered into a series of All-India federations, each aligned with one of the national political parties.

The three major national trade union federations in India today are the AITUC, which is controlled by the Communist Party of India, the Indian National Trade Union Congress (INTUC), which is Congress dominated, and the Hind Mazdoor Sabha (HMS), which is controlled by the Socialist party. Of the three the largest is INTUC, which has about 1.4 million members. Its relation to Congress is both a strength and a weakness. Congress has attempted to use its labor influence to prevent disruption of production by discouraging strikes and encouraging compulsory arbitration. At the same time, given the small size of the working class and its correspondingly weak electoral position, INTUC has succeeded in gaining extraordinary access to the highest levels of decision-making through the placement of its leaders in the Indian cabinet. Many INTUC leaders like V. V. Giri, currently the President of India, Khandubhai Desai and G. L. Nanda have served as labor ministers in the government of India where they played an important role in shaping Indian labor policy.

Agrarian Movements

The Indian peasantry which makes up about seventy percent of the Indian population continues to be dominated by localistic traditions. It functions in a segmented social system dominated by caste. Now, as in the past, power in the villages and small towns rests in the hands of the landlords, the small traders and the petty officials who wield the economic and political power of any one area. Since influence on this level was personal and local, there was traditionally little need for organization. Yet, since the masses among the peasantry tended to remain unorganized, they were just so much less able to formulate and articulate their demands so as to influence local power centers.[28] During the nationalist movement, the Congress leadership attempted to mobilize the peasantry from time to time but with mixed success. The left wing of the Congress in 1936 brought together a series of local peasant organizations to form an All-India Kisan Sabha as a way of pressing the Congress to commit itself to a strong program of land reforms. But since the Kisan Sabhas, like the trade unions, eventually became instruments of political mobilization used by political parties for electoral support, they had a limited impact on the structure of political power in the rural areas.[29]

Each of the major political parties has an adjunct peasant organization. The All-India Kisan Sabha eventually fell under the control of the communists, and the Kisan Sabhas have remained an instrument of the orthodox Communist Party of India. But until recently the organizations of the peasantry had made little progress in overcoming the traditional rural patterns. The green revolution, however, has begun to alter the old rural relationships drastically and the consequent growing polarization of the countryside has resulted in intense compe-

28. Weiner, *Politics of Scarcity*, pp. 12-17.
29. *Ibid.*, pp. 22-23.

tition among political parties in India to translate this localized discontent into political action. Among the most successful in mobilizing rural discontent has been the Naxalbari movement, a pro-Maoist revolutionary movement which developed in the state of West Bengal in 1967 and spread rapidly to the impoverished regions of Bihar, Orissa, Andhra, and Kerala. At its height the movement contained as many as 10,000 activists and attracted support from the frustrated youth and economically oppressed middle class in the urban areas as well as from the 80 million landless peasants of the countryside. The movement began to decline by the early 1970s for several reasons. Strong police measures resulted in the arrest of large numbers of Naxalite activists and their leaders, some of whom subsequently died, and the government of Mrs. Gandhi reduced the Naxalite appeal by at least temporily credible promises of social and agrarian reform. The creation of Bangladesh has also played a major role. Under Pakistani control East Bengal had served as a sanctuary for fugitive Naxalites and as a pipeline for arms supplies from Peking. The Indian role in the creation of Bangladesh, however, not only brought into being a government friendly to India but also increased the popularity of Mrs. Gandhi's Congress among the disaffected youth of Bengal who deserted the Naxalites to join the Congress. Their disillusionment was compounded by the Chinese support of Pakistan during the Bangladesh struggle. Thus, the Naxalite movement has lost both its leaders and its popularity. Unless the promised reforms are forthcoming, however, one would expect a resurgence of similar kinds of agrarian protest.

The power to enact land reform legislation in the Indian federal system, however, is in the hands of the state governments. Because state Congress leaders are heavily dependent upon the electoral support they receive from large and medium sized landowners, they have been much less enthusiastic about pressing for sweeping land reforms then has been the national leadership. Thus, Mrs. Gandhi's proposals tend to become diluted at the state level despite her preeminent position as leader of both the Congress party and the government of India.

In their most recent development, then, as in their previous history, interest 'groups in India have been molded by systemic factors into forms that are peculiarly adapted to the larger culture. The pattern of modernization and group mobilization, the strength and configuration of traditional antecedent loyalties, the development of strong institutional interests within the decision-making systems, and the degree of government intervention in social and economic affairs have combined to produce interest groups that are relatively weak. And yet, patterns of demographic change arising from urbanization, industrialization and colonization combined with the government's need to achieve consensus and support for public policy has led to the infusion of group demands in the policy process.

Modern voluntary associations in India have remained largely ineffectual for one or more reasons. Firstly, such organizations in India mostly grew out of the nationalist movement. Politicized today as then, they continue to lack autonomy and serve as agents of mobilization more than as structures of interest articulation. Secondly, the most potent interest articulators, even in post-independence India, have been the caste, community, language, and regional antecedents of modern associations. These persistent primordial loyalties tended to fragment membership and thus destroyed the ability of groups in the modern sector to formulate interests based on the needs which provided the impetus for their organization. In India, therefore, the strongest demands on government have originated with ethnic and cultural groups rather than with economic or class interests. Thirdly, though some modern associations have achieved a fairly representative membership, the powerful role of family, caste, and kinship structures within them has impeded the development of modern functional interests and organizational cohesion. Fourthly, the development of a strong bureaucracy imbued with a sense of independence, composed of members recruited for their ability to define the national interest and formulate policy in a rational way, has strengthened the position of institutional as opposed to associational interests in India. Finally, government intervention in all sectors of society has been so comprehensive and so overwhelming that fear of alienating government no less than over-regulation has placed limits on group activity.

Although obstacles to achieving a cohesive and effective collectivity have systematically inhibited the development of modern associations in India, the infrastructure for the development of autonomous structures of interest articulation has already come into being. Indian business has proceeded faster than any of the other interests in the modern sector. If business can so organize in India, it is not impossible that other interests will also in time be able to do so.

The structures of interest articulation reflect the ability of social and economic formations in the society to mobilize their potential resources, skills and membership. The process of pressing claims on the political system however, is dependent upon the nature of the party system and the structure of decision-making to which we now turn.

The Party System

Perhaps one of the most significant features of the Indian political system has been the resilience of the ruling Congress party. Since independence, except for a short interlude between 1967 and 1971, India has had a one-party dominant system in which the Congress enjoyed massive majorities in the national legislature and also controlled almost all of the state governments through its large majorities in the state legislatures. Congress dominance has rested on a variety of factors which go far beyond its legacy as the nationalist movement. Congress success has been based on strong leadership, a long history marked by a high level of institutionalization, an ability to manage internal conflict generated by competing demands, an integrative political style, and an ability to pre-empt the middle ground of the Indian political spectrum, which is reformist and slightly left of center. Congress support is widely based and although Congress is strong in almost all sectors of Indian society, it is especially strong in the smaller towns and rural constituencies, among the age group over 35, and among the middle and lower castes and less well educated.[30] It is weaker in the urban areas and among the more highly educated which partly reflects the alienation of the urban intellectuals and urban elites from the increasingly rural-based party.

The massive majorities which Congress has enjoyed in the national and state legislatures has never been matched by similar strength at the polls. The opposition in India has, in fact, been quite strong at the ballot box, and the total votes received by all the opposition parties has always exceeded that of the Congress. However, since the opposition has been fragmented into a multiplicity of parties, the Congress as the largest and best organized national political party has succeeded in winning the largest number of seats under the single member district plurality electoral system despite its inability to win an absolute majority of the total popular vote.

Political parties in India can be classified into national and regional parties and the national parties may in turn be given approximate location on a left-right ideological spectrum. Except for the Congress, all parties in India depend heavily on particular regional bases of support, but unlike the strictly regional parties they lay claim to being national parties and they do in practice take a national perspective on major issues. The regional parties, on the other hand, have been primarily concerned with exploiting local sources of discontent or pressing a variety of primordial demands based on language, caste, community, or region. Table I.1 indicates that regional parties and independent candidates have received roughly 22 to 27 percent of the vote since 1957. Among the most persistent and successful of the regional protest movements have been the Dravida Munnetra Kazhagam (D.M.K.) in Tamil Nadu and the Akali Dal in Punjab. The D.M.K.

30. Samuel J. Eldersveld "Elections and the Party System: Patterns of Party Regularity and Defection in 1967," *Asian Survey* 10 (November 1970): 1018-1020.

Table II.1

**Percent of Votes Polled by Major Parties in
India for Lok Sabha Elections 1952 to 1971**

Party	1952	1957	1962	1967	1971
Congress	44.99	47.78	44.73	40.73	43.70
Old Congress	—	—	—	—	10.50
Swatantra	—	—	7.89	8.68	3.10
Jana Sangh	3.06	5.93	6.44	9.41	7.40
CPI	3.29	8.92	9.94	5.19	4.80
CPI (M)	—	—	—	4.21	5.20
P.S.P.	—	10.41	6.81	3.06	1.10
SSP	—	—	—	4.92	2.40
Other & Ind.	48.66	26.96	24.19	23.80	21.80
	100.00	100.00	100.00	100.00	100.00

had its origin in the anti-Brahmin movement in the south prior to independence and has since become a champion of linguistic and regional demands which have taken the form of demands for greater autonomy within the Indian union. The Akali Dal has represented the interest of the Sikhs, a distinctive and militant religious minority located primarily in the Punjab.

The national political parties occupy the right and left of the ideological spectrum to either side of the centrist Congress. The three major political parties to the right of the Congress are the Swatantra party, the Bharitiya Jana Sangh, and the old Congress. The Swatantra party represents a mixture of former princes, sectors of India's modern industrial elite, and segments of the rich peasantry. While the party claims to stand for secularism, nationalism, and classical economic liberalism, the nature of its support base and its regional electoral strength tend to give the party a more traditional image as the representative of feudal princes and capitalists. The Swatantra party succeeded in winning 7-8 percent of the votes in the 1962 and 1967 elections but was reduced to a regional rump in 1971 when it was swamped by the Indira wave. Reduced to only 3 percent of the vote, Swatantra saw its representation in Parliament, as indicated in Table II.2, drop from 44 seats to 8.

The Jana Sangh is a militant Hindu nationalist party which has been classified as rightest more because of its stand on communal issues than because of its economic policies, which remain vague and poorly articulated. The Jana Sangh attracts its major support from the lower-middle class of the cities and small towns of the Hindi speaking areas of north India. From 1952 until 1971, the Jana Sangh had slowly been increasing its popular support from 3 percent in 1952 to 9.41 percent in 1967. Like the Swatantra party, it suffered a setback in the 1971 elections when, for the first time since independence, its vote de-

Table II.2

Lok Sabha Seats Won by the Major Political Parties in India from 1952 to 1971

Party	1952	1957	1962	1967	1970*	1971
Congress**	364	371	361	283	228	350
Old Congress	—	—	—	—	65	18
Swatantra	—	—	18	44	35	8
Jana Sangh	3	3	14	35	33	22
CPI	16	27	29	23	24	24
CPI (M)	—	—	—	19	19	25
P.S.P.	—	19	12	13	15	2
S.S.P.	—	—	—	23	17	3
Other & Ind.	106	73	60	80	79	65
	489	494	494	520	515	518

*This column represents the number of seats held by each Party following the split in the Congress.

**Mrs. Gandhi's New Congress is represented here as the mainstream of the Congress and therefore the figures for 1970 and 1971 are the seats held by the New Congress.

clined to 7.4 percent and its representation in Parliament dropped from 35 seats to 22. Some of the votes of the traditional right may have gone to the old Congress which split off from the parent body in 1969 and received 10.5 percent of the votes in the 1971 election.

To the left of the Congress stand two groupings of parties which constitute the communist and non-communist Left in India. The non-communist Left consists of the Samyukta Socialist Party (S.S.P.) and the Praja Socialist Party (P.S.P.). Both parties have merged and split several times over the past decades reflecting the divergent socialist perspectives which have existed within their ranks and which include Gandhian socialism, Marxist socialism, and democratic socialism of the British Labor Party variety. In addition to its endemic splintering, the non-Communist Left has also tended to get squeezed out as the Congress moved to occupy the left of center position of the Indian ideological spectrum with the adoption of the Avadi resolution in 1956 which committed the Congress to work for a socialist pattern of society. The S.S.P. has fared slightly better than the P.S.P. because of its more militant policy and tactics and its strong anti-English pro-Hindi policies which have won its support in the Hindi heartland states of the north. The total vote of the non-communist Left had declined from a high of 10 percent in 1957 to a low of 3.5 percent in 1971. Its representation in Parliament dropped from 33 seats in 1967 to 5 seats in 1971, as many members of the P.S.P. joined the ranks of the New Congress led by Mrs. Gandhi.

The communist movement in India has fragmented into three separate parties: the Communist Party of India (CPI), the Communist Party of India (Marxist) and the Communist Party of India (Marxist-Leninist). The CPI was founded in 1924-25 and even before the splintering began, the party was one of the least disciplined, most faction ridden communist parties in the world. The party was divided over the methods of struggle in the conquest of power, could not agree on the immediate objectives, and even fell out on deciding which classes were to be permitted to cooperate with the CPI. The Right, viewing imperialism and feudalism as communism's major enemies, called for a united front from above by which was meant an alliance with labor, certain bourgeois groups and anti-imperialist parties. The Left, to whom capitalism and the bourgeoisie were implacable enemies, called for a united front from below by which they meant an alliance with workers, peasants, and petty bourgeoisie. The Maoists considered imperialism and feudalism as the major enemies, as did the Right, but argued that the response should be a united front from below and not a united front from above. The CPI followed the leftist tactics during the 1947-1951 period, a strategy which brought the party into open conflict with the Congress government. In order to participate in the 1951 Indian election the party changed its tactics and declared that the CPI would confine its actions to those of a legal opposition party. It would seek to gain power through the ballot box. Tensions within the party continued to grow as a result of events in India and abroad during the late 1950s. After 1959, the stresses resulting from the Sino-Soviet dispute, the Sino-Indian border dispute and the policies of the Congress government combined to split the party wide open. Finally, in July 1964, the left wing broke off from the pro-Soviet CPI to form the CPI (Marxist) henceforth known as CPI (M). Later the left wing of the CPI (M) split off to form the CPI (Marxist-Leninist) referred to as CPI (M-L) or Naxalites. Although the pro-Soviet group retained control of the parent-party organization, the CPI (M) was strongest in those states where the party had the largest number of supporters—Bengal, Punjab, Andhra and Kerala.

The total electoral strength of the communist parties in India has hovered around 9-10 percent for the past decade. While the CPI (M-L) has shunned electoral politics in favor of a policy of armed struggle, the CPI and the CPI (M) have been in competition with each other in their attempt to increase their support. Despite its close association with Mrs. Gandhi's New Congress, the CPI saw its percent of vote drop from 5.19 percent in 1967 to 4.8 percent in 1971, although it increased its seats in Parliament from 23 seats to 24. The CPI (M), on the other hand, increased its strength from 4.21 percent of the votes in 1967 to 5.2 percent in 1970 and increased its representation in Parliament from 19 seats to 25 seats.

The dominant position which the Congress has enjoyed since independence was seriously threatened in 1967 only to be dramatically restored four years later. Electoral support for the Congress in post-independence India reached a high of 47.78 percent in 1957 and was followed by a steady erosion of Congress support to 44.73 percent in 1962 and 40.73 percent in 1967. The 1967 elections were particularly disturbing to the Congress, for the party saw its strength in the national Parliament reduced from 361 seats to 283 while the party lost control over half of the Indian state governments. The party was rocked by a strong anti-Congress wave which swept over the country as some traditional Congress supporters defected to opposition parties or refused to vote while, at the same time, the Congress failed to attract as large a proportion of new voters into its ranks as it had in the past. Congress support declined significantly among the young, the higher castes and higher income groups, and the alienated intellectuals. This erosion of Congress support was accompanied by a strong united front of opposition parties determined to bring an end to Congress rule and a severe breakdown of the Congress party's organizational unity, which resulted in widespread factional conflict and massive defections of disgruntled Congressmen.

Although the 1967 elections administered a severe blow to the Congress, survey data indicated that the election could not be interpreted as a realigning or critical election involving a major shift in partisan commitment. Realigning elections are usually indicated by massive increases in voter involvement, major shifts in partisan loyalties, or the emergence of new cleavages which restructure partisan commitment. None of these features was present in 1967. Voter involvement was high but not exceptional and did not indicate any massive surge to the polls to oust the Congress. Nor were there any massive shifts in partisan loyalties. Defections from Congress did occur but were not abnormally high. In fact, there were indications that party loyalty may have helped stem the flow of disgruntled Congress supporters to the opposition. Moreover, although Congress did not do as well among new voters as in the past, the party was still able to attract a reasonably high level of new voter support. Finally, there were no strong indications of the emergence of new cleavages that would have a realigning impact. In short, the evidence does not support labeling the 1967 Indian election as a realigning election. Nevertheless, the election may be considered one of the most significant since independence for its substantial impact both on the Congress and on the opposition.[31]

The elections of 1967 revealed a variety of potential threats to continued Congress rule. The existence of strong anti-Congress attitudes

31. *Ibid.*, 1027-1030.

reflected increasing voter dissatisfaction with Congress policy, program, and leadership. There was a genuine impulse toward reprisal among those who felt their personal economic conditions had deteriorated, and the party's failure to attract a larger share of the newly mobilized voters and especially the younger generation, were all cause for concern.

The election not only marked a temporary halt in Congress dominance but also resulted in severe strains within the Congress itself. The party became openly divided and factionalized at the national level as Prime Minister Indira Gandhi's management of party and government affairs was challenged by a group of senior Congressmen who appeared determined to replace her as prime minister. Finally, in 1969, the party faced an open split which resulted in the creation of two Congress parties, one led by Mrs. Gandhi and the other by Morarji Desai. While both claimed the mantle of legitimacy as the true Congress, Mrs. Gandhi's New Congress succeeded in retaining the loyalty of 228 of the 283 Congress M.P.'s in the national Parliament and most of the state party organizations. The old Congress won the support of only 65 members of Parliament and a handful of state leaders. Even so the split resulted in the first minority government in post-independence history, and Mrs. Gandhi was forced to depend on the votes of several opposition parties in order to remain in office. This untenable position lasted until 1971 when Mrs. Gandhi dissolved Parliament and called for a new election.

Not only did the 1967 election create a crisis in the Congress, it also brought the Indian political system itself under severe strain. While the opposition parties proved they could, when united, bring an end to Congress dominance, they revealed themselves incapable of sustaining their unity long enough to provide stable and effective government. Opposition governments were formed in over half of the Indian states. In states such as Tamil Nadu and Orissa, where a single party or a small coalition of parties replaced the Congress, stable and effective government was provided. In states where a opportunistic coalition of a dozen or so dissimilar parties took control, the result was neither effective nor stable government. The state of Bihar, for example, experienced seven changes of government from 1967 to 1971. Each government lasted only 4.2 months.[32] In general, coalition politics at the state level turned out to be a disaster resulting in endemic defection of legislators from one party to another, huge cabinets designed to please as many legislators as possible, politicization and demoralization of the state bureaucracies, paralyzed decision-making, increased corrup-

32. Iqbal Narain "Ideology and Political Development: Battle for Issues in Indian Politics," *Asian Survey* 11 (February 1971): 189.

tion and growing popular cynicism toward politics, political parties, and the political system itself, especially among the educated elite of urban India. Thus the situation in the states, no less than the problem of a minority government at the center, led Prime Minister Indira Gandhi to dissolve the national Parliament and seek a new electoral mandate.

India entered the 1971 national elections in an atmosphere of uncertainty and fear lest the pattern of coalition politics that had developed in the states since 1967 became a regular feature of the national scene as well. This fear of continued fragmentation was intensified by pre-election developments. The number of candidates, parties and independents increased until there were five candidates for every available seat. Moreover, for the first time since independence, no all-India party existed, and there appeared to be nothing to fill the void. Neither Mrs. Gandhi's New Congress nor the Grand Coalition of the old Congress, Jana Sangh, Swatantra, and SSP, was capable of placing candidates in every constituency.

At the same time, the 1971 elections were unique in that Prime Minister Indira Gandhi had decided to sever the national parliamentary election from the state assembly elections which were not scheduled until 1972. Her objective was to conduct a campaign that would be issue-oriented and free from the parochial pressures characterizing state elections. This strategy became known as the new politics. The new politics was based on leadership, ideology, and program rather than on traditional vote banks and dependencies. So right had Mrs. Gandhi been in her calculation that the 1971 election results became known as the Indira wave. The decline of the Congress was dramatically reversed and, instead of confirming an era of coalition politics at the center, the electorate restored Congress dominance along with strong government at the national level. Mrs. Gandhi's New Congress received only 43.7 percent of the popular vote but with 350 out of 518 seats in Parliament, Mrs. Gandhi was returned to power with a two-thirds majority despite the fact that the New Congress had not even contested 74 seats.

The national despair of the 1967 to 1971 period was thus overcome by a new sense of elan, a combination of relief, self-confidence and pride in the ability of the Indian political system to restore a strong, stable government. The success of the New Congress brought an end to splits and defections within its ranks and Congress even made significant progress toward restoring some of its old support, for the party of Mrs. Gandhi did extremely well in urban constituencies, Muslim constituencies, and among younger voters and independents. While some observers proclaimed the election results as a victory for the new politics, others argued that the Congress sweep could be attributed more to the pattern of alliances which had resulted in the Congress winning 79 percent of the seats it contested. Yet this triumph was achieved without the benefit of a national mass media, without a strong party organization, and without control of most of the state governments. Not only that, but the Indira wave of 1971 inundated the opposition for a second time a year later when the Congress succeeded in restoring its dominant position in most of the Indian states by winning 70.75 percent of the seats and 48.32 percent of the popular vote.

The restoration of Congress dominance which has thrown Indian opposition parties into disarray, generated high expectations that the leadership and policies of the New Congress would be able to solve India's major problems of unemployment, disparities between rich and poor, land reform, industrial and agricultural growth, and improving public sector performances. Yet despite its success at the polls, the New Congress faces a variety of systemic limitations on its capability to solve such problems. These institutional constraints include the inability of the central government to force the state governments to carry out its major reform policies, the inadequacies of the bureaucracy and their ability to gain substantially from redistributive policies through higher wages and larger payrolls, the failure of the public sector to generate needed surpluses, the lack of a wholly effective planning apparatus and the constraints of limited resources. These institutional constraints are exhibited in the structure of decision-making in India and the politics of planning.

Structure of Decision-Making

Not until the adoption of the Indian constitution in 1950 was the final structure of India's post independence government determined. The constitution created a federal democratic republic with a parliamentary form of government under which the executive authority of the union was formally vested in a president, though in practice these powers came to be exercised by the council of ministers with the prime minister at its head. The prime minister was appointed by the president, other ministers were appointed by the president on the advice of the prime minister. The council of ministers was collectively responsible to the Lok Sabha, the lower house of the bicameral Indian legislature. As a federal system, the constitution provided for a threefold distribution of power between the center and the states. The central Parliament was responsible for the union lists, the state legislatures were responsible for the state lists, and both were responsible for a concurrent list.

The Indian political system was modeled after the British pattern and the practice and traditions of the past two decades have confirmed its basic outlines. Although the executive authority of the union was vested in the president, who was given an impressive list of formal powers, in intent as well as in practice the president was expected to serve as a constitutional head of state exercising his powers only with the advice of the council of ministers. "The president," said Dr. B.R. Ambedkar, the chief architect of the Indian Constitution, "occupies the same position as the King under the English Constitution."[33] All four Indian presidents since independence, Dr. Rajendra Prasad (1950-62), Dr. Sarvapalli Radhakrishnan (1962-67), Dr. Zakir Hussain (1967-69), and V.V. Giri, elected in 1969 upon the death of Hussain, have accordingly acted as titular heads of state. Although collectively their actions would seem to have established the precedent that the executive power rests with the prime minister and his cabinet, there are some who feel that the president may still come to play a more powerful role should India develop a series of minority governments, succumb to excessive party fragmentation, or suffer from weak party leadership. So far, however, this has not happened.

The real powers have thus been exercised by the council of ministers with the prime minister at its head. India's three post independence prime ministers, Jawaharlal Nehru (1947-1964), Lal Bahadur Shastri (1964-66), and Indira Gandhi (1966-present) have all been relatively strong executives who have fairly constantly reinforced the preeminent role of the prime minister and the council of ministers. Although the prime minister is theoretically appointed by the president and the other ministers are appointed by the president on the advice of the prime minister, the selection of the prime minister and council of ministers has actually been dependent upon the forces operating within the dominant Congress party. Since the government is collectively responsible to the Lok Sabha and must command a majority to stay in power, the prime minister is de facto the leader of the majority party. During Nehru's tenure the prime minister was automatically re-elected by the parliamentary party at the beginning of each Parliament, but the selection of his successor was determined by the central and state leaders of the dominant Congress party. Similarly, in 1966, 1967, and 1971, Mrs. Gandhi's selection was determined by the internal distribution of power in the party and between the party and the Congress parliamentary party. Thus, the president of India has so far not been able to employ any discretionary powers in the process of selecting the prime minister and the council of ministers.

The precise role of the prime minister depends on the stature, personality, and effective power of the prime minister as well as on the qual-

33. M. V. Pylee, *India's Constitution* (New York: Asia Publishing House, 1962), p. 167.

ity of his cabinet colleagues. During the Nehru era decision-making was highly centralized, Nehru was in a position to obtain from the cabinet any decision he wanted, first of all because he could usually persuade others of his point of view but also because he was willing to be personally responsible for the results. Toward the end of his tenure, when his health was failing and confidence in his leadership had been shaken by the Chinese invasion which signaled the failure of his foreign policy, the decision-making pattern of the past became fragmented. The cabinet, its members no longer a compliant committee of ratification, came to play a more important role and other, more broadly based organs such as Parliament, the Congress Party in Parliament, and the decision-making structure of the mass organization came to play a more significant role as critics of policy initiatives taken by the executive.

Lal Bahadur Shastri and Mrs. Gandhi did not come to power with Nehru's overriding, automatic authority. Starting out as first among equals, each had to depend on consensus rather than charisma. When no agreement with the cabinet was possible, decision could not be forced by fiat. Issues had to be postponed with the result that problems piled up and tended to clog the operations of government. Under circumstances of divided leadership or no leadership at all, the civil service also ground to a halt, refusing to review or take any decisions on controversial issues. The split in the Congress party in 1969, which was followed by Mrs. Gandhi's overwhelming victory in the 1971 election, broke this stalemate. Forsaking traditional patterns of consensus decision-making, Mrs. Gandhi had begun the process of consolidating her position and centralizing the decision-making process in her hands.

The council of ministers in India consists of cabinet ministers, ministers of state, and deputy ministers who assist the ministers in carrying out their duties, doing as much or as little as the minister permits. Although decisions are taken in the name of the council of ministers, it is really the prime minister, the cabinet, cabinet subcommittees and individual ministers who make any given decision. The cabinet is an inner circle of the council of ministers consisting of the most prominent leaders of the majority party. The cabinet has four functions: it approves all legislative proposals of the government, it recommends major appointments, it settles inter-ministerial disputes, and it coordinates and supervises the execution and administration of government policies.[34]

The composition of Indian cabinets has varied over the last two decades. In the years preceding the first general election, India had a

34. *Ibid.*, p. 377.

national government in which prominent non-Congress party leaders and even representatives of various interests were given a place. Since 1951 Indian cabinets have been Congress cabinets whose membership has been determined by the necessity to represent the individuals of real stature in the party, the diversity of views in the party and the sectional and ethnic interests essential to continual party power. Thus, although the cabinet is theoretically collectively responsible, each cabinet minister tends to have a different perspective. Over the years some have been convinced socialists, others Gandhians, and still others have been conservatives, yet each has reflected one aspect of opinion within the multi-interest Congress. For this reason, while the policy of the government has remained constant under Congress rule, the policies of the individual ministries have tended to change with each minister.

In order to coordinate the functions of the various ministries, the cabinet has established a series of cabinet subcommittees. These cabinet subcommittees have been chaired by the prime minister or by one or another of a small handful of senior Congress ministers with the experience and esteem to play the peacemaker or arbitrator role and so to reconcile inter-ministerial conflicts and make final decisions. The number of the cabinet subcommittees has varied recently from 7 to 10. At times of crisis, small super-cabinets have emerged to handle crisis situations. In 1962 Nehru created the Emergency Committee of the cabinet composed of the prime minister and five senior ministers to deal with policy-making during the Chinese invasion. In her recent attempt to consolidate her control over the Indian government, Mrs. Gandhi created a third type of subsidiary body called the Political Affairs Committee whose function was to handle the functions of three major cabinet subcommittees—internal affairs, external affairs and defense. The Political Affairs Committee has become the most important decision-making body in India next to the prime minister herself. It is composed of a small group of senior ministers who are consulted on all major policy issues involving domestic affairs, regional international affairs, and security policy.

Although almost all policy initiatives emerge from the higher echelons of the executive, the details of most major domestic policy decisions in India are worked out according to a fairly regularized process. A commission of inquiry composed of distinguished citizens is appointed to investigate the problem. The commission takes public testimony from various groups and individuals and produces a report which includes a set of specific policy recommendations. The relevant ministry and the cabinet study the report, consider its recommendations and note public reactions, then draw up a draft Bill which usually includes most of the recommendations of the commission. The draft bill is next submitted to Parliament where it is usually sent to a select committee. It is at the select committee phase that interest groups have another opportunity to air their views on the pending legislation. The select committee report is debated in Parliament, and the bill is finally passed, usually in a slightly modified form. This step by step procedure was employed in the making of such major decisions as those involving states reorganization, monopoly legislation, patents and others, although it was not followed in the making of such major ideological reorientations as the nationalization of banks and general insurance, or the declaration in 1955 of the socialist pattern of society as the objective of Indian planning. On lesser matters the elaborate consultation process is dispensed with. Decisions are made by the prime minister, cabinet committees, the cabinet as a body or individual members of the cabinet.

Ministers of the government of India are responsible for formulating policy within their sphere of responsibility and for the execution and review of that policy. They are required to coordinate with other ministers in matters affecting the business allocated to another ministry and in some cases to seek the approval of the prime minister and the cabinet. Otherwise each minister expects a minimum of interference from his cabinet colleagues, who are likely to accept such working rules, for each of them has enough problems without creating additional burdens by interfering in the work of others. Since a minister has a great deal of freedom in shaping the policy of his ministry, policy has often changed with the appointment of a new minister. Even under Nehru individual ministers played important roles. A forceful minister could carry his point and have his way. In addition, the prime minister tended to gravitate toward a man who was on top of the job. Especially toward the end of the Nehru era, each minister was coming more and more completely to dominate his own department, and by resorting to private agreements with the prime minister and the finance minister, a minister could insure prior acceptance of his own approach.

The minister in charge of the ministry is assisted by a secretary who is the administrative head of the ministry and principal advisor to the ministers on matters of policy administration. The minister-secretary relationship consists of a very delicate balancing act. Which way the effective power shifts depends on the talent, skill and political standing of the minister. If the minister is competent, if he knows his job and is strong politically, then he runs his department. If not, he is heavily dependent upon the secretary for advice. Most ministers are almost totally dependent upon the secretary for advice, so that a secretary who violently disagrees with a minister can delay action through his detailed knowledge of substantive details, organization and procedure. Yet no secretary can stop a determined minister from embarking on a course of action. In fact, there is increasing evidence that ministers have again become assertive in policy-making. As the Administrative Reforms Commission observed:

> there is a disinclination among quite a number of ministers to welcome frank and impartial advice from the secretary or his aides and an inclination to judge him by his willingness to do what they wish him to do. Instances are not wanting of ministers preferring a convenient subordinate to a strong one and thereby making the latter not only ineffective but a sulky and unwilling worker. This has also bred a tendency on the part of an increasing number of civil servants to attempt to anticipate the ministers wishes and proffer their advice accordingly. A further development of this unhealthy trend is the emergence of personal affiliations leading to an element of "politicalisation" among the civil servants. All these cut at the root of the healthy relationship. . . . The Prime Minister should take special interest to curb this tendency, with the assistance of the cabinet secretary and the central personnel agency.[35]

Though the charisma and personal power of the prime minister are important in determining the locus of decision-making, the fact that policy, even in the Nehru period, was made at the highest levels and was rarely deflected by pressure from below or from the pluralistic interaction of groups, cannot be attributed merely to the banyan tree effect of which he was so often accused. The government did enjoy a near monopoly over policy-making and within it policy was indeed determined by a small leadership group, but the leadership and society shared many basic values of which specific policies were a logical outgrowth. Furthermore, the complexity of prospective legislation in major areas like labor policy and economic policy was so great that the ideas of the ministry tended to gain baffled acceptance. In addition, except in the case of ethnic and linguistic demands, which were pressed by well organized groups with strong local backing, the government could dominate policy-making in many areas because the countervailing forces to its initiatives were weak. Interest groups like labor and business were so dependent upon government benevolence and so vulnerable to its administrative actions that they were hesitant to pressure too extensively or to question its policies. Under these circumstances, groups in India have come to play at best a circumspect negative role in the decision-making process. They must exert themselves mightily for minor concessions.

The executive in India is responsible to Parliament and yet for a variety of reasons the executive has tended to dominate the formula-

35. S. R. Maheshwari, "The Minister-Secretary Relationship," *Journal of Constitutional and Parliamentary Studies* 4 (January-March 1970): 73.

tion of public policy. Throughout the Nehru era, the Congress controlled over 70 percent of the seats in Parliament and the opposition was dispersed among congeries of minor parties. Since most talented Congressmen had quickly been coopted into the ministerial ranks, a large proportion of the Congress members were simply ex-freedom fighters with little experience in legislative functioning. The Congress rank and file followed the advice of the leadership who commanded great respect in the party.

The government in these early days of independence introduced almost all the bills discussed in Parliament, and ministers bore the brunt of explaining and defending these policies. "The experience and equipment of the majority of members does not enable them to contribute a great deal, and one consequence is that ministers often feel somewhat lonely and isolated, dependent for encouragement, stimulus, ideas and arguments not on their back-benchers but on their civil servants."[36] Still, Parliament was given great respect and earned it by serving as a means of ventilating grievances, passing legislation and acting as a public forum.

Attempts to develop greater participation within the Congress parliamentary party by developing functionally specialized committees and state groups had very limited success. Even the party executive and the general body played only a minor role, for massive Congress majorities enabled the party to permit open criticism by dissident Congressmen on the floor of the house instead of confining it strictly to party forums. For all the latitude given to the expression of views, party discipline was effectively maintained at the time of voting. Thus, though Congress MP's exercised little real control over leadership, they provided the government with a solid majority to govern.

Parliament began assuming a more creative role in policy formation and decision-making in the late 1950s when, as a result of persistent efforts by Feroze Gandhi, a major scandal was uncovered which forced the resignation of T.T. Krishnamachari, one of Nehru's most trusted economic advisors. The Parliament became more restive and critical of government leadership following the first public disclosure of major Chinese border incursions in Ladakh and the trend which was already accelerating toward the end of the Nehru era received especial impetus following the Chinese attack in 1962.

As Parliament became more vocal, so did the Congress parliamentary party. Energized by the onset of the early rounds in the struggle for succession, the Congress parliamentary party became deeply divided over the selection of a deputy party leader to succeed G. B. Pant on his

36. W. H. Morris-Jones, *Parliament in India* (Philadelphia, Pa.: University of Pennsylvania Press, 1957), p. 324.

death in 1961 and eventually Nehru was forced to intervene. He succeeded first in postponing the issue and then in modifying the parliamentary party's constitution to provide for two deputy leaders, one
from each house. The parliamentary party executive next played an
important role in forcing the resignation of V. K. Krishna Menon from
the cabinet despite Nehru's desire to keep him on. The party held that
Menon, as defense minister, was responsible for the military setback
suffered by India at the hands of the Chinese and should therefore
resign.

Although on the death of Nehru the Congress parliamentary party
was formally responsible for the election of the party leader who, because of the Congress majority, would become the prime minister, the
Congress parliamentary party accepted the consensus of the party leadership as the basis for the selection of Shastri as Nehru's successor, but
the battleground in the fight between Morarji Desai and Mrs. Gandhi
in 1966 and 1967 was the parliamentary party itself. Finally, with the
Congress split in 1969, the parliamentary party became even more important in that its composition and the vote of each of its members
counted as never before. The possibility of defection in the face of a less
secure majority made the demands of individual MP's more potent
than ever before in the history of the Congress. The pattern of the
1950s, however, was restored as a result of the massive victory of Mrs.
Gandhi at the polls in the 1971 national elections.

Not only is Parliament's role in the decision-making process changing, but its composition and the kind of interests it represents are also
undergoing a transformation. Parliament is becoming more interest
based. Ethnic groups are no longer the only active and vocal groups in
Parliament. A farm lobby is beginning to emerge which, although still
not organized formally, is based on individual representation. As seen
in Table II.3 the proportion of agriculturalists in Parliament has risen
from 14.7 percent in 1951-1956 to 33.8 percent in 1971, as the richer
farmers have begun to take to politics. Moreover, though the proportion of businessmen in Parliament has ranged from 7 to 11 percent, the
1967 elections witnessed the entry into Parliament of individuals
representing the modern industrial sector rather than the traditional
bazaar merchants and traders. The modern professions, on the other
hand, have been on the decline. Thus, Parliament is becoming more
broadly based.

The increase in the strength of agrarian interests in Parliament reflects the substantial support which Congress has received from the
large and medium sized peasants who have gained substantially as a
result of the green revolution. These members of Parliament have
come to act as a commodity lobby to reinforce the substantial voice
already enjoyed by the chief ministers of the states as spokesmen for

Table II.3

Occupations of the Members of the Lok Sabha

Occupation	First Lok Sabha		Second Lok Sabha		Third Lok Sabha		Fourth Lok Sabha		Fifth Lok Sabha	
	No.	Per-cent	No.	Per-cent	No.	Per-cent	No.	Per-cent	No.	Per-cent
Full time Social & Political Workers	121	24.7	109	22.0	106	21.2	112	21.6	92	17.6
Lawyers	107	21.9	112	22.6	109	21.8	86	16.6	93	17.9
Scientists, Engineers, Doctors	21	4.3	15	3.0	20	4.0	23	4.4	16	3.1
Teachers	37	7.6	30	6.1	36	7.2	38	7.3	36	6.9
Business	53	10.8	47	9.5	55	11.0	58	11.2	39	7.5
Journalists	38	7.8	33	6.7	19	3.8	27	5.2	30	5.7
Agriculture	72	14.7	93	18.8	114	22.8	135	26.0	176	33.8
Services	24	4.7	22	4.4	24	4.8	25	4.8	12	2.3
Information not available	16	3.2	34	6.9	17	3.4	15	2.5	27	5.2
Total	489	99.8	495	100.8	500	100.0	519	100.0	521	100.0

Sources: S. L. Chopra and O.N.S. Chauhan, "Emerging Pattern of Political Leadership in India, *Journal of Constitutional and Parliamentary Studies* IV:1 (1970), 126. *Journal of Parliamentary Information* XVIII:2 (1972), 372.

agrarian interests. Despite the commanding position Mrs. Gandhi occupies in both party and government and despite her decisive role in selecting Congress chief ministers, she has not been able to reverse the pattern of center-state relations which emerged toward the end of the Nehru era. At the same time, however, some of the most important new programs which are part of her promise to abolish poverty require action by the state governments. The lowering of ceilings on land and the introduction of an agricultural income tax both fall under the jurisdiction of the states.

Patterns of decision-making in India have thus changed in response to changes in the political system and in the distribution of power within the political system. Independence had brought to power a strong, capable, and relatively united leadership backed by massive majorities in Parliament. Decision-making was highly centralized in the hands of the prime minister and a small inner circle of his cabinet, all of whom commanded a great respect because of their status as leaders of the nationalist movement. To change or to modify executive policy or legislative action it was necessary to convince the prime minister or one of his chief cabinet colleagues. The Congress majority in Parliament provided almost unquestioned support to the Congress government.

The passing of the old nationalist leadership resulted in a trend toward a more participant decision-making process. The prime minister, cabinet, and bureaucracy were forced to pay greater attention to pressures generated in Parliament and within the Congress party itself. The overwhelming 1971 election victory of Mrs. Indira Gandhi's New Congress, however, brought a return of Congress dominance, strong political leadership and a recentralization of decision-making. At the same time, however, it has also marked the beginning of greater concern on the part of the Indian electorate with government policy outputs. Thus, unlike the earlier years after independence, the government of India will be faced with increasing pressure from interests in the modern sector and less from the more familiar ethnic demands of the past. Emerging interests in the modern sector will focus greater attention on social and economic issues and government will be compelled to pay greater attention to these demands and the difficulties of balancing the demands for social and economic equality with the need for more rapid economic growth, increased employment and expanding productive facilities. In short, Indian politics will become more interest-based as pressures generated by emerging functional interests are felt at all levels of decision-making and groups increase their demands on the political system.

Public Policy and Performance: The Politics of Planning

The pattern of public policy in India was radically altered after independence. The British policy of laissez faire was replaced by a dedication to rapid economic development through centralized planning to create a socialist pattern of society or mixed economy within the framework of a secular, democratic political system. The most far-reaching redistributive policies were incorporated in the policies which implemented the philosophy and objectives of the newly created system of centralized planning. The basic framework of development was set out in the Industrial Policy Resolutions of 1948 and 1956. The Industrial Policy Resolution of 1948 provided for a mixed economy. Exclusive ownership was confined to three industries: munitions, atomic energy and railways. The government reserved for itself the exclusive right to start *new* ventures in six other fields: coal, iron, steel, aircraft manufacture, shipbuilding, telephone and telegraph materials, and minerals. So far as the existing private sector facilities were concerned, the government guaranteed that no redistribution through nationalization would take place for at least ten years. The advent of planning in March 1950 and the decision halfway through the First Five Year Plan to accelerate the growth of the economy through more rapid industrialization led to a restatement of the Industrial Policy Resolution of 1948. In late 1954, therefore, the cabinet declared that the Industrial Policy Resolution of 1948 "had to be interpreted in terms of the socialist objective." By December Parliament had passed a resolution making the "socialist pattern" the official policy of the government and a guide to the planning commission in drawing up the Second Plan.[37] The nature of the socialist pattern was spelled out more clearly in the Industrial Policy Resolution of 1956.

The new Industrial Policy Resolution expanded the scope of the public sector. The number of industries reserved for the public sector rose from six to seventeen. Included in this category were all basic and strategic industries, public utilities, and industries requiring large investments. Specifically, heavy industries such as iron and steel, machine tools and heavy electricals as well as mining fell under the jurisdiction of the public sector. A second category consisted of a concurrent list of twelve industries in which private sector investment was expected to supplement the dominant public sector enterprise. The concurrent list included the production of machine tools, essential drugs, aluminum, basic chemicals and sea and road transport. All other industries were to be left to the private sector. In addition, the Industrial Policy Resolution of 1956 guaranteed existing facilities

37. Kochanek, *The Congress Party*, pp. 164-181.

against nationalization, provided for expansion of existing facilities under certain circumstances, and permitted public-private cooperation in development of some of the reserved sector.[38]

Although the Industrial Policy Resolutions of 1948 and 1956 did not call for the nationalization of existing private productive facilities, they were redistributed in the sense that all subsequent planning was guided by the objective of achieving a socialist pattern of society, or a special kind of welfare state in which the public sector was given a dominant role. In practice, therefore, the Industrial Policy Resolutions were redistributive in three ways. Firstly, they defined spheres of activity for the public and private sectors in such a way that the economic future of India was taken from the hands of private capital and placed in the public sector. The Industrial Policy Resolution of 1956, in particular, contained a strong bias in favor of the public sector. Thus, although only about 10 percent of the total industrial output was in the public sector even at the end of the Second Plan, the public sector was so favored that it could not help but eventually close the gap between its total share of industrial investment and that of the private sector. Under the Second Plan public sector investment in organized industry was 56 percent of the total plan allocation for organized industry. Its share increased to 64 percent by the time of the Fourth Plan.[39] These targets, however, have not always been met.

Secondly, the Industrial Policy Resolutions were redistributive to the extent that the government nationalized most important financial and credit mechanisms in the society. In order to finance development and insure government's ability to dominate the commanding heights of the economy, the government nationalized the life insurance industry and the Imperial Bank of India, the largest private bank in India. Much later, it nationalized the remaining private sector banks along with general insurance. In addition the government introduced a comprehensive series of new taxes: a graduate surtax on dividends, compulsory deposits, a capital gains tax, wealth and expenditure taxes and gift taxes. Thus, through nationalization of financial and credit mechanisms and a severely progressive tax system, government policy was designed not only to attempt to produce redistributive justice but also to determine the precise sphere of all future private sector development.

Thirdly, the Industrial Policy Resolutions were redistributive in the sense that they led to a total reconstruction of the legal framework

38. Planning Commission, Government of India, *The New India* (New York: The Macmillan Company, 1958), pp. 387-396.
39. Planning Commission, Government of India, *Fourth Five Year Plan: 1969-1974* (Faridabad: Government of India Press, 1970), p. 51.

within which the private sector would have to operate. Constitutional sanctions and supreme court interpretation have given the government of India wide powers of economic regulation over the private sector. This power was utilized to pass the Industries (Development and Regulation) Act of 1951 which provides for the most complex and comprehensive system of control and regulation of private business in the world, in addition to creating the administrative institution for the coordination of public and private sector development. Thus, policies which are redistributive in their broadest social and economic implications give rise to subsidiary policies which are severally distributive, regulatory, or developmental in nature.

Though the Industries (Development and Regulation) Act of 1951 gives the bureaucracy vast powers to control and regulate private industry, its jurisdiction over the awarding of industrial licenses gives it a predominantly distributive impact. Under the Act all existing scheduled industries were required to register with the government, and a license was required before any new facilities could be built. Once registered the industries became subject to government regulations which included the power to investigate their operations and issue directives for changes, assume management and control of industries where warranted, and control the supply, distribution and prices of their production. Covered under the Act were 38 industrial categories involving over 150 articles of manufacture. Section 30 of the Act delegated to the central government the power to develop detailed rules for implementing the provisions of the Act, but preserved parliamentary control by requiring that rules be subject to parliamentary consent. The machinery subsequently created under the rules involves the activation of a complex system of inter-ministerial and inter-governmental coordination before a license for a new industrial undertaking can be granted.

The "discovery" that industrial licensing, by aiding predominantly the larger business houses, had led to increased concentration resulted in the government's enactment of a new monopoly law to control future growth. Ironically, the device that was to be relied on to inhibit monopoly under the new regulations was the very device which had earlier helped to create it. But under the new licensing system small and medium industry would not require a license to establish a factory which costs less than 10 million rupees. Only the top 20 industrial houses of India would have to apply for a license to set up a new unit or to expand an existing unit involving investment of less than 100 million rupees. Big business would then be expected to invest in industries requiring large capital outlays and long gestation periods before a return on investment could be expected. Moreover, under the new law loans obtained by big business houses for realizing this newly licensed capacity from public credit facilities were to be written with an option permitting conversion of loan value into equity, a proposal which had been raised before and which business had vigorously opposed. Thus, these credit institutions would be enabled to play an important role in control or management of the private sector facilities in which they had made a substantial investment.

Foreign Aid and Foreign Capital

Indian planned development since independence has raised its national product in real terms by about 85 percent of the 1950-51 level. However, due to a population growth rate of 2.5 percent the national product per capita has increased by only 30 percent during the same period. At the same time, net investment has been increased to 15 percent of the total national outlays and over half of the new investment is going into modern industry.[40]

The net national income in India has risen from $12.7 billion in 1951 to $37.2 billion in 1967-68, food production has more than doubled, and factory production has increased by over 185 percent. In the industrial sector, steel ingot production has increased from 1.47 million tons in 1950-51 to 6.5 million tons in 1968-69, fertilizer production has increased from 99,000 tons in 1951 to 1,954,000 tons in 1968-69 and the production of radios rose from 54,000 to 1,456,000 in the same period.[41]

The Fourth Five Year Plan which began in April 1969, aimed at an annual growth rate of 5.5 percent to achieve social justice and ever progressing self reliance. India was determined to do away with American P.L. 480 food imports by 1971 and to dispense with foreign aid by 1980-81. It remains to be seen, however, whether the conflicting goals of rapid growth and self-reliance can be achieved. Over the past two decades India's desire for rapid economic development led its leaders to turn to outside sources of support which in turn has enabled the great powers to penetrate into the subcontinent. Although the bulk of the resources for the Indian five year plans have been raised internally, foreign economic aid has played a very important role in Indian development. During the high point of the cold war India was considered to be a vital area by both American and Soviet leaders with the result that both countries were prepared to transfer large amounts of resources to India. From 1946 to 1969 India received a total of about $15 billion in aid from the West in the form of bilateral and multilateral aid. The largest portion ($8.3 billion) was provided by the

40. Wilfred Malenbaum "Politics and Indian Business: The Economic Setting," *Asian Survey* 11 (September 1971): 841-849.
41. *India News* 10 (January 21, 1971), p. 1.

United States in the form of loans and P.L. 480 food. Soviet bloc economic aid since 1955 has totaled $2 billion most of which was used to finance specific public sector projects. During the 1960s the Soviet Union also became India's major arms supplier.

Reduction in cold war tensions, increased problems at home, and the popular disillusionment with the Vietnam war led the United States to reduce its commitment in the Indian subcontinent. India in turn became more preoccupied with self reliance as a result of American suspension of aid during the 1965 and 1971 Indian-Pakistan wars. Thus, India's increased concern for self-reliance has coincided with a general decline in the willingness of the United States to continue its large aid program in India and elsewhere. To some extent India hopes to make up the difference with increased private foreign capital and soviet aid.

Despite the socialist rhetoric of Indian politics, approximately 95 percent of the output of organized industry in India in 1960-61 was still in the private sector. Foreign controlled assets represented a relatively small but important part of the total. In 1961 foreign capital controlled more than two-fifths of the total assets in the organized large-scale private sector. The bulk of this investment was new investment which had flowed in after independence. Foreign investment in 1961 was heavily concentrated in a small number of industries, some of which had been the long-standing original preserve of foreign capital, while others had grown up since independence. Three areas—tea, petroleum, and manufacturing—together accounted for three-fourths of the total foreign investment in India. Half of the investment in manufacturing was concentrated in a relatively small group of industries— chemicals and drugs, cigarettes and tobacco, jute textiles and light electrical goods. Generally speaking, older forms of investment like tea and jute manufacturing grew slowly or declined in relative importance after independence, for most fresh foreign capital was directed into petroleum and newer, technologically complex and patented manufacturing industries.[42]

Originally, foreign capital in India meant British capital. At the time of independence three-fourths of foreign investment in India was British. This British investment took two forms. One was the managing agency house, a unique organizational system which developed shortly after the end of the East India Company's monopoly of trade in 1833 and which played a dominant role in tea, jute and coal. The other form of British investment was the large multinational corporation which began investing in manufacturing enterprises in India during the inter-war years. Shifts in government policy after independence

42. See Michael Kidron, *Foreign Investments in India* (London: Oxford University Press, 1965).

affected most profoundly the more traditional forms of British investment, for a number of managing agency houses were sold to Indian
entrepreneurs, their capital being repatriated, while the remaining
rapidly consolidated, diversified and Indianized both capital and management. New capital has followed the modern corporate form.

Though British capital continues to play an active role in India, its
power and influence have been diluted, because the substantial influx
of foreign capital in the last 20 years has resulted in a greater diversity
of capital in terms of national origins arising from the development of
Indian affiliates by American, German, French, Swiss, Japanese and
Italian corporations. These affiliates were usually established in collaboration with the larger Indian business firms, thereby augmenting
the trend toward closer liaison between foreign and indigenous capital. Thus, despite the original hostility of the government of India and
the ambivalence of foreign investors, foreign investment in India has
increased in size, diversity, sophistication and national origins. It has
also played an important role in Indian development.

Public Policy and Performance: The Politics of Integration

The accelerated process of change brought about by British colonial
rule and British colonial policy tended to politicize the social disunities of the Indian sub-continent leading to serious problems of national integration. Most dramatic was the case of Hindu-Muslim
relations which deteriorated into the emergence of two competing
nationalisms. Although the social disunities of caste, language and
region which had existed for centuries also became politicized in the
late nineteenth century as traditional groups sought to gain higher
status by organizing and pressing their demands, they were for the
most part held in check by the nationalist movement. With independence, however, the demands of these antecedent groups came to dominate the political arena in such a way as to create severe crises of national, local and personal identity.

The implications of this translation of linguistic, caste, regional and
communal cleavages into politicized conflict have given rise to sharply
divergent interpretations. The urban nationalist elite tended to see the
demands of castism, linguism and communalism as a threat to national unity not only to the leadership's goals of economic and social reform but also to the very integrity of the country. Similarly, many
Western and Indian scholars agreed in interpreting these trends toward
the emergence of militant regional language and caste lobbies as a
danger to Indian unity and the emergence of authoritarian rule.

Another group of foreign and Indian scholars, on the other hand,
contended that the devisive impact of these conflicting group loyalties
was consistently overstated. Social segmentation by itself, they argued,

does not tell us very much about the patterning of social groups' participation in politics and its consequences for political integration. It is not simply the number of cleavages that count but the degree to which they have become politicized and the relationship of the cleavages to each other. National unity in India, it was argued, would not be vitally threatened by group conflict for a variety of reasons. Firstly, ethnic loyalties are too localized to take on an all-India character. This has been particularly true of caste associations, which are confined to particular regions within a state or at most within the state boundaries. Secondly, group cleavages in India have not been congruent but disassociated so that they cross-cut each other in a variety of ways. Thus, though the general level of conflict has been high, its intensity is substantially mitigated by the very diversity which gives rise to it in the first place. Thirdly, language and ethnic loyalties have not only been divisive. They have played an important role in initiating people into organized modes of participation and political activity, and so have helped to give new meaning to the idea of political community in India. Fourthly, the existence of cleavages cannot be viewed independently of the mechanisms within the society which may domesticate or intensify such conflicts. The leadership systems and interactional mechanisms of the political system itself play an important role in conflict management, mitigating as well as exacerbating any cleavages which may exist. Finally, it has been argued that misapprehension about social divisions in India are based on false conceptions of modern society and politics. "National associations based on religion, language, ethnicity and locality have not been assimilated or dissolved in modern nations; in fact they continue to play important roles in their society and politics."[43]

Language Politics in India

Language politics in India illustrates some of these generalizations. Next to the Hindu-Muslim antagonisms, the problem of language was among the most explosive issues faced by post-independence India. The language problem had two dimensions: the status of regional languages and the determination of an official language. The constitution of India lists 15 major languages. These languages are divided into two major linguistic strains: the Indo-Aryan languages of the north and the Dravidian languages of the south. Since most of these regional languages have a reasonably long history, one of the long-standing demands of regional Congress language leaders was to replace the administrative boundaries used by the British by the creation of unilin-

43. Rudolph, *The Modernity of Tradition*, p. 64.

gual states. In many ways British colonial rule had encouraged demands for linguistic states because of the early advantages accruing to Bengali, Marathi and Tamil, the regional languages of the three earliest British settlements in Calcutta, Bombay and Madras (Tamil Nadu).

Sub-national loyalties grew up almost simultaneously with the development of the nationalist movement. The Congress organization as early as the 1920s was based on linguistic rather than on British administrative units. Although the Congress leadership prior to independence exploited the linguistic issue against the British and supported the demands for the creation of linguistic states, the disruption of partition, the problems arising from the integration of princely states and the desire to consolidate national unity at the time of independence led the Congress national leaders to commit themselves to postponing the reorganization issue despite strong rank-and-file pressures. Demands for unilingual states, however, became incessant. They dominated the Indian political scene throughout the 1950s. So strong was the electoral appeal of regional linguistic oriented political parties that the Congress government was finally forced to concede the demand, first in Andhra, then for most of India in 1956 and later for Bombay, Gujarat and Punjab. Pessimists saw in these concessions the beginning of the balkanization of the subcontinent.[44]

By the early 1970s, however, regional linguistic solidarity appeared to be on the wane, for uneven economic development was bringing regions within unilingual states to demand separate political status as a means of coping with their problems. These regional parties were based on social and economic disparities rather than linguistic identity. Thus, while the creation of unilingual states has given a strong federal character to the Indian policy, their existence has not resulted in the political disintegration of the subcontinent along linguistic state lines. Unlike Pakistan where regional and language cleavages were congruent with totally different life styles, cultural identities, and attitudes, neither the north nor the south in India was sufficiently linguistically homogeneous to develop sectional separatist movements. Even the Dravida Munnetra Kazhagam (D.M.K.) in Tamil Nadu, the only major state party to develop such an orientation, has shifted from its separatist demands to a demand for greater states' rights. Overall, once unilingual demands had been met, the language problem ceased to be widely effective for purposes of mobilization and proponents were left without an issue that could be used for mass mobilization.

While the issue of linguistic states dominated Indian politics in the

44. Selig S. Harrison, *India: The Most Dangerous Decades* (Madras: Oxford University Press, 1965).

decade of the 1950s, the major issue of the 1960s was the official language question.[45] The linguistic diversity of India has made the problem of a national link language extremely critical. During the struggle for independence, English served this function. Yet, despite 200 years of British influence, English was spoken by only 2.5 percent of the Indian population. Moreover there were many Indians with strong convictions both before and after independence that an indigenous language had to replace English if true cultural freedom and national identity were to be achieved. The major claimant for the status of a link language to replace English was Hindi. However, although Hindi extended in its various dialects over several large northern states, it was spoken by only 30.4 percent of the Indian population. In the framing of the Indian constitution at the time of independence a clause was adopted which specifically acknowledged that the official language of the union should be Hindi in Deva Nagari script with international numerals, although for a period of 15 years (1950-1965) English was to continue to be used for all official purposes of the union. In addition, the clause provided that Parliament could by law extend the use of English after the 15-year period for such purposes as might be specified. At the end of the transition period Parliament adopted a bill which provided for the continued use of English in addition to Hindi for all official purposes of the union. However, the change in wording at that time from "English *shall* continue" to "English *may* continue" resulted in severe rioting and bitterness in the south and especially in the state of Tamil Nadu. In response to the strong objections of the south the central government modified the law to guarantee the continued use of English in addition to Hindi for all purposes of the union, both for the transaction of business in Parliament and for communications between the union and any state whose official language is not Hindi. In addition, a resolution was passed authorizing a three-language formula (English, Hindu and a regional language) for the school system and a regional language policy for civil service exams with a required knowledge of Hindi or English.

Despite intense conflict, the Indian leadership succeeded in keeping the dispute under control and ultimately in bringing about a compromise solution to both regional language and official language issues. While strong and vocal animosities are still often expressed toward Hindi, there is increasing evidence that Hindi has in fact been spreading quite rapidly as a second language in non-Hindi language

45. Jyotirindra Das Gupta, *Language Conflict and National Development* (Berkeley, California: University of California Press, 1970), and Baldev Raj Nayar, *National Communication and Language Policy in India* (New York: Frederick A. Praeger, 1969).

areas, although the growth of Hindi has also been accompanied by a resurgence of English. Thus, both link languages have gained numerically even while the regional languages have continued to serve the needs of the bulk of Indian society.

Linguistic movements have also served another important political purpose. They have acted as a mechanism for mobilizing people and increasing political participation. Studies of party activists have shown that many of them were recruited into politics as a result of these various language movements and now participate in one of the major Indian political parties.

Caste Politics

While the politics of language has had widespread appeal in the urban sectors of India where it was considered explosive because of its separatist overtones, the rural sector has tended to be dominated by caste politics as newly mobilized ascriptive groups have shifted their attention from education, community uplift and social status improvement to politics. The introduction of mass franchise in a highly segmented society in which mass media are largely absent, transportation networks underdeveloped, and party organization relatively weak presented substantial obstacles to marshalling popular support directly through the appeal of party leaders and party programs. As a result, the predominant vehicle for reaching the masses of the rural peasantry has been mobilization via the persuasive powers of local notables or caste elders. Traditional loyalties and dependencies thus become a part of modern politics.

One of the unique features of the traditional Hindu social order was the caste system. In theory the caste system divided society into four varnas: Brahmin, Kshatriya, Vaisya and Sudra. The Brahminical function was to provide authoritative interpretations of Hinduism and to serve as a priestly and learned elite. The Kshatriya was the prince or warrior who was responsible for political functions; the Vaisya conducted trade and commerce and the Sudra provided the work force. In addition to these four varnas there was an additional group now called Harijans or "scheduled castes" who though part of the Hindu social order were segregated from the other groups as a result of their low status and ritually polluting functions. These were the untouchables.

The four-fold varna structure existed in theory but not in practice. Caste in India was actually a far more complex phenomenon based on endogamous kinship groups called *jati* which were identifiable only on a local basis. Thus, caste consisted not of four but thousands of local jatis. These jati are often roughly grouped by varna status but such classifications tend to be clear only at the top and bottom levels.

Varna distinctions at the middle levels involve too many exceptions and qualifications to be useful for most purposes.

Although caste in India has often been portrayed as rigid and unchanging, studies have shown that an entire jati has been able to lose or elevate rank and status as a result of great religious movements, war or famine and by separation of more prosperous sectors from the bulk of the jati. In short, some mobility has always been possible but in a limited way. Overall, however, caste remains largely a local phenomenon centered around a village or a group of villages in the same area.

Like all other aspects of Indian life this traditional caste structure began to undergo certain transformations as a result of improved communication, economic change and Western education, all of which combined to open up opportunities for new patterns of interaction and association. Under the impact of these changes, advanced segments of similar jati undertook to upgrade their position in the caste hierarchy by adapting the attributes of higher castes and pressing the state to recognize their claims to higher status. In so doing, caste groupings took on the partial character of the more conventional voluntary association in which membership is not purely ascriptive, for their membership fluctuated according to their degree of political participation. Their leadership was no longer hereditary, the size of the unit greatly increased, and the group so organized and politicized became preoccupied with control or influence over those who held political power and not merely over themselves. In short, the caste association became a means of pursuing political power, social status and economic interest.[46]

These modern caste associations enabled the members of middle and lower castes to find a basis for self-esteem and to win social esteem. As a result they have contributed to structural change by helping to level the ritually based social hierarchy of the caste system. At the same time, they have contributed to the success of political democracy by providing the basis for communication, representation and leadership and by linking the masses to the new democratic political process. Subsumed within the larger ideology and program of the Congress and other political parties, caste leaders acted as brokers who integrated the group into the larger governing coalition. In short, caste was subsumed and integrated by leadership and policies.

Caste politics, however, appears to be a transitional phenomenon, for continued secularization through political involvement appears to lead to the encouragement of secular associations via a three-phase

46. Rudolph, *The Modernity of Tradition,* and Robert L. Hardgrave Jr., *The Nadars of Tamilnad* (Berkeley, California: University of California Press, 1969).

process. During the first phase, the pattern is one of polarization: an entrenched caste is challenged by an ascendent caste and conflicts become bilateral. A second phase follows in which caste fragmentation and factionalism develops. During the third phase increasing differentiation based on economic differences within the caste leads to a breakdown of homogeneity and a fragmentation of the group. In the ensuing system of mobility and cross-cutting loyalties caste loyalties lose their effectiveness.

Thus, language, caste and region have acted as forces for political mobilization and have translated mass franchise into political power for the masses of the formerly segmented, wider society resident in the countryside. As a result, there has developed an increased linkage between the urban elites and the segmented rural masses along with a widening of the social base of the Indian polity. The conflicts generated by this increased mobilization were managed by the Congress at both party and governmental levels. By mediating such disputes, Congress leaders were able to hold their broad-based coalition together. Thus, cleavages became domesticated rather than intensified. Disgruntled groups were free to mobilize, oppose government action, and make demands. Vociferous in pressing their demands as they might be, they were thereby encouraged to function within rather than against the emergent political system. Many individuals mobilized for some particularistic issue remained politically active even after the issue ceased being salient. Many of these activists even ended up in the Congress itself. Thus ascriptive associations played a critical role in the 1950s and 1960s in helping to integrate the segmented masses into the larger political system and in shifting political power away from the urban elites to more rural-based regional elites. At the same time, the cleavages brought about by the dispersion of political power, economic growth and development, and the more recent green revolution have begun to weaken these older loyalties and to give rise to embryonic modern classes. The result has been the beginning of a restructuring of social and political conflict in India.

Changes in rural India have now proceeded to the point where new tensions tend to take on more of a class than a caste character. The green revolution has resulted in severe economic polarization in the rural areas between the top 15.5 percent of the agriculturalists, of whom there are about 38 million largely from dominant castes owning over 15 acres of land, and the 84.5 percent who include smaller owners, owner tenants, sharecroppers, and the landless. Since many of the tenants, sharecroppers and landless tillers tend to belong to the lower castes, caste and class and their characteristic tensions may overlap and reinforce one another.

The polarization taking place in the rural areas has opened new opportunities for political mobilization. The New Congress is now competing with radical political parties in their attempt to transform these social tensions into political conflict and political support. So far the manifestation of characteristic class struggle activities has been sporadic and the opposition has succeeded in mobilizing rural discontent largely on a localized basis. As leader of the New Congress, Mrs. Gandhi has sought to mobilize these new rural tensions by promises of massive land reforms and a policy of *Gharibi Hatao* or the elimination of poverty. Thus, slowly, India is moving from a dual political culture in which segmented traditional loyalties dominate the bulk of the rural peasantry to a mass political culture in which loyalties transcend ascriptive groups.

Political elites are therefore attempting to appeal to this new type of Indian mass electorate by offering the leadership, philosophy and programs that appeal directly to the interests and values of the individual voter who thus becomes the unit of opinion gradually replacing the previously respected intermediaries, whose influence depended on traditional loyalties and dependencies. In the process, a more national, participatory political culture is slowly being wrought from the ebbing loyalties and identities of traditional man. Thus, the evolution of politically self-conscious participant communities has had an important impact not only on the patterning of cleavages and conflict within Indian society but also on the emergence of loyalties to larger political communities and increases in political participation.

Political Participation

Despite the high level of illiteracy in India, political consciousness has been relatively high and is increasing steadily under the combined impact of the politics of mass franchise and the devolution of political power. Both electoral statistics and survey data have revealed differential rates of participation in such activities as voting, attending political meetings, expressions of interest in politics and contributing to political campaigns. At the same time, studies of state politics and Panchayati Raj (local government) have demonstrated an increasing linkage between the political activity of the masses and modern politics. The most dramatic changes in political consciousness and political participation have taken place in the rural areas and among the poor and illiterate.

Political participation in the form of voter turnout has increased significantly in India in the past 25 years from a low of 45.7 percent in the First General Elections of 1951-52 to a high of 61.33 percent in the Fourth General Elections in 1967. Until the unusual mid-term parliamentary elections of 1971, there had been a steady progression of increased voter turnout. In 1971, however, the trend was broken when despite Mrs. Gandhi's popular appeal only 54.73 percent of the eligible voters showed up at the polls. This decline of 6.6 percent reflected the impact of holding national parliamentary elections independent of state assembly elections in which state candidates help to increase voter interest by raising regional and local issues, mobilizing the electorate more effectively through local interests and communities, and intensifying campaign exposure and contact.

Although voter participation has been on the rise in all states, it has varied considerably from state to state. In general, voter turnout has tended to correlate with the level of modernization of the state as measured by per capita income, urbanization, literacy and mass communications. The higher the level of modernization the higher the turnout. Participation also varies, however, according to the level of factionalism in the constituency, the effectiveness of local party organization and the degree of party competition.

Voter turnout has also tended to vary in terms of the level of education. Unlike most developed Western democracies, voter turnout in India among the higher educated groups tends to be lower than among the illiterates or the poorly educated. Primordial group pressure and the festival atmosphere of elections in the rural areas tends to result in high voter turnout among the rural poor and illiterates. In contrast a sense of alienation, frustration and futility tends to color the intellegentsia's view of electoral participation.

It is not that the intellectuals are uninformed or uninterested in politics. In fact the more highly educated sectors of Indian society exhibit a higher level of knowledge about policies, programs and leadership; they are more vocal and critical of government performance; and they express greater subjective interest in politics than do the illiterates. However, they do not translate this intense interest in politics into active participation in the form of voting, attending political rallies or contributing money to political campaigns.

The assumption, therefore, that increased education will produce a more participatory and democratic political system and foster democratic values may prove to be incorrect as intellectuals grow increasingly unhappy with the pace and direction of modernization and impatient with the development of parochial loyalties and pork barrel politics which they see as a threat to national unity and survival. They do not form a bulwark against the establishment of an authoritarian regime but in fact might be the first to assist and welcome such a change, for they, more than anyone else in the society, resent the emergence of a mass political culture and the participatory style of the political arena they themselves created.

Political participation in India has increased since independence not only because of the politics of mass franchise but also as a result of the devolution of political power from the center to the states and from the states to the districts and below. As we have seen, the great movements based on language, caste and region have politicized larger and larger sectors of India's formerly segmented rural society and has resulted in a political devolution of power from the center to the states. The state assemblies and the members of the legislative assemblies (MLAs) are the meaningful levels of democratic government to the Indian masses and not the central cabinet and Parliament.

The introduction of the system of Panchayati Raj designed to introduce self-government at the district, block, and village level has had the effect of not only expanding democratic participation in the rural areas but has also ensured the development of closer linkage between the MLA and rural India, thus making the state assemblies the focal point of democratic politics. The MLA must ensure effective contact with the masses in his constituency in order to guarantee a solid local base of electoral support. The MLA in turn acts as a broker in attempting to assist his constituents in acquiring developmental benefits and in aiding them in their relations with the state bureaucracy when they get into difficulties or need something from the government. Thus, the MLA tends to act more as a provider of direct benefits such as helping to secure permits, licenses, jobs and places in colleges rather than as a policy-maker. However, it is also because of the close relationship between the MLA and local politics that the system of localism and rural dominance became projected into the state assemblies. It is precisely this parochialism and style of pork barrel politics which the intellectual elite detest so much and it is also the process by which caste, community, language, region and other primordial loyalties become translated into political action to affect the distribution of benefits.

So far however, the system has worked to the benefit of only certain sectors of the rural society—that is, the middle level peasantry and petty landlords who control the local Congress party machine. Political participation, however, has begun to awaken the masses of small landowners, tenants and the landless who have now become available for mobilization and political parties are working to win their allegiance. Thus, the politics of mass franchise and the existing distribution of rural power are surely going to come into conflict and the new political consciousness of the rural masses, illiterates and the poor must be channeled into political participation within the system or lead to mass upheaval.

Future Perspectives

India's location as a land bridge between the Middle East and Asia placed the subcontinent in the direct path of the expansion of the West into Asia. The British were able to establish hegemony over almost the entire subcontinent in the wake of the breakup of the Moghul Empire. Through direct control over most of India and indirect control over the princely states, the British impact colored all aspects of Indian political, economic and social life. British colonial rule and British colonial policy thus provided a stimulus for change.

Indian interaction with the West was also influenced substantially by the nature of its own traditional heritage which proved to be remarkably resilient in adjusting traditional institutions to modern use. The long, continuous, cultural tradition provided a variety of dominant and latent themes and mechanisms which could be utilized in the process of change. The amorphous nature of Hinduism, Indian tolerance of ambiguity, the strong desire to maintain harmony, the belief in the efficacy of norms and law and the tradition of a learned and civilizing elite all contributed Indian elements to the amalgam of ideas and political institutions which the Indians were prepared to borrow from the British including the press, voluntary associations, and the British parliamentary system based on mass franchise. For example, this synthesis of Western and Indian values was reflected in the early religious reform movements of the nineteenth century and in certain elements of Gandhianism in the twentieth century.

Deeply concerned with preserving national unity despite India's past political disunity, the leadership which developed out of the nationalist movement was equally skilled in the techniques of conflict management and political organization. Leaders preached the theme of national unity and stressed the desirability of substituting persuasion and compromise for repression. Opposition parties as well as Congress played an important role in the tasks of political socialization, recruitment, interest articulation and aggregation, and in many cases the opposition served as feeder organizations for the dominant Congress party. Elites did not remain closed, for competition within the elite resulted in increased mobilization and integration of new elements in the society. Thus, India appears to be successfully handling its crises of identity, integration, and participation all at the same time. To a large extent this accomplishment was confirmed by Mrs. Gandhi's election sweep in 1971 and 1972 which restored popular confidence in the Indian political system.

The major concerns in India in the 1970s have shifted from unity to problems of security, development and penetration, all of which focus on governmental performance. Three major military conflicts since 1962 have resulted in a major change in the leadership perception of its security needs, but especially since preoccupation with Pakistan has been replaced by an obsession with China. There is a new emphasis on long term security planning and maximum defense preparedness, for some of the idealism of Nehru's foreign policy has been replaced by a stress on the need to increase India's military and economic power in the world. These changes in Indian perceptions are occurring at a time of major realignment of the global international system which so far has not provided a place for India. Talk of a pentagonal pattern of the United States, the U.S.S.R., Europe, Japan and China would appear to imply that the world is not yet willing to recognize any change in the status for India. To gain this status will require one of several developments: the acquisition of nuclear weapons, a rapid surge of economic development, or the development of alignments independent of the super powers.

Mrs. Gandhi's electoral victories in 1971 and 1972 combined with the Indian successes in Bangladesh have created a new elan in India and a renewed commitment to establishing a redistributive justice. Yet the high aspirations which have emerged must still function in a system in which government has very limited capabilities to satisfy these aspirations because of economic and institutional constraints. Although Mrs. Gandhi now has the majorities to push through major constitutional changes which will enable her government to enact a series of laws which have a high symbolic effect, the basic problems of organization, planning, resources and more effective political and bureaucratic leadership at the state and national level remain to be solved. State governments need stronger and more effective leadership to enact and implement basic land reforms, development and social services. The bureaucracy must be made more innovative, less subject to rapid expansion as a way of creating employment and must exercise self-restraint in its demands for higher incomes. The public sector will have to begin to generate the surpluses essential for increased growth, and growth in turn must take place both in terms of GNP and per capita income. Finally, the party system must become more highly organized and based less on charisma if the system is to survive.

In short, the emphasis must shift away from immediate consolidation to long-term development and evolutionary growth if the pressures generated by rapid change are to be controlled and channeled into the creation of a society firmly based on social justice.

Table II.4
Fourth 5-Year Plan, Proposed Expenditures, by Public and Private Sectors, 1969-70 to 1973-74, India (in 10 Millions of Rupees)[1]

Head of development	Public sector				Private sector		Public and private sectors		
	Total outlay	Current outlay	Investment	Percentage distribution of total outlay	Investment	Percentage distribution	Total Investment	Total outlay	Percentage distribution
Agricultural and allied sectors	2,217	550	1,667	15.4	1,800	18.0	3,467	4,017	16.5
Irrigation and flood control	964	14	950	6.7	—	—	950	964	3.9
Power	2,085	—	2,085	14.4	50	0.5	2,135	2,135	8.7
Village and small industries	295	111	184	2.1	500	5.0	684	795	3.3
Industry and minerals	3,090	35	3,055	21.5	2,150	21.5	5,205	5,240	21.5
Transport and communications	3,173	40	3,133	22.0	1,010	10.1	4,143	4,183	17.2
Education	802	539	263	5.6	50	0.5	313	852	3.5
Scientific research	134	41	93	0.9	—	—	93	134	0.5
Health	437	305	132	3.0	—	—	132	437	1.8
Family planning	300	250	50	2.1	—	—	50	300	1.2
Water supply and sanitation	339	2	337	2.4	—	—	337	339	1.4
Housing and urban development	171	—	171	1.2	2,680	26.8	2,851	2,851	11.7
Welfare or backward classes	134	134	—	0.9	—	—	—	134	0.5
Social welfare	37	37	—	0.3	—	—	—	37	0.2
Labor welfare and craftsmen training	37	18	19	0.3	—	—	19	37	0.2
Other programs	183	70	113	1.2	—	—	113	183	0.7
Inventories	—	—	—	—	1,760	17.6	1,760	1,760	7.2
TOTAL	14,398	2,146	12,252	100.0	10,000	100.0	22,252	24,398	100.0

[1]Rs7.5 equal US$1.
[2]Exclusive of transfers of public funds.
Source: Adapted from India, Planning Commission, *Fourth 5-Year Plan 1969-74, Draft*, p. 48.

Data

area: 1,266,000 sq. mi.
population: 1971 547.949 million rank—2
birth rate: 41 per 1,000 (1968) rank in 1961—35.5 (AH)
infant mortality rate: 145 per 1,000 (AH) 1968
capital city: New Delhi
percent urbanization: 19.91* 80.09% rural (1971 census)
newspapers per 1,000: 13 based on circulation of 402 of 636 dailies in 1968
  (UNSY)

distribution of work force: 1967 (AH)

agriculture—	73.2%
industry—	10.8
transport and communications—	5.9
services (banking and insurance, public administration, defense, et al.)—	9.9
	total 99.8%

religious composition: 1971 (OHT)

Hindus	82.72%	453,292,000
Muslims	11.21	61,417,000
Christian	2.60	14,223,000
Sikh	1.89	10,378,000
Buddhist	.70	3,812,000
Jain	.47	2,604,000
Other	.41	2,220,000

major exports: 1968 (AH)
  jute
  tea   cotton + jute + tea = 40% of exports
  iron ore
  cotton

major trading partners: per cent of exports, 1968 (AH)

Great Britain	19.15%
United States	17.29
Japan	11.38
Soviet Union	10.10

---

*definition of urban area—towns, localities having 5,000 or more inhabitants, density equal to or greater than 1,000 per sq. mi., pronounced urban characteristics, three-fourths of male population employed in other than agriculture (UNDY)

104

size of military: 1.2 million

literacy rate: 1969, 25% (AH)

per capita GNP: United Nations 1967 estimate in US$ at market prices, $84.00 (UNSY)

name of present head of regime and how came to power: Indira Gandhi, election.

Sources

(UNSY) *United Nations Statistical Yearbook 1970.* New York: United Nations, 1971.

(UNDY) *United Nations Demographic Yearbook 1970.* New York: United Nations, 1971.

(AH) *Area Handbook for India 1970.* Rinn-Sup Shinn (et.al.). Washington, D.C.: United States Government Printing Office, 1971.

(OHT) *Overseas Hindustan Times,* July 1, 1972, Report of 1971 Census.

Selected Readings

Austin, Granville. *The Indian Constitution*. New York: Oxford University Press, 1966.

Bailey, F. G., *Politics and Social Change: Orissa in 1959*. Berkeley, California: University of California Press, 1963.

Basham, A. L., *The Wonder That Was India*. New York: Grove Press, 1954.

Baxter, Craig. *The Jana Sangh: A Biography of an Indian Political Party*. Philadelphia, Pa.: University of Pennsylvania Press, 1969.

Brecher, Michael. *Nehru: A Political Biography*. New York: Oxford University Press, 1959.

_____, *Nehru's Mantle: The Politics of Succession in India*. New York: Praeger, 1966.

Carstairs, G. M., *The Twice-Born*. Bloomington, Indiana: Indiana University Press, 1958.

Das Gupta, J., *Language Conflict and National Development*. Berkeley, California: University of California Press, 1970.

Erdman, Howard L., *The Swatantra Party and Indian Conservatism*. Cambridge: Cambridge University Press, 1967.

Gandhi, Mohandas, *An Autobiography, or The Story of My Experiments with Truth*. Ahmedabad: Navajivan Publishing House, 1927.

Harrison, Selig S., *India: The Most Dangerous Decades*. Princeton, N.J.: Princeton University Press, 1960.

Kochanek, Stanley A., *The Congress Party of India*. Princeton, N.J.: Princeton University Press, 1968.

_____, *Business and Politics in India*. Berkeley, California: University of California Press, 1974.

Morris-Jones, W. H., *Parliament in India*. Philadelphia, Pa.: University of Pennsylvania Press, 1957.

Nehru, Jawaharlal, *The Discovery of India*. Garden City, N.Y.: Doubleday, 1959.

Overstreet, Gene D., and Windmiller, Marshall, *Communism in India*. Berkeley, California: University of California Press, 1959.

Rosen, George. *Democracy and Economic Change in India*. Berkeley, California: University of California Press, 1967.

Rudolph, Lloyd I. and Susanne H., *The Modernity of Tradition*. Chicago, Illinois: University of Chicago Press, 1967.

Seal, Anil, *The Emergence of Indian Nationalism: Competition and Collaboration in the Later Nineteenth Century*. Cambridge: Cambridge University Press, 1968.

Shils, Edward. *The Intellectual Between Tradition and Modernity: The Indian Situation. Supplement I, Comparative Studies in Society and History.* The Hague: Mouton, 1961.

Smith, Donald E., Ed., *South Asian Politics and Religion.* Princeton, N.J.: Princeton University Press, 1966.

Stern, Robert W., *The Process of Opposition in India: Two Studies of How Policy Shapes Politics.* Chicago, Illinois: University of Chicago Press, 1970.

Weiner, Myron, *Party Building in a New Nation.* Chicago, Illinois: University of Chicago Press, 1967.

_____, *The Politics of Scarcity.* Chicago, Illinois: University of Chicago Press, 1962.

_____, ed., *State Politics in India.* Princeton, N.J.: Princeton University Press, 1968.

3   Pakistan and Bangladesh

Robert LaPorte, Jr.

The political systems of Pakistan and Bangladesh provide two of the most interesting and perhaps tragic examples of post-World War II decolonization and nation-building. Both systems began as one unit: the Islamic Republic of Pakistan formed from the division of British India in 1947. With the departure of the British, the new leaders of independent India and Pakistan had to grapple with the problems of governing without the British presence to interfere with their plans. Pakistan found the problems of governance to be extremely complex and difficult since public expectations had been aroused to the point that the meagre resources of the new nation would be severely pressed to meet the demands of a rising population. An analysis of the political and social developments must take place within a framework of limited resources, increasing popular demands, and a considerable amount of elite misunderstanding and conflict.

The intention of this chapter is to survey the evolution of Pakistan and Bangladesh from a number of standpoints. Firstly, their relative economic position vis-à-vis the industrialized world and other nations of Asia, Africa, and Latin America will be considered and the themes of economic underdevelopment and dependency will be examined. Secondly, as an introduction to the evolution of political processes and institutions, the historical perspective and the colonial legacy will be briefly presented. Thirdly, the theme of political instability and continuity will be discussed as a framework for understanding the evolution of political and economic forces in Pakistan and Bangladesh. Fourthly, an analysis of elites and their economic and political power will be presented as a means of analyzing political development in the two nations. Finally, a concluding note is added to indicate what the future may hold for the citizens of both nations.

Pakistan, Bangladesh, and the Third World

Undivided Pakistan spatially contained somewhere between 110 and 115 million people prior to 1972 and the dissolution of the nation into two separate political entities. Almost every broad political study of this country has begun with two prominent features—the religious nature of the union of East (now Bangladesh) and West Pakistan (the territory which retained the title of Islamic Republic of Pakistan) and the unique geographic aspects of this union. Except for the State of Israel, no other modern nation appealed to a religious faith as the common denominator for its establishment. The uniqueness of Pakistan was further illustrated by the dominant role of geography—Pakistan was a nation composed of two distinct, geographic socio-cultural units (more if one includes the diversity found in West Pakistan) separated by a thousand miles of Republic of India territory. Although commented upon *ad nauseam*, these two aspects are critical to an understanding of politics in Pakistan, and will be discussed fully later. For the time being, it is important to examine in brief the macro dimensions of this nation state in terms of (1) economic underdevelopment, and (2) economic dependency. In this analysis, the extent to which Pakistan and Bangladesh conform to some general Third World "model" will be examined.

Economic Underdevelopment

If the risks involved in using macro-economic measures such as the inability to control for micro-economic distortions of sub-national units producing at a rate much greater than national calculations would reveal are accepted, then one can state that there are "rich" and "poor" nations. Within this framework, Pakistan and to a greater extent, Bangladesh, certainly belong to the latter category as when it was the fifth most populous nation in the world, its GNP of approximately $10 billion was one one-hundredth that of the United States. Per capita income, another measure used by economists to determine stages of economic development, while not the lowest in the world is, at about $90, at the lower end of what has been maintained as the world poverty line.[1] In the immediate area of South and Southwest Asia (including India, Sri Lanka, Afghanistan, Iran, Turkey, Syria, and Iraq), only

1. The "world poverty line" has been discussed by many individuals. For example, one scholar maintains that a per capita income of less than $300 constitutes poverty. See David Simpson, "The Dimensions of World Poverty," *Scientific American* 219 (Nov. 1968): 22, 27-35; and Gunnar Myrdal, *Asian Drama: An Inquiry into the Poverty of Nations* (New York: Pantheon, 1968), 3 volumes.

India and Afghanistan have lower per capita income figures. Although noncash or nonmonetary transactions are not included in this figure such an average indicates that individuals and families may consume even fewer resources than this figure would maintain.

Admitting the unreliability of economic measures and the possibilities for distortions included in economic analyses of underdevelopment, there is considerable agreement that Pakistan and Bangladesh are two of the poorest nations in the world. As subsequent discussion will reveal, this position has prevailed even with undivided Pakistan's relatively high economic growth rate, increases in industrial development and production, and increases in agricultural output during the decade of the 1960s. Hence, using economic measures, it can be readily concluded that Pakistan and Bangladesh conform to the Third World stereotype with regard to economic "underdevelopment."

Other economic characteristics which have come to be identified primarily with the nations of Asia, Africa, and Latin America can be found in the examination of the national economies of Pakistan and Bangladesh. The preponderance of their work force engaged in agriculture, for example, is one indicator.[2] Secondly, only 9.7 percent of the population reside in urban centers of 100,000 or more as of 1969. An additional indicator of an underdeveloped economy is the greater extent to which the agricultural population contributes to a subsistence (and/or regional) market, rather than a commercial (and/or national) market. Of the 12.1 million landholdings in both countries, 9.6 million or 79.5 percent are less than 13 hectares in size; an overwhelming majority of these 12.1 million are less than 5 hectares. These miniplots of land combined with the given agro-technology in both nations means that the commercial market contribution of the majority of agriculturalists is negligible. Land size and land technology, including the "green revolution," dictate an economic description which is within the Third World stereotype.

Related to economic macro measures of underdevelopment are those measures which indicate the socio-economic status of Pakistan and Bangladesh. Such statistics as infant mortality rate per thousand (142 as of 1965), life expectancy (as of 1962, 53.7 years for males and 48.8 years for females), literacy rate (as high as 48 percent for urban males and as low as 5 percent for rural females as of 1962—which averages out to about 20 percent for the total population), per capita caloric intake daily, as well as public sector expenditure per capita (for both

2. As of 1965, 67.5 percent of the total work force was engaged in agriculture, fishing, forestry, and hunting industries. See United Nations, International Labour Office, *Yearbook of Labour Statistics* 1970 (Geneva: ILO, 1970), p. 232.

countries it was $38 per capita in 1967—for New Yorkers, it was $950 per capita as of 1968) underscore socio-economic underdevelopment. Aggregate analyses of socio-economic conditions in Pakistan and Bangladesh reaffirm the qualitative indicators of both nations' positions vis-à-vis the Third World. In short, using macro-economic indicators, Pakistan and Bangladesh emerge as two of the poorest of the poor nations of the world. The ratio of resources to population is unfavorably fixed to the disadvantage of the average citizen—truly a situation which underscores Myron Weiner's description of the Indian political system.[3]

Economic Dependency

To state that both countries are economically dependent upon any one foreign power is to slightly distort the present state of affairs. Pakistan is vulnerable, however, to economic conditions derivative of its position as a producer of raw materials (as opposed to a processer and manufacturer of finished products) and its strategic geographical location. Its vulnerability is further complicated by its historical role in the Cold War—it was a nation in search of strategic military materials at a time when the United States was desirous of establishing military alliances against the "Communist threat." The influence of the internal variable of a raw producer economy coupled with the external variable of U.S. willingness to use Pakistan as a pawn in Cold War strategy, therefore, leads to the initial assessment of a dependency condition.

When the sources of external financing of public operations in Pakistan and Bangladesh are surveyed, it is possible to estimate the extent to which many past, present, and future endeavors undertaken by both governments have been or are being underwritten by external sources. Economic dependency results when threatened or actual suspension of economic and military assistance actually deters the government of Pakistan from pursuing a particular policy. The extent to which Pakistan has reached the state where this has occurred is not yet known. In other words, economic dependency upon external resources can be shown; the extent to which demands of these external resources can force governmental decision making into certain channels is not so easily demonstrated despite claims made by certain scholars.[4] A brief

3. Myron Weiner, *The Politics of Scarcity* (Chicago: University of Chicago Press, 1962).
4. The thesis of some radical scholars is that the U.S. has fashioned Pakistan, through its aid and assistance, into the kind of raw producer nation which compliments U.S. industrial needs and desires. It is not as simple as that, as will be related later. For information relating to this radical argument, see the well-argued "Pakistan: The Burden of U.S. Aid," by Hamza Alavi and Amir Khustro, *New University Thought* (Autumn 1962).

examination of the economic and military relationships which have evolved within this notion of economic dependency follows.

Having received little from the division of assets of the British Empire in India, Pakistan faced an immediate need for external resources to satisfy certain national "needs." These needs included military assistance to develop an armed force capable of maintaining the territorial integrity of Pakistan from its principal adversary, India, and economic and technical assistance to encourage and support elite desires to modernize and industrialize the western portion of the country.

Military aid and economic assistance to Pakistan from its principal donor, the United States, began within three years of each other. The first economic assistance agreement between the United States and Pakistan was signed on February 2, 1951, and was a technical assistance agreement of modest magnitude. Prior to this date, foreign assistance to Pakistan had been largely part of the Colombo Plan operations. After 1951, however, the United States gradually assumed the role of major donor. As a result of the failure of the 1951 monsoon and the resulting "famine scare" of the following two years, the United States in 1953 began in earnest to extend rather large amounts of financial and commodity assistance to Pakistan. Well before Ayub assumed power in 1958, the United States was the prime donor country—a situation which was assisted by Pakistani military authorities in their roles as national defenders. Military aid, as referred to above, was a product of U.S. estimates of "security needs" in the Middle East—Pakistan being considered as a key to both the CENTO and SEATO "security systems." Responding to favorable overtures by the United States, the government of Pakistan applied formally to the U.S. for military aid on February 22, 1954. This was granted by the U.S. three days later. This began the massive armament of the Pakistani military forces by the United States with weapons assistance which has been used in two wars against India (September 1965 and December 1971) and one civil war against East Pakistan (March-December 1971).

It is not enough to indicate that external resources (primarily from the U.S.) have been critical to the financing of both civilian and military operations; some quantitative data are required. In the words of the government of Pakistan:

> Foreign assistance has played a significant role in economic development in the earlier part of the 1960s. Foreign loans and credits have financed about 35 percent of total development expenditure and 48 percent of total imports during 1959-60 to 1967-68. The country has tried to put these loans to productive uses . . . Unfortunately, since 1965, the international climate for foreign assistance has deteriorated, the availability of credits has become uncertain, and the overall terms of credit have become harder . . . Recent developments make it imperative for the

country to reduce its dependence on foreign assistance as quickly as possible, despite its growing economic capacity to absorb larger resources from abroad.*

What is said about the 1960s is also true of the situation prior to that time. Although the first foreign assistance from the Colombo Plan countries was not major, it was not insignificant. The following table indicates the magnitude and type of assistance given to Pakistan. As Table 1 reveals, although 75 percent of the external assistance Pakistan has received came after 1960, $1.4 billion (of which 60.4 percent was in the form of grants)—a not insignificant amount of assistance—was received and used in the decade of the 1950s, a period in which Pakistan was still trying to establish a viable planning and implementing system.

Table III.1

**Foreign Economic Assistance to
Pakistan, 1952-1968
(in million U.S. dollars)**

Time Period	Type of Assistance		Total Assistance	Percentage of Total
	Grants	Loans		
Pre-First Plan (1950-55)	$ 250	$ 121	$ 371	6.8
First Plan (1955-60)	573	417	990	18.0
Second Plan (1960-65)	340	2,037	2,377	43.1
Third Plan (1965-68)	104	1,666	1,770	32.1
Totals	$1,267	$4,241	$5,508	100.0

Source: Ministry of Finance, Pakistan Economic Survey, 1968-69 (Islamabad: Government of Pakistan Press, 1969), p. 180.

In regard to military assistance, the case of Pakistan is one which might best be described as "shifting dependency"; that is, original dependence upon British arms and training from 1947 to 1954 (and beyond if one includes the influence of Sandhurst graduates as well as graduates of the Indian Military Academy on the development of the Pakistani Army); shifting to dependence on the United States with the signing of the first military assistance program in February 1954 and continuing until 1965; and shifting finally to a "multi-national" dependency which translates as receiving military arms and other assistance from the Peoples' Republic of China, certain Western European

*Government of Pakistan, Ministry of Finance, Pakistan Economic Survey, 1968-69 (Islamabad: Government of Pakistan Press, 1969), p. 192.

countries, and the United States. Pakistan's military assistance situation in the early 1970s is one where reliance is still upon the United States for spare parts for lethal weaponry, combined with reliance upon its new supplier, the Peoples' Republic of China. Neither the Chinese nor the Americans can assert control over the Pakistani armed forces, as demonstrated in the civil war in East Pakistan.

In summary, with regard to the question of economic dependency both in terms of economic-financial assistance for civilian activities and military assistance (arms and training), Pakistan is in a transitional period; it recognizes that external sources are disappearing and that a period of "hard times" might prevail if resources cannot be found to replace a diminished U.S. commitment. Likewise, with military assistance, the Pakistanis recognize that they must either substitute Chinese arms for existing U.S. weaponry (which might not be feasible) or begin to divert internal resources to fabricate the spare parts needed to maintain their current weapons level. Hence, Pakistan shares with other Third World nations the attribute of economic dependency—however, a somewhat unique one.

Historical Perspective and the Colonial Legacy

The historical roots of Pakistan and Bangladesh are, of course, those of modern India as well. Separate histories of pre-Independence Muslim Indians and Hindu Indians are, in reality, an emphasis on separate communal developments within a common historical framework. The modern Indian is a product of both Islamic influence and British rule and the modern Pakistani and Bengali Muslim have in the same way been influenced by their contacts with Hindu Indians during the period of the British Raj. Since another chapter has treated historical developments on the Indian subcontinent (see Chapter 2), this section will emphasize the development of distinctly subcontinental or South Asian Islamic traditions and concepts which have influenced modern Pakistani and Bengali Muslim politics, administration, and economics.

The beginnings of Islam in the subcontinent can be traced to the early expeditions of Arabs under Pulakesin II who invaded the area near the present city of Karachi around 637 A.D. This initial expedition led to Arab conquests of the provinces of Sind and Baluchistan. Eventually, Punjab was conquered by the Sultans of Ghazni and its subsequent occupation "paved the way for that final struggle which overwhelmed the Gangetic Kingdoms some two-hundred years later."[5] From the early Arab invasions through the governments of the Turko-

5. R. C. Majumdar et al., *An Advanced History of India* (London: MacMillan and Co., Ltd., 1965), p. 276.

Afghans (which lasted until the end of the fourteenth century), the establishment of Islam in the subcontinent within the confines of present-day Pakistan (Sind, Baluchistan, Northwest Frontier and Punjab) was accomplished. The Mughuls continued to extend the rule of Islam and dominated Indian history until the modern colonial era.

The period of Indian history loosely called the era of the Mughul Empire began with the first Battle of Panipat (1576 A.D.) and ended with the Battle of Plassey (1757 A.D.). In the Battle of Panipat, the first Mugul Emperor, Barbur (1483-1530), succeeded in securing a foothold in the Punjab. In the second conflict, Robert Clive secured British preeminence over European rivals and signaled the beginning of British dominance in the subcontinent. Such historic figures as Humayun (Barbur's son), Akbar (the great Mughul Emperor who united all of India and ruled from 1556-1605), Jahangir, Shah Jahan ("The Builder" who was responsible for the Taj Mahal, the Shalimar Gardens, and the Red Fort in Delhi, among other works), and Aurangzeb ("The Puritan", whom some historians credit with the disintegration of the Empire because of his persecution of Hindus and other non-Muslims) are part of this richly dramatic period. Islam under the Mughuls flourished as the religion of the privileged and the rulers and converted great numbers of Indians, both willing and unwilling. The great impact of Islam and its expansion during this period is found in the existence of 120 million Pakistanis and Bengali Muslims and the millions of Muslims who remained in India after partition. Islam became the second largest religion in the subcontinent and its interaction with Hinduism has produced the particular societies that one finds in the three countries. The fortunes of Muslim elites declined under the British ascendency.

During the early British period (up to the 1800s), the English who served in India maintained a certain respect (based on fear during the early eighteenth century) for the Mughul Empire and Islamic customs and traditions. However, by the time Lord Cornwallis had assumed the Governor-Generalship of British India, a change in British attitudes was evident toward all things Indian (both Muslim and Hindu). The English now exhibited a contempt for the indigenous culture, manifest in the various British attempts to alter ("reform") or isolate the traditions and values of both Muslims and Hindus. The Muslims, as the dominant political elite prior to the British, stood to lose the most. Some scholars, for instance, maintain that Hindus had become accustomed to adapting to foreign rulers since the advent of Islam and therefore the transition from Mughul to British rule did not cause great handicaps to the Hindu elite's participation in politics and administration, at least in comparison to the relative problems of Muslim participation. Muslims were not as readily adaptable to the changes in government and did not compete successfully with Hindus for posts the British "reserved" for the natives. Just as Indian (Hindu) nationalism was fed by economic, political, and social discontent and deprivation on the part of elites, likewise, Muslim nationalism reflected the Muslim Indian elite dissatisfaction with their calculations of what the opportunity costs would be in a Hindu-dominated, independent India. The British clearly favored Hindus over Muslims (except for certain segments of the military), since they found Hindus more adaptable to western education and culture, a preference evident in the preponderance of Hindus in both civilian and military bureaucratic positions at partition. The British period brought a decline in the influence of Islam in India and, consequently, a decline in the relative position of Muslim elites near British power. Muslim nationalism has, in part, continued to reflect the glories of the Mughul past and the fear of Hindu domination.

Although Muslim nationalism might be traced further back in time, the Central National Muhammadan Association (founded in 1885) represented one of the first, albeit elitist, organized efforts of Indian Muslims to represent their interests to the British Raj. To a great extent, the Muslim Nationalist movement followed the advice of Sir Syed Ahmed Khan, a nineteenth century Muslim intellectual, who encouraged Muslims to adopt and adapt to the modern technology and education brought into India by the British. A direct confrontation demanding a separate nation did not develop until the twilight of British rule.

Clearly, a separate Muslim identity in India was fostered, in much the same way as the Indian nationalist movement developed, as a means to oust the British so that Indians could secure positions in government and the economy which were reserved during British rule for the British alone. Of course, the economic, political, and social causes were presented within an ideological-historical argument appealing to the more abstract, loftier human motives. But the root causes for Muslim nationalism are eminently visible in the Indian Muslims' individual and collective forecasts of their position within a society dominated not by the outsider, the British, but by descendents of former subjects, the Hindus.

The creation of an independent Muslim homeland in the subcontinent became an objective of the Muslim League (an elitist organization founded in 1906) in 1940 with the passage of the Lahore Resolution at the Muslim League convention held in that Punjabi city. Some claim the name, "Pakistan" (country of the pure), owes its origins to the famous Muslim philosopher and poet Muhammad Iqbal and became the designation for the Muslim ideal. The driving force in successfully securing the areas of East Bengal, West Punjab, Northwest Frontier,

Sind, and Baluchistan (plus those Princely States found within these areas) from the British and the Indian National Congress was Mohammad Ali Jinnah, known as the Quaid-i-Azam or "Great Leader." Jinnah, a member of the Congress movement until 1921, inspired both Muslim elites and masses and persevered to achieve an independent Pakistan.

After agreement had been reached on the partitioning of British India into independent India and Pakistan, the details of the division of assets of the British Empire were worked out between Indian, Pakistani, and British politicians and civilian and military bureaucrats. A series of committees were established prior to partition, to ascertain and agree upon what share should be assigned to each nation. This first major interaction between the two new nations seems to have set the tone of relations that India and Pakistan would maintain with each other over the next twenty-five years. Administratively, Pakistan received less than its share in terms of any proportionate division of government personnel. For example, only 82 Indian Civil Service (ICS) officers chose to opt for Pakistan, of over 540 Indians in this elite bureaucratic cadre. In addition, Pakistan received a disproportionate number of lower level bureaucrats who faced the immediate prospect of unemployment in their newly chosen land. With regard to materials and supplies, again, Pakistan did not fare well. Although agreement had been reached as to a fair share of military supplies for Pakistan, most of those materials were not delivered. Pakistan did not begin an independent existence with the material and personnel advantages of India. The division of assets and liabilities left Pakistan with the lion's share of the latter; those resources which remained after 200 years of British exploitation of the subcontinent went overwhelmingly to India.

Pakistan began its national existence with great problems and disadvantages but soon experienced the even more traumatic period following partition. Even today, after the exodus of 10 million Bengalis to India as a result of the 1971 civil war, the partition of British India remains as the largest uprooting of peoples in recorded history. For both Indians and Pakistanis, memories of partition loom large. The total number of individuals who left their ancestral homes in Punjab, Bengal, United Provinces, and other parts of British India has been estimated as between 10 and 15 million. The total number of refugees who initially resettled in three districts in West Punjab alone has been estimated at several million. Karachi became a refugee-dominated city over night. The number of people murdered on both sides of the border has been estimated in the millions. Neither the moral persuasion of Jinnah or Gandhi nor the strength of combined Indian and Pakistani military and civilian police forces could stay the slaughter. Certainly, the events of partition did not contribute to the establishment of friendly relations between the two nations.

Partition also had another impact—it forced the integration of Princely India with British India on both sides of the border.[6] Integration of these states, however, did not offset the division of Punjab and Bengal. The partition of the Punjab and Bengal had economic repercussions for both regions. East Pakistan (formerly East Bengal and now Bangladesh) had been the primary supplier of raw jute and rice to what became the Indian state of West Bengal. For East Pakistan, the loss of commercial and port facilities and services in Calcutta meant economic dislocation and hardship until the development of replacement facilities in Chittagong. In Punjab, North India lost the agricultural resources of the vast, irrigated districts of West Punjab, while Pakistan had to resettle the several million Muslims who fled to these districts from East Punjab.

The British colonial period contributed to the present inequities that exist in the political, economic and social systems in both Pakistan and Bangladesh. Cultural intrusion and colonialism are a part of the British legacy, as are the English language and western philosophical values. The British, for instance, introduced the military and bureaucratic structures and forms which have been maintained in Pakistan and Bangladesh. Colonial strategy, tactics, and ethics initiated and inculcated by the British established the precedents for political and economic exploitation in the two nations. Indeed, it might be argued that the British in undivided India taught too well their concepts of colonial governance, control, and exploitation to the elites of Pakistan, Bangladesh, and India and it is these legacies rather than British ideas of democracy and popular government which have been more effectively maintained in the nations of South Asia.

Political Instability and Continuity

In a formal, constitutional sense, Pakistan's existence has been marked by political instability. In a non-legal, nonconstitutional sense, Pakistan's history since independence reveals a steady, constant evolution of military-civilian bureaucratic decision-making (resource allocation for the political system as a whole) and politics which was evident shortly after partition. The theme of the dominance of the military-civilian bureaucratic coalition, a coalition of non-representative-type political actors, over decision-making in Pakistan has often been

6. Princely India refers to those semi-autonomous states in pre-partition India which the British ruled indirectly through the residency system. British India, of course, refers to those parts of India under direct administration of the British.

stressed, although many works by political scientists and modern historians on Pakistani politics tend to discuss the intricacies and shifting coalitions between and among Pakistani political parties. This is not to denigrate the study of political parties, legislatures, voting behavior, or the representative-type political actors; but given Pakistan's particular political evolution, the period has yet to arrive when it can be accurately stated that decision-making is dominated by a political party apparatus. This could of course, be qualified by the recent emergence of political parties and party leaders such as the Awami League headed by Mujibur Rahman in Bangladesh and the Peoples' Party led by Z.A. Bhutto in Pakistan, currently in control of decision-making.

Despite the fact that the western model of mass democracy has not been useful in analyzing political and social developments in undivided Pakistan, it is still necessary to recapitulate the main events of the constitutional instability which has dominated the political processes in Pakistan. Pakistan has had no political institution comparable in organizational terms to the Indian Congress Party. The emergence of Pakistan, as was discussed earlier, was the result of elite manipulation of an age-old issue—Muslim-Hindu conflict. The movement for Pakistan was elite-based and without a broad mass base capable of long-term, effective struggle against British colonial rule.

Pakistan emerged as a separate nation as a result of Mohammed Ali Jinnah's skillful maneuverings between the British and the Indian National Congress leadership. The paternalistic leadership, however, did not foster any type of collective parliamentary bargaining politics. Ironically, the period from 1947 to 1958 has been labeled the "Parliamentary Politics" period by many authors. It is appropriate to examine this period as a clue to successive periods.

The Parliamentary Period, 1947-1958

With the partition of British India, each of the two major entities, India and Pakistan, established separate central governments and began to administer public goods and services in the name of their two separate populations. Both India and Pakistan used, as their legal bases, the Government of India Act of 1935 and the Indian Independence Act of 1947. The former statute provided for parliamentary federalism as the means for organizing public power and the latter gave dominion status to India and Pakistan. This patchwork legal basis for both countries was viewed as a temporary measure until the constituent assemblies of the two nations could devise permanent replacements in the form of constitutions. India accomplished the constitutional task in less than three years; Pakistan took until 1956 before a "revised" Constituent Assembly[7] could produce a more complex constitution. Hence, the bulk of the period from 1947 to 1956, was involved in trying to reach some constitutional consensus. During this time, the only institutional developments that occurred were within the civilian and military bureaucracies; cabinets and prime ministers came and went but the civil servants and military leaders retained positions of importance and power in the new state.

The instability of the parliamentary period is underscored by the frequent changes of prime ministers, especially during the last part of this period. From 1947 until the coup in October 1958, Pakistan had a total of seven prime ministers; from September 1956 until October 1958, the rate of change increased so that four individuals occupied this position. One individual, I. I. Chundrigar, had the distinction of holding office for only two months. On the other hand, the chief executive (known as Governor-General until 1956 and thereafter as President), initially thought to be primarily a symbolic and politicially inactive position, has had relative stability of occupation. Part of this stability has been laid to the fact that the "Father" of Pakistan, Mohammad Ali Jinnah, chose to become Governor-General rather than prime minister and thus initiated a tradition of strong, paternalistic executive rule. There were four Governors-General/Presidents during the parliamentary period.

During the 1947-1958 period, no general election was held nationally in Pakistan. The indirect elections of the 1930s and 1940s (with the exception of the East Bengal election in 1954) were the only ties between the members of the Constituent Assembly and the public. Clearly, electoral politics were not part of the Pakistani political process. Elite-based political parties were, for the most part, the only kinds of parties in Pakistan during this period. Although some leftist movements (such as those which Maulana Abdul Hamid Khan Bhashani has led from time to time) have attempted to link provincial or national leadership with the masses, for the most part these were the exceptions rather than the rule during this period.

The Constituent Assemblies were composed of constantly shifting party coalitions and parties. Crossing the aisle was a common practice, as was physical violence during the sitting of the Assembly. What was true for the center was also true for the provincial assemblies. As one scholar observed:

7. "Revised" in the sense that by this time, many original Members had died or had been displaced by the Governor-General of Pakistan. Actually, the second Constituent Assembly "drafted" the 1956 Constitution since the first Assembly had been dismissed by Governor-General Ghulam Mohammad in October 1954.

... [The system of] political parties in Pakistan bears little resemblance to that of most other democratic countries. Politics has begun at the top ... politics is made up of a large number of leading persons who, with their political dependents, form loose agreements to achieve power and to maintain it. Consequently rigid adherence to a policy or a measure is likely to make a politician less available for office. Those who lack fixed ideas but who control legislators, money or influence have tended to prosper in political life. . . . political parties . . . have not turned their attention toward the primary voter. This has not been necessary [since the] national legislature has never been chosen by popular vote.[8]

Although one might question the extent to which political instability during the 1947-58 period was unique to the Pakistani form of parliamentary politics, it certainly exhibited a considerable amount of maneuvering and many political party inconsistancies. Whether the unprincipled behavior of Pakistani landlords, lawyers, and civil-servants-turned-politicians led to the October 1958 coup in a cause-and-effect fashion is open for debate. But it cannot be denied that the military bureaucrats in league with President Iskander Mirza chose to move and perform the coup in the name of ending parliamentary corruption and immorality. It can be asserted that the instability of this period and the inability of the civilian politicians in and out of parliament to appease the military-civilian bureaucratic coalition did contribute to the abandonment of the parliamentary democratic facade. The end of the parliamentary politics period ushered in the First Martial Law Period.

The Ayub Khan Era, 1958-1969

The proclamation of martial law within a particular nation-state is considered to be an indication of an emergency situation. In most societies it has been employed as a temporary measure, a device to govern during emergencies caused by natural or man-made disasters. In Pakistan, however, the imposition of martial law has become a convenient means of government succession. During the last 13 years, Pakistanis have lived under martial law for a total of almost eight years.[9] Clearly, in Pakistan the extraordinary became the usual. The exception was the relatively but not completely disorder-free period of "normal" government operations from March 1962 until March 1969. The First Martial Law Period (October 1958 to March 1962) was a period of unchecked

8. Keith Callard, *Pakistan: A Political Study* (London: Allen & Unwin, 1957), p. 67.
9. This calculation includes the 44 months of martial law imposed by Ayub (October 1958 through March 1962) as well as the imposition of martial law and its various modified forms under Yahya and Bhutto (March 1969 until June 1972).

executive rule by President Mohammad Ayub Khan. During this pe-riod, the central government attempted to discourage anything ap-proaching parliamentary politics and succeeded in encouraging "new" participants in overt political decision making—the newly emerging industrialist class and military-turned-civilian politicians. Ayub also continued to rely upon the Civil Service of Pakistan (CSP) as an in-strument of the vice-regal, colonial-style regime he inherited and encouraged.

One articulated goal of the First Martial Law Period was to "sta-bilize" the nation politically. Maintaining that Pakistan was "given a system of government totally unsuited to the temper and climate of the country,"[10] Ayub sought to "guide" his fellow Pakistanis in much the same fashion as other paternalistic despots have attempted to do both in the past and present. The "proper" government for "illiterate and primitive" Pakistanis, maintained Ayub, was one which consulted with only those localized, Ayub-designated rural elites through the Ba-sic Democracies scheme[11] and, of course, the other, less traditional elites of the cities and small towns. This conceptual, governmental framework was phased into operation with the promulgation of the 1962 Constitution in June of that year.

The 1962 Constitution was an attempt to institutionalize one-man rule through a strong presidential form of government. In Ayub's words:

> The President should be made the final custodian of power on the coun-try's behalf and should be able to put things right both in the provinces and the centre should they go wrong. Laws should be operative only if certified by the President . . . No change in the constitution should be made unless agreed to by the President.[12]

10. Mohammed Ayub Khan, "Pakistan Perspective," *Foreign Affairs* 38, 2 (July 1960): 550.

11. This was a system of indirect elections which formed the electoral base for the national assembly, the provincial assemblies, as well as the Office of President. There were a total of 80,000 "Basic Democrats" elected by the population as a whole. These "Basic Democrats," in turn, elected the Presi-dent and various legislators. Even with this system of indirect elections, the government felt compelled to "insure" that Ayub and his hand-picked can-didates always won by imposing many legal and illegal constraints on balloting.

12. "A Short Appreciation of Present and Future Problems of Pakistan" (Memorandum written by General Mohammed Ayub Khan, Defense Min-ister, October 4, 1954), cited in Karl Von Vorys, *Political Development in Pakistan* (Princeton: Princeton University Press, 1965). Similarly, see Mo-hammed Ayub Khan, *Friends Not Masters* (New York: Oxford University Press, 1967).

The 1962 Constitution departed radically from the 1956 document. A "controlled" National Assembly was provided for and similar bodies were installed in the provinces. Debate and discussion were the only powers permitted the legislators; power of the purse remained with the Chief Executive and his appointed Governors of both provinces. The 1962 Constitution attempted to formalize the power of non-representative elite groups (civilian and military bureaucrats) and curtail the influence of both old and aspiring parliamentary politicians. Through a mixture of legal and illegal means, Ayub maintained order from 1958 until the fall of 1968.

During the period from October 1958 to March 1969, Pakistan experienced an economic growth that was spectacular for Asia in gross, quantitative terms but which occurred within a context of increasing economic inequality between a minute upper class on the one hand and a small middle and an enormous lower class on the other. Macrogrowth was meaured at around 6 percent per year for the decade of the 1960s. Prior to the fall of 1968, the Ayub era was proclaimed by both domestic and foreign observers as an era of great economic growth, if not prosperity for the masses. This optimism faded into the background amid the apologetic reversals of the regime's leading economic advisers and planners.[13] Social change (defined here as the redistribution of societal goods and services to previously excluded classes or as change in class structure) was minimal, although a new business and industrialist class was fostered through government-encouraged and subsidized private industrial development. This government-sponsored "change," however, benefited those who already had a large share of the economic pie. Although the Ayub regime had begun to encourage agricultural development by the Third Five Year Plan (1965-70), this, like Pakistan's industrial development, tended to aid the traditional middle and upper classes in the rural areas. Little if anything was done for the embryonic urban proletariat[14] or for the

13. Two influential economists during this period were the Chief Economist of the Planning Commission and the Director of the Harvard University Development Advisory Service (principal source of economic advice to the Government of Pakistan). At a conference on "Economic Growth and Distributive Justice in Pakistan" held at Rochester, New York in July 1970, both individuals while defending economic policy decisions during the Ayub period admitted that these decisions failed to provide for equity in economic resource allocation and distribution.

14. Shortly before Ayub's resignation, the Planning Commission admitted that real wages of industrial workers had declined during the 1960-68 period while the new industrial class had been given generous tax concessions.

large group of landless or land-poor rural proletariat.[15] Politically, this period witnessed a formalization of centralized, executive rule—the remedy offered by the opponents of parliamentary government during the 1950s—and was officially adopted by Ayub and incorporated as the ideological foundation to achieve political stability. The liberal use of a number of restrictive measures,[16] including the suppression of opposition, was the means and, finally, one of the ends of the Ayub regime. Let us examine the pluses and minuses of this era more closely, looking first at economic activity, then social change, and finally political change.

As previously mentioned, economic growth during the Ayub years was outstanding by any quantitative measure. In examining the data, one finds that from 1959-60 to 1966-67, Pakistan averaged a yearly growth in GNP of about 5.17 percent.[17] Compared to the eight-year period from 1950-51 to 1957-58, in which the average increase was 2.19 percent per year, Ayub's claims of quantitative economic growth are justified. In regard to another gross indicator, per capita income, there was no growth during the period 1950-51 to 1957-58 but a 20.1 percent increase from 1959-60 to 1966-67. More important, during the four years prior to 1957-58, population increase equaled or surpassed the increase in GNP, while at no time did this occur during the Ayub period. In short, quantitative indicators of economic growth supported Ayub's claim that Pakistan under his rule enjoyed a respectable—indeed laudable, for South Asia—period of economic development.

Gross measurements do not, however, tell the whole story. Qualitative inequalities as reflected in income distribution among economic/social classes more accurately reveal who received the lion's share of

15. Ayub's land reform claims did not include this group. Furthermore, as the events in early 1969 revealed, a major geographic area of discontent was rural East Pakistan. See *New York Times*, March 20, 1969, pp. 1 and 16.
16. There were a number of "legal" weapons which the government could use to suppress political actions and utterances: First, the Martial Law Regulations promulgated in October 1958—many of them either incorporated into the 1962 Constitution or in force even after the Constitution was adopted; second, the Elective Bodies Disqualification Order of 1959; third, the Press and Publication Ordinances of 1963, providing stringent controls over newspapers; finally an abandonment of judicial review which existed prior to 1958. It is noteworthy that the Martial Law regime of General Yahya Khan incorporated many of these devices. See "Prepared Statement by President Yahya Khan at his First Press Conference," April 10, 1969.
17. The following analysis is based upon statistics found in Government of Pakistan, Ministry of Finance, *Pakistan Economic Survey, 1966-67* (Karachi: Manager of Publications, 1967), pp. 1-5 of the Statistical Section.

the increase in national economic well-being. An extremely small number of families owned the major share of industrial investment made during Ayub's period—a fact admitted by Ayub's own Planning Commission prior to the 1968-69 disturbances. This problem was further recognized, albeit belatedly, in the government's January 1969 announcement of the objectives of the Fourth Five Year Plan 1970-75 —"To synthesize the claims of economic growth and social justice through the pursuit of pragmatic policies" and "to direct the forces of socio-economic change in the interests of all the people."[18]

Ayub's approach to economic development was marked by the fostering of a private sector through state subsidies and other encouragements, emphasizing gross economic increase without regard to income redistribution or other considerations of social justice. The heavy burden—the costs of change—was squarely placed upon those who could least afford to carry it. As various historical and contemporary experiences have amply illustrated, populations cannot be persuaded to make sacrifices if the burdens and rewards are not shared equitably. Pakistan's elites were educated to this fact when the demands of the polity were expressed violently in the streets of urban and rural Pakistan.

In the area of social change, Ayub and his administration engaged in rhetoric and symbolic manipulation. Twenty-eight "reform" commissions were established, and from the beginning the term "revolutionary" was widely employed. Some minor changes did occur. But to maintain that the sum total of these economic, social, and political adjustments constituted a "revolution" is a totally misleading use of the term. An examination of some of these "reforms" will illustrate the point.

The problem of land distribution and tenure was attended to early in the Ayub regime with the establishment of the Land Reform Commission on October 19, 1958. The Commission's Report, issued on January 20, 1959, offered only mild remedies for this major socio-economic problem, and was accepted by the President with only a few minor changes. Although many of the more archaic, feudal aspects of landlord-peasant relationships were abolished, there was no large-scale land expropriation and redistribution. Few large landowners lost land, and few, if any, landless peasants received it. The consensus from most sources is that the regime chose not to erode its landholding support base by imposing government expropriation of land.[19] Recently,

18. Government of Pakistan, Planning Commission, *Objectives of the Fourth Five Year Plan, 1970-75* (Karachi: Manager of Publications, January 1969).
19. Many general officers as well as members of the middle and junior grade officer ranks come from landowning families in West Pakistan—a most important political reason for Ayub's conservative approach to land tenure change.

efforts in support of agricultural development (under the Third Five Year Plan, 1965-70) emphasized the development of middle and upper-middle class "farmers," while carefully reassuring the status of the already powerful, large landowners. This gradual modernization-from-above approach to agricultural development[20] illustrates the conservative character of Ayub's land program. Social change in terms of land tenure revisions and redistribution was virtually non-existent under Ayub.

The regime also gave attention to improving the position of women in Pakistani society and protecting children from exploitation within the family. The result was the enactment of the Muslim Family Laws Ordinance No. VII of 1961—a legal vehicle which discouraged the practice of polygamy, promoted women's rights, and was regarded as the first step toward modernization of family life. However, since its enforcement was vested in committees of the Union Councils—the lowest tier in Ayub's Basic Democracies Scheme—its implementation has been less than rigorous. Only to the extent that symbolic endorsement of new principles contributes to the implementation of these principles can a case be made for social change having occurred in this area.

In a third area, education, Ayub was most unsuccessful. If the literacy rate may be used as a crude measure, the Ayub regime barely kept up with population increase. Some increases occurred in capital construction for primary and secondary education, but the goal of universal primary education is still a distance away. University education was viewed as posing particular hazards for the regime. Ayub was never popular with university students; as early as 1961-62, he had to close the universities in East .Pakistan because of student demonstrations demanding the release of H. S. Suhrawardy from house arrest. Student violence in opposition to the Ayub regime constantly threatened the operations of universities in both Wings.

Thus, in these three areas of possible social change—land distribution and socio-economic relations in the countryside, family and social relationships, and education—Ayub's words exceeded his deeds. As in the case of economic policies, social planning reflected a preference for preserving elite privileges; changes that did occur were of a minor, gradual nature and did not infringe upon the prerogatives of the conservative coalition that supported Ayub.

20. The Third Five Year Plan emphasized tube-well construction, fertilizers, improved "miracle" seeds, and other technical solutions. This "Rostowian" approach did not consider redistribution or criteria of social justice. See: Government of Pakistan, Planning Commission, *The Third Five Year Plan, 1965-70* (Karachi, 1965). During the first few months of the Bhutto regime, an agrarian reform program was announced; however, the impact of this program on large landholdings appears minor.

It was clear from the beginning that Ayub sought to scrap the legal-constitutional system inherited from the British. In its place he created a presidential system, with the President wielding centralized power and the legislatures (National and Provincial Assemblies) reduced to debating clubs. Legally, Pakistan remained a federal republic, but in reality decision-making was an exclusive function of the President and his chosen advisors. Provincial autonomy, for all intents and purposes, was nonexistent. Ayub created an electoral college (the Basic Democracies scheme) for the indirect election of the President and the members of the National and Provincial Assemblies.

The changes that were not made are equally important: No efforts were made to curtail the informal but extremely influential roles of the military and the civilian bureaucracy.[21] In fact, the coup led by Ayub expanded the role of the military[22] and set the precedent for open military intervention into what had been, at least formally, civilian affairs. Although ushered back to their barracks by the end of November 1958, the military maintained their importance through Ayub and his colleagues during the entire eleven years; and in the crises of 1968-69, these "specialists in violence" again became the men of the hour. In effect, Ayub formalized the "Garrison State" nature of the Pakistani system. He made manifest what had already been implicit during the 1950s—the dominant roles of the military and the civilian bureaucracies in Pakistan.

Ayub's political coalition differed from those of his parliamentary predecessors, and that in itself was political change. He drew his support first and foremost from the military; then from the civilian bureaucracy, the new industrial-entrepreneurial class, and part of the traditional rural elite (large landowners in West Pakistan and the middle-class, Basic Democrat-types in East Pakistan). His opponents included the law profession (including many disenfranchised, if not politically

21. Although there was some indication very early in the Martial Law period that Ayub would "clean out" the civilian bureaucracy and reduce the power exercised by CSP officers, the CSP soon "proved" its value to Ayub. Just as the CSP had adapted to parliamentary politics, so it adjusted to the post-1958 Garrison State.

22. Both in constitutional-legal terms and in practice, the military and civilian bureaucracies received symbolic and real rewards. The 1962 Constitution ensured (for the length of its existence as the basic legal document for the state) continued military control over the military ("Constitution of the Islamic Republic of Pakistan," Article 238), Ayub's constitution also guaranteed the privileges which the CSP possessed throughout the 1950s. Yahya maintained military control and civil service privileges but Bhutto's Constitution eliminated the civil service guarantees.

ostracized, former parliamentarians and other politicians), university students and most of the intellectual community, some large landowners in West Pakistan, an assortment of religious leaders, the urban middle class in both Wings, and, as evidenced by their street violence, the urban and rural proletariat. Numerically, Ayub probably had more opponents than supporters at the end. But, as will be suggested and discussed shortly, it was not numbers that terminated his tenure. It was defection by members of his support coalition, in particular, the military, that determined the end of the regime.

In the final analysis, political change under Ayub was revolutionary in word rather than in action. It is true that he abolished the parliamentary system, but he did not radically change the composition of the political elite—those who directly and indirectly influence political decisions in Pakistan. Civil Service officers, large landowning representatives, the military bureaucracy, and some lawyers continued to influence government actions and programs. Ayub emphasized, institutionalized, and legalized the very same sources of political power that had been present but latent during the period from 1947 to 1958.

In analyzing Ayub's descent and the accompanying succession of General Yahya Khan, an obvious limitation of knowledge must be recognized. No one except the General and the Field Marshal, and perhaps their immediate colleagues and aides, knows exactly or fully what happened or who said or did what during those final months. With this qualification, we shall examine Ayub's descent from power, beginning with a discussion of the reason offered by the U.S. news media and opposition parties in Pakistan.

According to some reports, it was months of urban unrest and student demonstrations for "democracy," culminating in a general strike, that forced Ayub to resign. Four months of intermittent rioting by urban workers and students indeed revealed the unrest and dissatisfaction among both groups, but the fact remains that Ayub had never relied upon, nor in all probability did he expect or need, any measure of support from either group. In the 1965 indirect elections, his poorest showing was in urban areas. Indeed, in West Pakistan, his stronghold, the only Division in which he was defeated was Karachi, the largest urban area in the Province. In East Pakistan, the two Districts won by Miss Jinnah, his opponent, were Dacca and Chittangong—both urban areas. The urban areas were not, therefore, regarded as strong support bases for Ayub, and since the urban proletariat, refugees, and middle class were not critical segments in his political coalition, their dissatisfaction could not have critically affected the then existing power relationships within the regime.

As noted above, there were very few years during Ayub's tenure that did not witness student demonstrations against the government.

Ayub's anti-intellectualism,[23] although not directly related to his problems with students and the intellectual community, certainly did not
facilitate his understanding of either group or of the motivations behind student unrest. But there is no evidence that he depended upon
student support for his regime or that student unrest in 1968-69 could
have deterred him from maintaining firm control over decision-making when similar disturbances in earlier years had not.

A third cause, related to the above, has also been promoted—the so
called "growing strength" of the opposition leadership. This line of
reasoning attempts to link opposition political party leaders to student
and urban unrest in a leader-follower relationship. The proposition
that a popular call for democracy was stimulated by particular political parties or leaders does not bear up under analysis. The opposition
parties were only "patron" operations which formed around a strong
personality. To conclude that Ayub would step down because of the
"growing strength" of elite-based, mutually hostile, political parties
whose leaders independently demanded his abdication is not convinc-
ing. Student and urban unrest *led* rather than followed political party
leadership.

What did cause Ayub to resign, and to what extent did the violence
of 1968-69 contribute to his decision? The underlying causes were partly personal, partly nonpersonal, the latter reflecting changes in
the power and political relationships between Ayub and his support
coalition.

In examining the nonpersonal causes, it is necessary to reemphasize
the importance of Ayub's support from the military and civilian bureaucracy. The military executed the coup which brought Ayub to
power, maintained control during the month of October 1958, and
then returned to the barracks. This does not mean that the military
reverted to an apolitical role. Rather, while it remained in the background and refrained from intervening, it contributed indirectly to the
maintenance of the regime. However, while Ayub publicly had no differences with his former colleagues in the military and gave them symbolic, constitutional-legal rewards, he granted them less materially (as
measured by defense expenditures) than they had received during the
parliamentary period. This is clear if one compares defense expenditures for the years prior to 1959-60 and after that date (excluding the
years 1965-66 and 1966-67, since these were clearly "abnormal" years
due to the Indo-Pakistani War in the fall of 1965). Table 2 reveals that
total expenditures for the years prior to 1959-60 were $1,823.0 million,
of which $1,020.1 million, or about 56 percent went for defense. Com-

23. For an example, see his description of John F. Kennedy in *Friends Not
    Masters*, p. 139.

parable figures for the 1959-60 to 1964-65 period were $2,645.2 million, of which $1,393.9 or about 52.7 percent was spent on defense. Examining these figures another way, while total expenditures during the 1959-65 period increased by 48.2 percent, defense expenditures increased by only 21 percent. Comparable figures for the period prior to the 1958 coup show an increase of 54.5 percent in total public expenditures and 53.8 percent in defense expenditures.

One interpretation of these financial data is that Ayub the President was not as generous to the military as Ayub the Commander-in-Chief, and that this generated some ill feeling among the military. If a scapegoat was sought to assume responsibility for Pakistan's military reversals during the 1965 war, Ayub as the allocator of scarce resources in Pakistan was a vulnerable target. Until 1965-66, for instance, defense expenditures had increased at a much slower rate than total public expenditure, reaching a low of 46.1 percent of total expenditures in 1964-65, the eve of the Indian conflict. In comparison, defense expenditures increased under Yahya and have not decreased under Bhutto. Yahya's regime expended a total of about $578 million in 1969-70—an increase of about 11 percent over the previous year.

Another possible, and related, area of conflict between Ayub and the military was Ayub's agreement to the Tashkent settlement of January 10, 1966. Most observers contend that the Pakistani government could not have obtained Indian agreement to troop withdrawals without this settlement. At the same time it is also apparent that public opinion in Pakistan, or a large segment of it, opposed the settlement (Bhutto's ouster as foreign minister was laid to his differences with Ayub over this issue). It is probable that a major share of this discontent and unhappiness resided in those who were most "embarrassed"—the Pakistani military.

A third indicator of the military's unhappiness with Ayub was the emergence of Asghar Khan, a former air marshal, as an active and vocal opponent of the Ayub regime in the fall of 1968. It is unlikely that Asghar would have ventured into politics without some indication that a portion of the military agreed with his dissatisfaction with Ayub.

With these indirect but important indicators of the military's dissatisfaction with Ayub during the latter years of his tenure, it is possible to conclude that by the fall of 1968 Ayub could no longer depend upon the unified, solid support of the military. The erosion of this source of support is the single most important non-personal reason for his retirement announcement. Had Ayub not considered the military to be a critical support base for maintaining his regime, or had these indications of support erosion not been as visible, he might have held onto his office longer, or at least he might have attempted to do so. In

Table III.2

**Defense Expenditures as Percentage
of Total Government Expenditures,
1948-49—1971-72
(in million U.S. dollars)**

Year	Defense Expenditures	Total Expenditures	Defense as % of Total
1948-49	97.2	136.6	71.1
1949-50	131.7	180.0	73.3
1950-51	16.8	266.6	51.3
1954-55	133.7	246.7	54.1
1955-56	193.2	301.8	64.2
1956-57	168.2	279.4	60.2
1957-58	179.4	319.6	56.1
1958-59	209.9	410.9	51.0
1959-60	219.7	388.7	56.5
1960-61	234.2	398.8	58.7
1961-62	232.8	417.2	55.6
1962-63	200.4	377.0	53.1
1963-64	242.9	490.8	49.5
1964-65	265.7	576.0	46.1
1965-66	601.1	1,094.4	54.9
1966-67	482.8	792.7	60.9
1967-68	460.0	858.3	53.59
1968-69	510.9	920.2	55.52
1969-70	578.8	1,073.6	53.91
1970-71[a]	715.8	1,274.2	56.17
1971-72[a]	896.8	1,511.4	59.33
1972-73[b]	890.5	1,565.1	56.89

a. Revised Figures
b. Estimates as of July-August 1972

Source: Government of Pakistan, Finance Division, *Pakistan Economic Survey, 1971-72* (Karachi: Manager of Publications, 1972), pp. 94-95.

other words, the 1968-69 violence in the streets and Ayub's reaction to it reflected his precarious standing vis-à-vis the military, which in turn caused him to reevaluate his position and subsequently announce his retirement.

Another nonpersonal factor in his decisions of February and March was his inability to develop an effective, institutionalized base of political support outside the military and civilian bureaucracies. The complex set of activities through which he attempted to establish such a base began in 1959 with the promulgation of the Basic Democracies scheme. Following that, using cajolery, patronage, and other devices, he tried to develop civilian, non-governmental support, first through a non-party institution (among the Basic Democrats) and then with political party trappings (the Pakistan Muslim League of 1962). Neither approach really achieved the objective. Furthermore, as the violence in March 1969 revealed, the "Ayub men" in rural East Pakistan discovered that Ayub was really powerless to protect them. The targets of mob violence were government officials and, more importantly for Ayub, his Basic Democrats. Therefore, not only was Ayub unable to develop meaningful political support outside the government, but what support he had cultivated was reduced to a fraction after the March 1969 riots. By that time, Ayub could rely on only a handful of faithful supporters (those he could physically protect) and, to a limited extent, the military. And, as indicated above, it is suspected that the military (in the personages of the General Staff) had already formally informed Ayub that they could not support him indefinitely. Facing these realities, Ayub retired from the presidency on March 25, 1969, appointing Yahya as Chief Martial Law Administrator.

The role of the civilian bureaucracy throughout this critical period appears to have been one of effective neutrality. Although the Civil Service of Pakistan had worked out its modus vivendi with the Ayub regime, it was not a personal, individualized arrangement but an institutional one. That is, even though Ayub was the leader of the 1958 coup and the effective ruler of Pakistan from 1958 to 1969, the civilian bureaucracy's accommodation with the regime was an institutionalized arrangement designed to outlast any one military-turned-civilian leader. Hence, although some CSP officers might have personally regretted Ayub's departure, the collective bent of the CSP and other civilian bureaucrats was to ensure a smooth transfer of leadership.

The mechanics of the succession or transfer of power from Ayub to his hand-picked successor were quite mundane. Although the popular press in the United States paid attention to the statements of parliamentarians, politicians, and other self-styled leaders outside the government, Ayub's round table discussion revealed what everyone knew —that there was no viable, effective alternative to a military-directed succession. By their inability to agree among themselves, those politicans and party leaders who met with Ayub merely underscored this political fact of life. Hence, using excuses of further street demonstrations, unrest in the East Pakistan countryside, and "threats" (real and imagined) of economic stagnation, Ayub resigned. He formally communicated this intention to Yahya, and in the same letter declared martial law and appointed Yahya the Chief Martial Law Administrator. He announced all of the above in a radio broadcast to the nation—his last formal paternalistic action, which paralleled events in the October 1958 succession. The action had, perhaps, its own constitutional-legal basis. Under the 1962 Constitution, the President had been given emergency powers. Certainly, this transfer of the Presidency was as legal as the 1958 action and similar to the legality surrounding the imposition of Presidential Rule in any of India's states. Yahya accepted the call, abrogated the 1962 Constitution, banned all political activity, dismissed the National and Provincial Assemblies, issued Martial Law Regulations, and finally, on April 1, 1969, retroactively proclaimed himself President of Pakistan.

Succession via martial law is much less complicated than other forms of constitutional transfer of power. Theoretically, it permits the new executive a greater degree of discretion in keeping or discarding whatever he wants of the old regime. Given the actual circumstances of this succession, however, and as will be discussed below, Yahya, having been selected by his predecessor, came to power saddled with some commitments to the status quo. His discretion, therefore, was limited. As a preface to an elaboration of the case at hand, let us examine what Yahya (and later Bhutto) inherited.

Reassessments will, of course, be made of Ayub's regime in the light of recent events, and it is clear that this era of Pakistani history was a dramatic one which will have an impact on future generations of Pakistanis. By working within the constraints imposed by capitalistic economic development theory and thereby avoiding the important issue of inherent conflict between quantitative economic growth and social justice, Ayub was able to achieve impressive economic gains and to defer the problems of redistribution of these gains to his successor. Thus, having increased the gulf between rich and poor in Pakistan, he presented his successor with an explosive situation. Ayub's economic legacy, therefore, is mixed—impressive industrial growth and the beginnings of a "revolution" in agricultural production, both supported by a highly exploited rural and urban working class, which was increasingly demanding greater, more equitable distribution.

Ayub's social legacy must be viewed within the context of Pakistani economics. Social demands, too, would have to be dealt with by Ayub's successors. Readjustments in the prevailing social relationships, if they are attempted, will affect the positions of presently powerful segments in Pakistan—in particular, the military, the civilian bureaucracy, the new industrialist class, and the traditional landlord class. These segments overlap, of course, with interconnections existing between the military and the landlords, the civilian bureaucracy and the industrialist class. Except for the development of a new industrialist class via government subsidies, Ayub's regime did not tamper with the prevailing socio-political power distribution. Ayub, in fact, diversified the exploiting classes by adding the industrialists to the existing military, civilian bureaucracy, and large landlords. While there was a readjustment or reshuffling of elite activities, no attempt was made to provide new avenues of social mobility for the middle and lower classes. As shown above, the "costs" of this elite modernization were borne by the middle and lower classes, those least able to afford it.

The political legacy has already been discussed at some length. Within the framework of a highly centralized, strong executive system, Ayub's Garrison State formalized, and in a sense legitimized, the dominant roles exercised by non-representative political actors. In addition, Ayub's political legacy included his political support coalition—the military, the civilian bureaucracy, the new industrial-entrepreneurial class, and a segment of the traditional rural elite including large landlords in West Pakistan and, until the emergence of Bangladesh, upper and middle-class Basic Democrat-types in East Pakistan.

The Yahya Khan Interlude, 1969-1971

With the downfall of Ayub, the issue of regional economic disparities came to the forefront. This issue, however, was not the only one facing Pakistan. In fact, the broader one of developing a "suitable" governmental form to replace the bankrupt Ayub presidential scheme *appeared* to have more immediate visibility. These were not, of course, inseparable issues; East Bengali leaders such as Sheikh Mujibur Rahman of the Awami League maintained at the time of Yahya Khan's ascendency to power that any new governmental form would have to accommodate the demands for autonomy of the eastern half of the country.

With General Agha Muhammad Yahya Khan's assumption of power through the Second Martial Law promulgation (March 25, 1969), citizens of Pakistan were told that the generals were not desirous of maintaining their power, that they were willing to permit a return to civilian rule—provided that Pakistan's "integrity" and sovereignty remained intact. What the military decision-makers appeared to be offering at this point in time was the opportunity of greater civilian participation in government so long as no threatening moves were proposed that would essentially dilute the "character" of Pakistan as defined by the military.[24] In mid-1969, a timetable was established for the return to civilian rule. Yahya agreed to consider the readoption of a federal parliamentary system similar to that which existed during the pre-Ayub period; the "reform" nature of the Second Martial Law Period appeared to attempt to start satisfying both the demands for more

24. This definition would certainly preclude any de facto separation of the two wings of the country; that is, the military would not permit civilians in government whose "loyality" they suspected. A "prime suspect" at this time was Sheikh Mujib.

equitable income distribution *and* the demands of the East Pakistanis for greater economic autonomy within a one-nation framework.

On November 28, 1969, General Yahya announced his political timetable; full political activity, subject to "certain guidelines," would be permitted after January 1, 1970, and general elections would be held on October 5, 1970.[25] The national assembly elected as a result of this first general election in Pakistan's history would have 120 days to draft a new constitution. (General Yahya reserved the right to "authenticate" the constitution before it would be adopted.) As the election date approached, political activity intensified. The two political parties most active were the Awami League, led by Sheikh Mujibur Rahman, and the People's Party of Pakistan, led by Zulfikar Ali Bhutto.

The general election for National Assembly seats took place as scheduled and the electoral results sent shock waves through the nation. The Awami League captured all but two seats in the East (167 seats) and about 72 percent of the vote, whereas the People's Party with 81 seats (out of 138 in the West) became the majority party in the West. Hence, by the end of 1970, Pakistan had completed, successfully, what some observers considered the critical first step in the restoration of electorally-based civilian government.[26] But the process of transfer was not effected with the electoral victories of Mujib and Bhutto. Indeed, the election resulted in heightened tensions between civilian and military-bureaucratic leaders and between the civilian leaders of the East and the West. The election results in the East had underscored the Awami League's demands for greater regional autonomy. It appears that certain members of the Awami League felt they had successfully translated "ballots into bullets" and, certainly, that West Pakistan (the generals and other influentials) would not intervene in force after finding out the magnitude of electoral support that existed for the Awami League's demands.[27]

From the elections in December 1970 to the military occupation of the East (and the accompanying action against the "miscreants") in late March 1971, events accelerated and appeared to control the political actors in this tense drama. January and February saw riots and violence in Dacca with a death toll from military-civilian clashes es-

25. Because of the severe flooding in East Pakistan during August, 1970, the general election was later rescheduled for·December 7, 1970. Provincial assembly elections were held on December 17, 1970.

26. Craig Baxter, "Pakistan Votes-1970," *Asian Survey* 22, No. 3 (March 1971), p. 217.

27. This dangerous reasoning, perhaps, contributed to unpreparedness of Awami League leadership for the Army's coercive actions which commenced on March 25, 1971.

timated at over 300. On February 13, 1971, Yahya Khan announced the date for the National Assembly meeting as March 2, 1971, only to have Bhutto declare, two days later, that he and his followers would boycott this meeting. After meeting with Bhutto and the Pakistani generals, Yayha announced on March 1 a postponement of the Assembly meeting and appointed Lt. General Tikka Khan (later to become Chief of Staff of the army under President Bhutto) as the Military Governor and Martial Law Administrator for the East to replace the civilian Governor of the beleaguered province.[28] Wide-spread rioting and further conflicts between the authorities and the masses in East Pakistan greeted this move and only through the intervention of Awami League "law and order" committees did the province maintain a semblance of civil order. On March 7, Sheikh Mujib responded to Yahya's moves with a set of demands for East Pakistani autonomy only somewhat short of a declaration of secession and independence,[29] withstanding the immense pressure for such a step both within and outside his party. Further, Mujib threatened to boycott the National Assembly meeting rescheduled for March 25 unless Yahya terminated martial law.

On March 10, President Yahya Khan announced his intention to fly to Dacca to meet with Mujib. Meanwhile, reports circulated that Sheikh Mujib had "ordered" the East Pakistani Government to take orders from him and not the central authorities; Government workers were instructed to stay away from their jobs and a member of the East Pakistani judiciary refused to swear in Lt. General Tikka Khan as military governor of the province. From March 16 (the date of Yahya's arrival in Dacca) to March 21, discussions between Yahya, Mujib, and some minor West Pakistani politicians were held. During these discussions, in an attempt to meet one of Mujib's demands, Yahya agreed to establish a commission of inquiry to probe the army's activities during the civil disobedience campaign the Awami League had launched in response to the postponement of the National Assembly meeting in early March. But Mujib then declared that "the people of Bangladesh

28. Later, on March 6, Yahya set March 25, 1971, as the date for the first meeting of the Assembly. At the same time, he issued this warning: "No matter what happens, as long as I am in command of Pakistan's armed forces and head of state, I will insure the complete and absolute integrity of Pakistan. I will not allow a handful of people to destroy the homeland of millions of innocent Pakistans." See *Washington Post*, March 7, 1971.

29. Specifically, Mujib made two demands, (1) that the army be withdrawn to their cantonments and (2) that President Yahya Khan end immediately Martial Law and turn over the powers of government to elected representatives. See *Washington Post*, March 8, 1971. Needless to say, neither demand was met.

shall not cooperate with such a commission."[30] Yahya's position on the discussions was that any agreement on the future of Pakistan must have the "full endorsement" of all major political leaders in Pakistan.[31] This ran counter to the Mujib position of a loose confederation providing maximum autonomy for the East with or without "full endorsement" of all Pakistani politicians. While these negotiations were taking place, the Awami League was organizing and consolidating its de facto control over the province.

On March 21, Bhutto arrived in Dacca to take part in the Yahya-Mujib discussions. Bhutto was the last but electorally the strongest West Pakistani politician to come to Dacca to discuss the fate of the nation. Rumors of settlement, tentative agreement, and even permanent accord between Mujib, Yahya, and Bhutto circulated widely, but other reports also circulated to the effect that a troop build-up in East Pakistan was occurring.

On the night of March 25, 1971, the army was ordered to move out of the cantonments in force to put down what President Yahya Khan described as an "armed rebellion" but what others have described as the legitimate attempt of Bengalis to assert their rights won in the December 1970 elections. Presidential action beyond the deployment of the military involved the outlawing of the Awami League and the banning of all political activity in both West and East; Yahya's proclamation to the nation was simple: "I have ordered the armed forces to do their job and fully restore the authority of the Government."[32] In doing so, all Awami League leaders were either arrested, killed, or forced to flee into exile. Sheikh Mujib was charged with treason,[33] arrested at his Dacca residence, flown to Rawalpindi, and reportedly

30. *Washington Post*, March 19, 1971. The Sheikh's objection was that the proposed Yahya commission would be established by and responsible to Martial Law authorities; hence, this would prevent inquiry into "actual atrocities."

31. This was a reference to the absence of Bhutto's endorsement. In fact, it appears that Yahya knew Bhutto would veto Mujib's loose confederation plan.

32. "President's Broadcast," *Pakistan Affairs* Special Issue, No. 18, (Washington: Embassy of Pakistan), March 31, 1971.

33. This was not the first time that the Sheikh had been charged with treason. In August 1967, the Ayub Government "disclosed" what has been called the Agarthala "conspiracy" Case. This "conspiracy" involved a group of retired naval officers (Bengalis) together with soldiers (Bengalis) who were charged with conspiring with India. Mujib, along with other Awami League leaders, were implicated. The Sheikh chose to refer to the case as the "Islamabad Case" since, according to him, "that is where this conspiracy was hatched."

tried by a secret military tribunal. Hence, a second climax in the series of events following Ayub's ouster had been reached; the momentous decision had been made to use the army to force a recalcitrant, strongly regionalistic (or nationalistic) East Pakistan to remain within the one-nation framework.

Immediate disorder and confusion reigned in Dacca and other parts of East Pakistan. The East Pakistani Rifles, other Bengali regular soldiers, and the police were disarmed and incarcerated by the military. Some of these professionally-trained individuals evaded arrest and fled to India, later to form the core of the Mukhti Bahini, which operated as guerrilla units within the military-controlled areas of East Pakistan during the period from the crackdown to the Indian invasion. The bombardment of Dacca University and other civilian areas of the city led to charges of bloody, inexcusable repression of civilians—a policy attributed largely to General Tikka Khan and other "hardliners" in the Pakistan army. By the end of April 1971, the army had secured the major cities of East Pakistan including rebel strongholds along the border. Guerrilla units were formed in the less secure parts of East Pakistan and in India, and reports filtered in of active Indian support for the Mukhti Bahini. Also in April, President Yahya was forced to declare a six-month moratorium on external, bilateral debts—an indication of the shaky financial position of the Pakistani Government.

The period from March to November 1971 was one of Indian and Pakistani rhetorical thrust and counter thrust. Actions by the Mukhti Bahini continued on an increased scale and, of course, the refugee flow maintained at high level. Pakistan's strategy seemed to be one of subduing East Pakistan physically and, then, through the activities of so-called "peace committees" to develop civilian support within the province for the government's program of suppression and control. During this period, U. S. Congressional action was taken to terminate all military and economic assistance to Pakistan; relations between the Soviet Union and India culminated in the signing of a twenty-year "peace, friendship, and cooperation" treaty (August 9, 1971); and the Indians were increasing their active support of Mukhti Bahini incursions into East Pakistan.

The situation in the East continued to deteriorate. On November 27, Indian troops made their first major "incursion" into East Pakistan in support of Mukhti Bahini units. The following day, President Yahya declared a national emergency which would provide for even greater press censorship and civilian mobilization. Several more Indian "defensive incursions" occurred.

On December 3, 1971, a full-scale, two-front war broke out between the two countries. V. V. Giri, the Indian President, declared a state of national emergency and the Indian Parliament passed the Defense of

India Act giving emergency powers to the Government; international airlines terminated all commercial flights to the subcontinent; India declared an air and naval blockade of both East and West Pakistan; and most observers awaited a replay of the 1965 war. During the early days of the fighting, even before India's formal recognition of Bangladesh and, consequently, Pakistan's break in diplomatic relations with India, the speculation widely voiced was that India was intent upon dismembering Pakistan. India successfully isolated the 70,000 Pakistani troops in East Pakistan, severing Pakistani control over the East. The traumatic outcome of this undeclared war was the partition of Pakistan and the formation of a new nation, Bangladesh. Whatever the primary motivation for India's role in these events, the dismemberment of Pakistan was the achieved reality.

Several years ago, Wayne Wilcox, in a definitive study of the emergence of Pakistan as a modern state, wrote: "If Pakistan is to become one nation, it requires years of common history and experience under gifted leaders, who, while maintaining a consensus within their own circles, recognize their obligations to the broader public."[34] After twenty-four years of political independence marked by numerous governments, three wars with India, a civil war, and several major natural disasters, the East-West union known as the nation-state of Pakistan had been shattered and two distinct political entities had emerged. The Western wing retained the title of the Islamic Republic of Pakistan, while the former East Pakistan is now recognized as the Peoples' Republic of Bangladesh. The "years of common history and experience under gifted leaders," one might argue, never materialized. The triumph of the politics of regionalism over the politics of consolidation and integration long prophesied by the skeptics of such a geographically bifurcated political union was consummated in 1971.

The Return to Civilian Rule: The Bhutto Government in Pakistan and the Mujib Government in Bangladesh

Although the return to civilian rule in Pakistan coincided with the emergence of an independent Bangladesh and, hence, the development of two separate political systems, the two "new" nations shared several similar problems during the first years of separate existence. Pakistan inherited a war-strained economy (the nation had approached international bankruptcy as well as suffered a dislocation of its economy through the loss of East Pakistan as a market for finished and semi-finished products made in the West) and a demoralization of its population as a result of the abandonment of the idea of Pakistan as *the*

34. Wayne A. Wilcox, *Pakistan: The Consolidation of a Nation* (N.Y.: Columbia University Press, 1963), p. 221.

homeland for Muslims in the subcontinent. Furthermore, the political questions of governmental form, constitution making, and political participation which had been deferred during the Yahya interlude once again surfaced to face the Bhutto regime. In Bangladesh, a war-ravaged economy coupled with similar political questions emerged to challenge the ingenuity of Sheikh Mujibur Rahman and his Awami League supporters.[35] The tasks of economic and political develop-ment, therefore, were similar in both countries.

In Pakistan, economic and domestic political problems confronted the new regime. Politically, Bhutto's problems included: the search for national identity; the development of political rules of the game; con-sensus development regarding a new constitution; relations between the center and the provinces (legal, political, and economic); the roles of political parties, the military, and the civil services; and the extent to which political participation of formerly excluded groups in Pakistan society (peasants and urban workers, for example) would be encour-aged. In many ways, these were not "new" problems since previous regimes had been unsuccessful in resolving them. The identity crisis which the secession of Bangladesh had exacerbated involved a basic questioning of what Pakistan really was since the idea of a Muslim homeland in the subcontinent did not appear logical if *most* Muslims in the subcontinent now resided *outside* Pakistan in India and Ban-gladesh. Bhutto's attempts to resolve the illogics of post-1972 Pakistan was a combination of postponement, temporary solutions, and perma-nent arrangements. For example, the question of national identity was deferred during the first year (1972) by Bhutto's refusal to recognize the new Government of Bangladesh. China was a partner to this since United Nations membership for Bangladesh was held up by a Chinese veto in the Security Council. The development of new political rules of the game involved the imposition of temporary, somewhat chang-ing "solutions" in that periods of relative freedom of expression (on the part of opponents or competitors to the Bhutto Government) alter-nated with Government repression and harassment of these critics (newspaper editors and opposition party leaders have been jailed or accused of treasonous "plotting" in newspapers favorable to the gov-ernment). A new constitution was adopted which appears to be a com-promise between both the government and the opposition and this document may be a relatively permanent arrangement. Other political problems such as relations between the center and the provinces re-main unresolved. The government saw fit in 1973 to enforce presiden-tial rule in the two provinces, Northwest Frontier and Baluchistan,

35. President Bhutto released Sheikh Mujibur Rahman from custody in early January 1973, permitting the Bengali leader to return to Dacca via London.

which were controlled by opposition party coalitions. Bhutto appeared, however, to become a deft political "manager" in that both military and civilian bureaucratic rivals and opponents were successfully isolated and removed from positions of public power, including those military leaders who "promoted" Bhutto in the first place—Lt. General Gul Hassan and Air Marshal A. Rahim Khan. In addition, the first year (1972) also witnessed the emergence of Bhutto's own men as political supervisors over the civil service—a situation which had never occurred even during the parliamentary politics period.

Economically, President Bhutto also moved to offset the effects of the bifurcation. After the seizure of the management of 20 private firms with assets of at least $200 million, Bhutto abolished the managing agency business practice,[36] nationalized the insurance industry, devalued the rupee (from 4.75 to 11 per U.S. dollar), all within a framework which attempted to reassure both domestic and foreign investors that the new regime would not undertake any "radical" departures from the capitalistic mode of development followed by previous regimes. In addition to these actions, Bhutto also attempted to improve the marketability of Pakistani goods—the devaluation was one necessary step but export diversification programs and reduction of imports on such items as tea were encouraged without the imposition of rationing. Labor unrest was quickly met by the use of police and military units in support of civilian authorities in such cities as Karachi and Lahore. In short, Bhutto attempted to meet economic problems in a fashion similar to preceding regimes, but attempted them in a manner calculated to create the least opposition.

Social reforms were set aside to await a later date. In fact, the two non-elite groups who were strong supporters of the Pakistan Peoples' Party (PPP) in the December 1970 elections (landless and land-short peasants and industrial workers) appeared to be unaffected economically or politically by the return to civilian rule. The middle-class professional, on the other hand, was given an increased sense of participation through the individuals appointed by Bhutto to his cabinet and to various other government agencies nationally and provincially. The PPP became the most important national group or coalition, and the

36. The managing agency practice or institution was a means of direct control of certain industrial firms by "managing agencies" who were contracted by manufacturing or industrial firms to handle their management problems. The result was more "profit-taking" than management. The Government's abolition was advocated as a means (1) to loosen the economic hold maintained by the family groups and (2) to permit the Government to realize more revenue from taxes on various industrial firms since the managing agency commission was chargeable to the expense account of the managed firm.

extent to which it was composed of small-town and urban middle-class professionals indicates that the regime became the vehicle for the emergence of these middle-sector groups in Pakistani society. This is not to say that the traditional political elite (landlords, soldiers, civilian bureaucrats) and economic elite (industrialists) are out; rather their role became reduced at least in the short-run and the lower middle classes have achieved some measure of prominence under Bhutto.

The Pakistan of the 1970s is not the Pakistan of the 1950s and 1960s territorially or spiritually. Economically and politically, it has undergone changes which offer both promise and problems. Adjustment to the new geography and geopolitics of South Asia will take a long time; the extent to which Pakistan developed into the polity, economy, or society envisioned by its founders has been limited by the events of the early 1970s.

For Bangladesh, the political problems were similar but not as staggering as Pakistan's since the euphoria of recent independence from Pakistan was still fresh and considerable consensus existed over national leadership in the person of Sheikh Mujibur Rahman and his Awami League. Economically, the problems were relatively greater than those which confronted Bhutto in Pakistan.

Politically, Sheikh Mujib as both *Bangapita* (Father of the Bengali nation) and *Bangabandhu* (friend of Bengal) had little opposition to the imposition of his rule.[37] Within nine months of his release from Pakistan, the Constituent Assembly of Bangladesh passed his Constitution for the People's Republic of Bangladesh—a document which provided for a unitary parliamentary system in which the practice of changing one's political party affiliation (at least among public officials) could be costly.[38] Fourteen months after Mujib's release, the first general election of independent Bangladesh occurred and, as expected, the Awami League won an overwhelming majority of the 300 seats in the National House. Opposition parties in Bangladesh cannot yet muster electoral support in any significant strength. Although charges of corruption and favoritism, as well as black-marketeering, have been leveled against Awami League leaders (with the exception of Mujib), the political hold of the Awami League is formidable

37. Rounaq Jahan, "Bangladesh in 1972: Nation Building in a New State," *Asian Survey* 13, 2 (February 1973): 206.
38. This unique constitutional feature (Article 70) is as follows: "A person elected as a member of Parliament at an election at which he was nominated as a candidate by a political party shall vacate his seat if he—(a) resigns from that party; or (b) votes in Parliament against that party." The attempt is thus made to discourage the frequent party desertions which occurred during the parliamentary politics period 1947-58 of undivided Pakistan.

in the short run. Although former leaders of the Mukti Bahini (the guerrilla movement which fought against Pakistani army regulars during the
civil war) have become disenchanted with the Awami League
(some have been arrested by the regime), organized opposition has not
yet developed.

Economically, the situation in Bangladesh was more serious. Famine and threats of famine have occurred from time to time since independence and although Bangladesh did not become the "international basket case" reportedly prophesized by one U.S. official, economics dominated the thoughts of many citizens:

> Even without the massive destruction of 1971, Bangladesh would have
> been an intolerably poor land . . . The structure of the economy was
> primitive, with large-scale economy contributing a mere six percent of
> the Gross Domestic Product. Nearly half the population had a deficiency
> in calorie intake, and the literacy rate was as low as 17 percent. While the
> economy was underdeveloped to begin with, the destruction incurred in
> 1971 was extensive. A United Nations report estimated the cost of re-
> construction in Bangladesh at U.S. $938 million. . . . The cost of living
> jumped . . . nearly 50 percent (from January to October 1972) . . . As 1972
> drew to a close, the major problems in the economic front remained
> rising prices—especially food prices—labor unrest, multiplication of
> middlemen and heavy dependence of foreign aid.[39]

In the short run, the Awami League and the Sheikh himself have done
little to improve the situation. In fact, many within the Awami League
have taken economic advantage of their positions and the situation.

With the end of "internal colonialism" as practiced in East Pakistan
by the westerners, the new leadership of Bangladesh lost its political
target. Dwelling upon events of the past will not provide solutions for
present and future economic ills; the substitution of an Awami League
official for a West Pakistani as an exploiter of human resources will
not be any more palatable to the newly independent masses of
Bangladesh.

Elites and Decision-Making in Pakistan and Bangladesh

As in other newly independent nations, institutional development depends upon many variables, most of which are related to inherited
power configurations and forces. Essentially, we are looking at the
fundamental relationship between the governed and the governors—
and this relationship, it might be argued, was not profoundly altered
as a result of the independence movement. The British "sahib" was

39. Rounaq Jahan, "Bangladesh in 1972," pp. 208-209.

replaced by the Indian, Pakistani, or Bangladeshi "sahib." In general, those elites who emerged immediately after 1947 have fundamentally maintained their positions of power over the twenty-five year period. It is important, therefore, to examine the nature of elites and inter-elite conflicts as a means of understanding the evolution of economic and political forces in modern Pakistan and Bangladesh.

Institutional and Traditional Bases of Power

One scholar gives us this simplified description of the institutional bases of power in Pakistan:

> In Pakistan, political power has been concentrated on the bureau-cratic-military elite who were the successors of the British raj. In the 1950s they functioned with a parliamentary facade of politicians and ministers drawn largely from landlord interests, but there was no gen-uine general election in Pakistan before 1970, and the government has been a military dictatorship since 1958. The main beneficiaries of in-dependence have been (a) the bureaucracy and military themselves who have enjoyed lavish perquisites and have grown in number, (b) the new class of industrial capitalists, (c) professional people whose numbers have grown rapidly and (d) landlords in West Pakistan.[40]

This interpretation, perhaps, indicates greater gains to the profession-als (basically part of the small middle class) than were received since it was from this source that opposition to Ayub developed in 1968 and provided the basis of support and second-level leadership for both the PPP and the Awami League. Certainly, power does rest most visibly with the civilian and military bureaucracy but events of the past few years have altered the monopoly of power which these two institutions exercised previously.

In analyzing the institutional bases of power in Pakistan, one finds that while civilian and military bureaucrats have dominated national (and provincial) decision-making since independence, it is landed wealth that has interconnected these two institutional bases. That is, few individuals from non-landed families have achieved prominence in government decision-making as either civilian or military bureau-crats; wealth in land or some relation to wealth in land appears to have been a requisite for political elite standing. The linkages between Pa-than, Punjabi, Sindhi, and Bengali families have never been thor-oughly established although limited investigation has revealed impre-cise links between some 200 families. The implication is that the polit-

40. Angus Maddison, *Class Structure and Economic Growth: India and Pakis-tan Since the Moghuls* (N.Y.: W. W. Norton & Company, Inc., 1971), p. 136.

ical elite of Pakistan prior to the Bangladesh crisis was drawn from these 200 families.

Wealth based on industrial holdings has not been a primary source of political elites. That is, the so-called "20 families" (or 37 families as some scholars have maintained)[41] have not produced notable civilian or military bureaucrats nor even politicians. With regard to politicians, during the Ayub period only a handful of members of the "Lucky 20" families stood for election in 1965. At present, however, it appears that the role of this class might be changing since certain younger members of these families have been elected to provincial assembly seats in Punjab.

The interconnection between forms of wealth (principally between landed and industrial-commercial holdings) has not been documented. There are reasonable suspicions that such linkages do exist and that the newly established industrial class has sought to strengthen these linkages by securing agricultural land for various economic or symbolic (status) purposes.

Newer Sources of Power

Although the new industrial class has not yet participated directly in political decision-making, this does not mean that they have not influenced these decisions. The separation of politics from economics is more analytical than real. The leading industrial families were a support base for Ayub, Yahya, and, probably, also for Bhutto and Mujib as well. Prior to the December 1970 elections, these industrialists tended to be concerned primarily with managing their newly acquired

41. The first reference made to these "Lucky 20" families was made by the then Chief Economist of the Planning Commission, Mahbubal Haq, in an address to the West Pakistan Management Association in April 1968. He maintained that twenty families controlled 80 percent of Pakistan's banking and 97 percent of its insurance business; in addition, the 20 families had direct control of the bulk of large-scale business and commerce activities and indirect control of a number of other concerns. These families included: Adamjee, Dawood, Habib, Saigol, Colony, Mohammad Amin, Mohammad Bashir, Valibai, Ispahani, Bawany, Jalil, Hyesons, Marulabaksh, Batalo, Adam, Wazir Ali, Fancy, Habibullah, Habib, Dada, and Rangoonwala. Most of these families settled in Pakistan as "refugees" from India and a considerable portion are Gujarati speakers. For additional information on these families, see Hanna Papanek, "Entrepreneurs in East Pakistan," in *Bengal Society*, edited by Robert Beech (East Lansing: Asian Studies Center, MSU, 1971), "Pakistan's Big Businessmen: Separatism, Entrepreneurship and Partial Modernization," (unpublished paper, March 29, 1971), and "Pakistan's New Industrialists and Businessmen: Focus on the Memons," (unpublished paper, 1970).

holdings and concerns and engaging in "political intrigue" to secure government favors for their family concerns. Familial prohibitions against direct political involvement ("the spouting whale gets the harpoon" notion) appear to have prevailed in many of the wealthy industrialist families just as similar prohibitions existed in the civil service-land-owning families against going into business. This is not to say that some type of "joint venture" cannot be undertaken. Industrial wealth has been linked to the civilian and military bureaucracy (and indirectly to landed wealth) in joint partnerships which were promoted during the Ayub and Yahya regimes. These partnerships were formed principally between retired generals or central civil service personnel and industrialists; the former providing the contacts and licenses required to do business and the latter the capital and managerial talent required to make the business successful. The most prominent and successful, as well as the only Pathan in the "Lucky 20" list, is Lt. General (Ret.) M. Habibullah Khan Khattak, who for a time served as Ayub Khan's Chief of Staff prior to 1958. Habibullah followed this pattern of joint partnership with a retired civil servant and a Karachi businessman in launching his business career. Furthermore, even though Bhutto's nationalization program has theoretically infringed upon the activities of these industrialists, there are indications that the government of Pakistan is acknowledging the usefulness of these industrial families by appointing members of the families, as well as managers from foreign firms, to the managing directorships of some of the nationalized firms.

Although the industrial families' relations with the civilian and military bureaucracy as they existed during the Ayub-Yahya years may have changed, the industrialists appear to be maintaining themselves in spite of the Bhutto government rhetoric, programs, and the effects of the Bangladesh partition. Pakistan industrialists are still important economic elites and are able to exercise considerable influence over political decision-making.

Some attention should be paid also to the middle-class professionals who appear to be the major source of PPP and Awami League support both in the urban and small town areas of Pakistan and Bangladesh. These include the lawyers, doctors, engineers, government bureaucrats (outside the central services), university professors, and teachers—individuals who possess college or professional degrees of some sort or another. These individuals have positions and status apart from traditional, land-based sources and represent the small but developing urban bourgeoisie. Along with university students, these professionals were directly involved in the demonstrations which contributed to the downfall of Ayub. They were attracted quite early to either Bhutto or Mujib and considered the PPP or Awami League as alternatives to the existing military rule. It is, perhaps, from this class or sector of society that new leadership in Pakistan and Bangladesh might develop as alternatives to traditional political elites. Both the Bhutto and Mujib cabinets, as well as sizable portions of the National and Provincial Assemblies in Pakistan and Bangladesh, now include representatives from this level of society.

Inter-elite Conflict

Very little discussion has taken place concerning religion and religious elite leadership. Although religious leaders (pirs, mullahs, and ulemas, for example) are important, their influence is confined primarily to rural areas. National decision-making is the area for the westernized, secular elite for the most part. One might maintain that religion plays less of a role nationally in Pakistan than it does in Israel. Conflict between westernized, secular elites and religious elites does take place but generally not over matters such as economic development, military and defense spending, export and import licensing, or other questions relating to allocation of national resources. Rather, the conflict centers on the "Islamification" or "westernization" of Pakistani society—issues of importance in terms of social policies relating to family affairs (the Muslim Family Laws Ordinance promoted by Ayub is the best example) or rural life of the masses in general. One might even speculate that since the raison d'etre of Pakistan—a homeland for Muslims in the subcontinent—has been severely questioned by the Bangladesh issue, the importance of religion in Pakistani society will become progressively less. Its importance has never been as great in East as in West Pakistan and very probably will be even less a factor in national decision-making in Bangladesh.

The major conflict that has occurred and which continues is that among secular elites and is rooted in issues of ideology and geography. In the Pakistan that remains, political elites divide along center-provincial lines. The interests of the Punjab (the richest province as well as the most populated), which has controlled the central government, are opposed to the provincial interests of the Sind (with the exception of Karachi), Northwest Frontier, and Baluchistan. Prior to the December 1971 war, one found the elites of East Pakistan (Bengal) aligned with those of the smaller provinces (at that time, all four western provinces were one unit). The accusations and demands of the Awami League during the 1960s related to the extent to which West Pakistan had "colonized" East Pakistan and was using the latter as an earner of foreign exchange, through the export of jute, and a captive market for the products of the industrializing western wing. The foreign exchange earned by East Pakistan was being used to finance the industrialization of the Punjab and part of the Sind (Karachi). This geo-graphically-based elite conflict had cultural roots as well—the Urdu-Punjabi speakers claiming preeminence over the Bengali, Pushtu, Sindhi, and Baluchi speakers. With the loss of Bengal, Pakistan still must resolve the regional-provincial issues which tend to dominate the attention and energies of the political elite.

Ideological cleavage also exists in Pakistan within the political elite but is more evident in Bangladesh. The disenfranchised elites of East Pakistan felt that once the westerners were removed from Bengal, they could then rightfully assume the vacant positions in government and the economy. The more ideologically leftist elite in Bangladesh, how-ever, have been attempting to disabuse the Awami League moderates and conservatives of the notion of merely assuming existing positions without first restructuring society along more collective lines. The po-tential for violence accompanying this conflict is great. "Business as usual" is not being accepted in many parts of Bangladesh and it ap-pears that the central government under Mujib's leadership faces many difficulties for the long run.

These geo-culturally inspired conflicts eventually led to the bifurca-tion of Pakistan. The decision to attempt a non-political solution to the set of complex political-economic problems in East Pakistan may be recorded as one of the greatest mistakes in the history of South Asia. To a great extent, this conflict stems from the politico-economic-cul-tural configuration which is rooted in the historical-colonial legacy of Islam and the British in India. Undoubtedly, ideological conflict will more and more characterize the efforts to find direction in both coun-tries—conflict which has emerged as a by-product of independence rather than from the subcontinent's efforts to gain independence from the British. Both types of conflict relate to power and position—con-trol of decision-making apparatus and the coercive forces of society are the objectives of both. In both cases, the non-elites have played little if any role. It has been a case of inter-elite struggle and conflict, with the masses as non-participants except when they stray into the path of the army or police. Decisions have been made in their name and, rhetori-cally, in their "best interests" but have not involved them or their representatives. Until December 1970, the average Pakistani was less involved in politics than his neighbor in India. Now this has changed. The implications of this change are still not fully manifested.

Pakistan and Bangladesh: The Future

Although many questions regarding the future of both political sys-tems remain unanswered, it is certain that separation of Bangladesh from Pakistan did not solve all the problems of either nation. The immediate euphoria which developed with the successful invasion and conquest of East Pakistan by the Indian and Mukhti Bahini armed forces in December 1971 gave way shortly to the depression of attempting to reconstruct and rebuild the war-shattered economy within a framework of limited external assistance, a large measure of government corruption, and disorganization. For Bangladesh, most questions regarding the future are economically inspired—how to divide the existing meager resources among the great and growing masses and how to parley those meager resources into increased future production. Bangladesh is a symbol of over-population in the world. It has the world's highest man-land ratio and is almost completely devoid of natural resources. It has fertile soil, a climate which can produce multiple crops per year, and the over-abundant human resources of a Third World nation. For the immediate future, the population of Bangladesh must share the austerity and not the wealth if further violent change is to be avoided. Political stability now centers in the person of Mujib and even he cannot maintain stability indefinitely on charisma alone. For Pakistan, economics are important and alternative markets for its raw and finished goods must be found to replace the loss of Bangladesh. National identity is the grave question. What is the purpose of Pakistan now that the idea of a Muslim Homeland in South Asia has been destroyed? One scholar wrote the following summary of Pakistan in 1963:

> National unity, a free society, economic development, a welfare state, national security—all these problems are intimately bound up with the need for constitutional stability . . . it is to be hoped that the political leaders profit by the lessons of the past and press their views within the existing order.[42]

Today, the same issues confront both Pakistan and Bangladesh and the same hope is offered for their future.

42. Richard S. Wheeler, "Pakistan," *Major Governments of Asia*, edited by George McT. Kahin, 2nd ed.; (Ithaca, N.Y.: Cornell University Press, 1963), p. 526.

Selected Readings

Abbot, Freeland. *Islam and Pakistan*. Ithaca: Cornell University Press, 1968.

Ahmed, Muneer. *The Civil Servant in Pakistan*. Karachi: Oxford University Press, 1964.

Alavi, Hamza, "The State in Post-Colonial Societies—Pakistan and Bangladesh," *New Left Review* 74 (July-August 1972).

Ali, Tariq. *Pakistan: Military Rule or People's Power?* New York: Morrow, 1970.

Ayub Khan, Mohammad. *Friends Not Masters*. New York: Oxford University Press, 1967.

Beach, Robert, ed. *Bengal Society*. East Lansing: Asian Studies Center, Michigan State University, 1971.

Bhutto, Zulfikar Ali. *The Great Tragedy*. Karachi: Vison Publications Ltd., 1971.

Binder, Leonard. *Religion and Politics in Pakistan*. Berkeley: University of California Press, 1961.

Birkhead, Guthrie S., ed. *Administrative Problems in Pakistan*. Syracuse: Syracuse University Press, 1966.

Braibanti, Ralph. *Research on the Bureaucracy of Pakistan*. Durham, N.C.: Duke University Press, 1966.

Burki, Shahid Javed, "Social and Economic Determinants of Political Violence—A Case Study of the Punjab," *Middle East Journal* (Autumn 1971).

———."Twenty Years of the Civil Service of Pakistan: A Reevaluation," *Asian Survey* 9 (April 1969).

Callard, Keith. *Pakistan: A Political Study*. London: Allen & Unwin, 1957.

Feldman, Herbert. *From Crisis to Crisis: Pakistan, 1962-1969*. Karachi: Oxford University Press, 1972.

———. *Revolution in Pakistan: A Study of Martial Law Administration*. London: Oxford University Press, 1967.

Gankovsky, Yu. V. *The Peoples of Pakistan*. Lahore: People's Publishing House, n d.

Jahan, Rounaq. *Pakistan, Failure in National Integration*. New York: Columbia University Press, 1972.

Lewis, Stephen R. Jr. *Economic Policy and Industrial Growth in Pakistan*. Cambridge: M.I.T. Press, 1969.

Malik, Hafeez. *Moslem Nationalism in India and Pakistan*. Washington, D.C.: Public Affairs Press, 1963.

Muqeem Khan, Fazal. *The Story of the Pakistan Army*. Lahore: Oxford University Press, 1963.

Papanek, Gustav F. *Pakistan's Development: Social Goals and Private Incentives.* Cambridge: Harvard University Press, 1967.

Sayeed, Khalid B. *Pakistan: The Formative Phase,* 1857-1948. London: Oxford University Press, 1960.

————. *The Political System of Pakistan.* Boston: Houghton Mifflin Co., 1967.

Siddiqui, Kalim. *Conflict, Crisis and War in Pakistan.* New York: Praeger Publishers, 1972.

Von Vorys, Karl. *Political Development in Pakistan.* Princeton: Princeton University Press, 1965.

Wheeler, Richard S. *The Politics of Pakistan: A Constitutional Quest.* Ithaca: Cornell University Press, 1970.

Wilcox, Wayne A. *Pakistan: The Consolidation of a Nation.* New York: Columbia University Press, 1963.

Ziring, Lawrence. *The Ayub Khan Era: Politics in Pakistan, 1958-1969.* Syracuse: Syracuse University Press, 1971.

4   Malaysia

Gordon P. Means

The Social Dimension

Malaysia is a country divided by race, culture and language, but united by economic and political necessity. Its society is frequently characterized by such terms as "plural," "communal," or "segmental,"[1] because it is composed of a number of ethnic-cultural groups each of which tend to live in distinct communities with a distinctive life style and each tending to dominate or monopolize certain sectors of the economic or political system. The segmented communal compartmentalization of society has given the total social and political order a "caste" character in the sense that persons born in a particular community have tended to assume roles and functions traditionally performed by their communal group. Although each ethnic-cultural community has its own social, political, and economic institutions, no communal group exists as an autonomous self-sustaining social unit. Instead, each community is dependent on other communities for some goods and services. While some institutions reinforce communal bonds, other institutions bridge the ethnic-cultural divisions of Malaysian society. Furthermore, the processes of modernization have in-

1. See: Leo A. Despres, *Cultural Pluralism and Nationalist Politics in British Guiana* (Chicago: Rand McNally & Co., 1967); Arend Lijphart, *The Politics of Accommodation: Pluralism and Democracy in the Netherlands* (Berkeley: University of California Press, 1968); J. S. Furnival, *Colonial Policy and Practice* (London: Cambridge University Press, 1948); and Alvin Rabushka and Kenneth A. Shepsle, *Politics in Plural Societies: A Theory of Democratic Instability* (Columbus, Ohio: Charles E. Merrill Publishing Co., 1972).

duced increasing cultural diversity within each community, partially blurring the lines of communal compartmentalization. Similarly, communal groups have become increasingly interdependent in the larger economic and political system. Thus, for purposes of analysis of Malaysian society it is possible to stress the cultural ethnic divisions, which are most pronounced at the local and sub-unit level, or one can emphasize the processes of integration and nation-building by concentrating on supra-communal institutions and the functional integration of these segmented communities into the wider economic and political system of the country. In reality, unity and diversity are opposite sides of the same coin, and both sides must be examined for a realistic appraisal of Malaysian social and political processes.

The three major ethnic-communal groupings of Malaysian society are the Malays, the Chinese, and the Indians. In addition, Malaysia contains a number of smaller communities, such as Ceylonese, Eurasians, Europeans, and various tribal people. Each of the major com-

Table IV.1
Community Composition, Malaysia, 1970

		%	% urban by community
Malays	4,550,807	43.6 ⎫	
Indonesians	265,168	2.5 ⎬ 46.8	15.0
*Aborigines[a]	70,937	.7 ⎭	
Chinese	3,555,879	34.1	46.3
Indians	942,944	9.0	34.7
Dayaks	386,260	3.7	2.2
Kadazans	184,512	1.8	3.4
Other natives	337,395	3.2	5.7
Others	145,628	1.4	31.2
Total	10,439,430		26.7

Source: 1970 Population and Housing Census of Malaysia, Community Groups (Kuala Lumpur: Jabatan Perangkaan Malaysia, 1972), pp. 24 and passim.

a. The census defines a "community" as "a people who are bound together by common ties of language, religion, custom or allegiance." Yet the Aborigines are classified as Malays even though most Aborigines differ from Malays in language, religion and custom. The grouping of Aborigines and Indonesians with Malays is probably based on political considerations, with the government seeking to amplify the size and influence of the Malays.

munities has a fairly small modernized and western-educated element, usually in elite positions. While the masses of each community are undergoing social and cultural changes, they remain more traditional in their attitudes, culture, and behavior patterns. As a result, within each community considerable cultural diversity is to be found, to a large extent differentiated by social stratification. The cultural distance between the elite and the masses within each community is substantially greater than normally found in western society. Between communal groups cultural differences are less at the elite level than at the lower levels of the social stratification system, where traditional communal values and "primordial sentiments" are more intense. As a consequence, the linkages which bridge communal divisions in Malaysian society tend to be provided by westernized communal elites interacting in brokerage roles primarily through economic and political institutions. For the common man, interactions with members of other communities are much more likely to be casual, perfunctory, or impersonal transactions which do little to challenge the cultural autonomy of each community at its mass base. Although government policies are attempting to break down some of the cultural and economic compartmentalization of Malaysian society, it remains essentially as depicted in this somewhat oversimplified, heuristic model of Malaysian society.

Functional specialization on the basis of ethnicity is not always apparent by looking at occupational statistics, because the categories frequently bridge ethnic divisions. For example, Malays, Chinese, and Indians all participate in business activity, but some businesses such as auto repair and tailoring are primarily Chinese, while others such as handicraft stores are primarily Malay. Even so, the occupational statistics presented in Table IV.2 reveal some of the disproportionate ethnic distribution of functions in the Malaysian economic system.

Education

Ethnic-cultural differences in occupational and status roles may be explained in part by ethnic differences in educational background. In Malaya[2] there have been four separate school systems organized according to the language medium used for instruction. The government operated a Malay-medium school system which was free and ostensibly compulsory for Malays, but only extending through the primary level. The curriculum in these Malay schools was devoted to teaching the "three Rs" and providing rudimentary instruction in Islam and a few general knowledge subjects. While the Malay schools

2. Malaya refers to the area of the former Federation of Malaya, or peninsular Malaysia, now called West Malaysia. It is comprised of nine Malay states and two non-Malay states, the former British crown colonies of Penang and Malacca. Malaysia refers to the Federation of Malaysia formed in 1963 by the union of Malaya with Singapore and the two Borneo states of Sarawak and Sabah (formerly North Borneo). Singapore withdrew from Malaysia in 1965 to become an independent state.

Table IV.2

**Economically Active Population By Race And
Industry With Selected Subdivisions,
1957 (thousands)**

Industry	Malays	Chinese	Indians	Others
AGRICULTURE, FORESTRY,				
FISHING	749	310	174	10
rice	381	9	.5	6
vegetable growing	23	54	1	.1
rubber	260	200	150	2
coconut	26	4	9	.1
MINING	10	39	6	1
MANUFACTURING	26	97	10	1
COMMERCE	32	127	32	3
OTHER INDUSTRIES &				
SERVICES	180	174	80	38
government services	17	5	8	2
police	43	4	2	1
armed forces	15	2	3	24
Total	1,023	771	312	56

Calculated from: *1957 Population Census of the Federation of Malaya, Report No. 14*, (Kuala Lumpur: Department of Statistics, 1960), pp. 102-110.

raised Malay literacy, they did not prepare their students to continue to higher education, or to acquire technical commercial or professional skills. Rather, Malay schools were geared to the life style of rather traditional Malay peasants. Consequently, Malays who attended such schools have tended to retain much of their traditional peasant culture and have not acquired the skills or motivation to compete in the modern sectors of the economy or participate in commercial or professional pursuits.

A system of Chinese-medium schools was first established in the 1890s through the efforts of Chinese voluntary associations dedicated to preserve Chinese culture. Initially various Chinese dialects were utilized, but after 1917 nearly all Chinese schools adopted the Chinese national language of Kuo-yu, which is the Mandarin of public life in China. These schools generally employed teachers trained in China and utilized Chinese text books, with a curriculum heavily oriented to Chinese history, literature and politics. As the government began to be concerned about the political indoctrination in Chinese schools, it subjected them to closer supervision and forced them to give greater emphasis to subjects related to Malaya. As these controls were extended, the government also began to provide assistance to Chinese schools through grants-in-aid, so that government supervision and government financial support went hand-in-hand. Quite naturally, the Chinese schools have been at the forefront of political movements to preserve Chinese identity and to promote Chinese culture and language. The most articulate spokesmen for a militant form of Chinese chauvanism have been those Chinese who are products of and the supporters of the Chinese-medium schools.

In comparison with the Malay schools, the Chinese schools have included more science subjects and have provided some training in technical and quasi-professional subjects. Furthermore, the Chinese schools extended through the secondary level, and after 1955, with the establishment of Nanyang University in Singapore, the products of these schools could obtain higher education in the Chinese medium without going to China or Taiwan. In short, the Chinese schools have provided the educational background for its students to fill semi-skilled, urban-based occupational roles in society.

After the First World War, the importation of Indian laborers for rubber estates and the construction of railways prompted the government to promote the formation of Indian vernacular schools. Rubber and palm oil estates employing a substantial Indian labor force were required to provide Indian vernacular schools for the children of their workers. Such schools were assisted by government grants. The instruction was in Tamil and of extremely poor quality. The drop-out rate was so excessive that even in 1957 over half of the students in Indian estate schools were in the first or second year of school, and only 5.2 percent were in the final sixth year. Obviously, such schools have not provided the opportunities for rural Indians working as estate laborers to escape their lowly social and economic condition.

The English-medium schools have been the most important in their impact on the country. The first English-medium school was founded in 1816 by the British administration, but English education proceeded very slowly for the next fifty years. However, with the arrival of European and American Christian missionaries who began building their own English-medium schools, the government found it convenient and economical to provide government assistance to the mission-operated schools. After the turn of the century, the English school system expanded steadily so that by 1938 Malaya had 105 government and government-aided English schools, in addition to a number of lesser quality private (non-aided) English schools. After the war, English schools expanded at a phenomenal rate to become second in enrollment only to the government Malay schools.

The popularity of the English schools derived from the occupational opportunities and status roles available to the English-educated. Besides being the vehicle for the introduction of western values and

Table IV. 3

Historical Trends in School Enrollment
by Media, 1947-1968

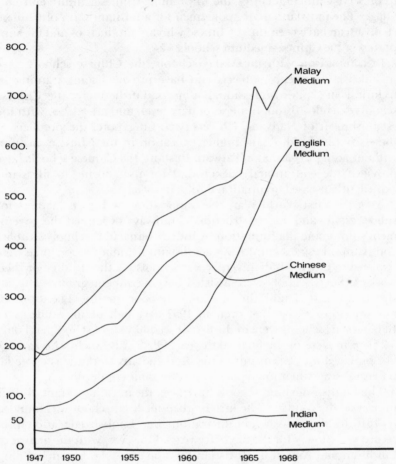

Source: Calculated from Ministry of Education Malaysia, *Education in Malaysia* (Kuala Lumpur: Dervar Babasa dan Pastaka, 1970), pp 11-12.

technology, these schools maintained the highest standards and the most extensive system of secondary education which provided access to higher educational institutions in Europe or, after World War II, at the University of Malaya. The products of these schools have provided a pool of candidates for elite positions in government administration, commerce, the professions, and more recently, politics. Although all ethnic communities could attend English schools, cultural, psychological and economic obstacles created differential access among the ethnic communities to English education. Furthermore, because English schools were first built in urban areas, the opportunities afforded by English education were largely filled by the urban-based immigrant population of Chinese and Indians. Consequently, the Chinese and Indians were proportionately over-represented in English-medium schools and thus they have tended to dominate the more advanced technical, commercial and professional sectors of the economy.[3]

Table IV.4

Student Enrollment In Malaya In English-Medium Schools By Race 1962 (thousands)

	Malay	Chinese	Indian	Others	Total
English Primary Schools	63	113	56	4	238
English Secondary Schools	56	89	21	1	168
Total	119	202	78	6	406

Source: Compiled from figures obtained directly from the Ministry of Education in a private letter.

Migration and Settlement

Demographic and settlement patterns differ for each ethnic community, reflecting their different styles of life and their immigration and migration trends. Being the indigenous people, the Malays are found in the better agricultural areas suitable for wet rice cultivation and along the coasts where fishing and coconut cultivation sustain their traditional life styles. Over the past several centuries, Malay communities, particularly along the West Coast, have had substantial infusions of immigrants from Sumatra and from other areas of Indonesia. Cultural, religious, linguistic and ethnic affinity between these immigrants and local Malays facilitated their assimilation into Malay society. Malay internal migration between states remained rather low during the colonial period, but gradually over the last few decades the attractions of city life have produced an increasing influx of rural

3. See: Fredric Mason, *The Schools of Malaya* (Singapore: Donald Moore, 1954); Ministry of Education, Malaysia, *Education in Malaysia* (Kuala Lumpur: Dewan Bahasa dan Pustaka, 1970); International Bank for Reconstruction and Development, *The Economic Development of Malaya* (Baltimore: The John Hopkins Press, 1955), pp. 439-501; John W. Henderson et al., *Area Handbook for Malaysia* (Washington, D.C.: U.S. Government Printing Office, 1970), pp. 167-194.

Malays to urban areas. Although Malays have found jobs in the government, the police, the armed forces and the many industries established after independence, they remain a minority in the urban areas, usually living in distinctively Malay segments of the towns.

All the immigrant communities were attracted to Malaya in part because of economic opportunities, and thus they tended to enter the sectors of the economy which were the most dynamic and where fortunes could be made. Even before the British extended their rule over the Malay states, substantial numbers of Chinese flocked to the rich tin fields of Perak and Selangor. Indeed, the severe conflicts which developed over the control of the tin fields created civil disorders which were beyond the capacity of the Malay sultanates to control. Ultimately, the ensuing anarchy prompted the British to intervene and in 1874 to initiate the British system of indirect rule through Malay Rulers supported by British power and subject to British administration. Once the British became responsible for law and order and administration, new economic opportunities and unrestricted immigration policies combined to stimulate a new influx of immigrants.

On their own initiative, the Chinese introduced an immigration scheme to subsidize the passage of Chinese peasant laborers to Malaya. In return for his boat fare, the Chinese peasant would contract with a Chinese labor broker to work as an indentured laborer for a year or two until his debt had been repaid with interest. The labor broker who recruited the laborer and paid his passage, in turn, contracted with Chinese mine and estate operators to provide cheap and dependable coolie laborers. This system of immigration of Chinese contract laborers continued from the early years of the nineteenth century until the First World War, when it was abolished by government action. However, limitations on Chinese immigration were not initiated until 1933 when the depression created unemployment and a labor surplus in Malaya.

The early Chinese immigrants to Malaya were overwhelmingly adult males who arrived usually with the intention of making their fortune and eventually returning to China. Yet in time, they found that return to China was difficult, either because they remained poor or because they had become prosperous and did not want to abandon their investments in the country. The imbalance in the sex ratio in the early years stimulated the immigration of Chinese brides, or of family members remaining in China. Gradually over the years the demographic characteristics of the Chinese community became more normal both in regard to age and sex distribution, indicating the more stable attachments of the Chinese to Malaya.

Indian immigration to Malaya remained at a fairly low level until after the turn of the century when the country experienced a severe

Table IV.5

The Growth Of Chinese Population In
Malaya And Malaysia

Year	States Included in Count	Total
1750	Malacca	2,161
1842	Penang and Malacca	16,597
1901	Penang, Malacca, Singapore, Perak, Selangor, Negri Sembilan, Pahbang	584,036
1931	All Malay States and Straits Settlements	1,708,966
1947	Malaya and Singapore	2,614,667
1957	Malaya and Singapore	3,424,351
1970	Malaysia (excluding Singapore)	3,555,879

Source: M. V. del Tufo, *Malaya, A Report on the 1947 Census of Population* (Singapore: Government Printing Office, 1948) Appendix C, pp. 584-588; *1957 Population Census of the Federation of Malaya*, Report No. 14 (Kuala Lumpur: Department of Statistics, 1960), p. 51; *Singapore Annual Report 1958* (Singapore: Government Printing Office, 1959), pp. 27-28; *1970 Population and Housing Census of Malaysia, Community Groups, op. cit.*, p. 24.

labor shortage due to the rapid growth of the rubber industry and large government investments in rail and road construction. To encourage the immigration of Indian laborers, the governments of the Federated Malay States and the Straits Settlements established an Indian Immigration Fund to provide free passage for Indian laborers from Madras to Malaya. Government subsidy of Indian immigration continued from 1907 to 1938, so that South Indian Tamils became a primary labor force for European-operated rubber and palm-oil estates and for public works and the Malayan Railways. In addition, many Indians came to Malaya through the financial backing of the typical Indian extended joint-family enterprise. Those Indians who came without government assistance usually settled in urban areas and entered such occupations as trading, shopkeeping, and banking. As a result, Indians who settled in the cities tended to be from upper-middle castes, and included representatives from most areas of India, while those who became rural estate and construction workers tended to be from the lower rungs of the Indian caste structure and were predominantely Tamils from the area around Madras. Although Indian immigration produced some imbalance in sex ratio and age distribution, a fairly high proportion of Indians came to Malaya as family units. After the Second World War the age and sex distributions for Indians have become quite characteristic for a stable community.

Both the Chinese and the Indians settled in towns and in areas of the country first opened to mining and rubber production. The more de-

Table IV.6

**The Growth Of Indian Population In Malaya,
Singapore And Malaysia**

	Singapore	Malaya
1881	12,138	44,000 (est.)
1901	17,845	119,000 (est.)
1911	28,454	268,269
1931	50,860	621,847
1947	68,978	599,616
1957	124,084	820,270
1970		Malaysia 942,944

Source: Kernial Singh Sandhu. *Indians in Malaysia, Immigration and Settlement 1786-1957* (Cambridge: Cambridge University Press, 1969), p. 183; see table IV.1 above.

veloped sectors of Malaya are found in a belt along the west coast from Penang to Singapore which is serviced by a good road and rail transportation system. The highest population density is found within this belt, and in most of the districts along the west coast the combined Chinese and Indian population is quite dense, varying from about 35 to 65 percent of the total. Similarly, the Chinese and Indians have always been concentrated in towns and cities. Because modern roles, skills and life styles are disseminated from the cities, the proportion of each community living in urban areas provides a rough index of the relative exposure of each community to modernizing influences.

Table IV.7

**Degree Of Urbanization By Community And Year
For West Malaysia**

	1947	1957	1970
Malays	7.3	11.2	14.9
Chinese	31.1	44.7	47.4
Indians	25.8	30.6	34.7
Others	46.2	49.3	40.8
Total	15.9	26.5	28.7

Source: 1970 Population and Housing Census of Malaysia, Community Groups, op cit., p. 33.

Social Changes in Malaysian Society

All communities in Malaysia have experienced dramatic changes during the last half century. The country has progressed from a rather traditional, peasant-oriented, colonial dependency to one of the most economically developed countries in Asia. The most significant changes have been those generated by the cumulative effects of education, economic growth, and the infusion of modern values and attitudes arising from intensive contacts with exogenous cultures, primarily British, but also to a lesser extent European and American.

The British impact on Malaysia has been so pervasive it is impossible to trace all its manifestations. Yet a few aspects of Malaysia's British legacy can be briefly noted. When the British established their colonial system, they created a legal system based on the principles of common law as modified by British colonial experience elsewhere, primarily in India. Although the British became a privileged political and administrative elite, and maintained a social and cultural distance from the people under their authority, British administrative and legal institutions tended to give greater emphasis to equalitarian and universalistic norms, than to particularistic norms of privilege and status. This trend was more pronounced in the Crown Colonies of the Straits Settlements, where all British subjects, whether indigenous or immigrant, were treated equally before the law and enjoyed equal legal, if not political, rights. However, even in the Malay States, the legal principles of equality were modified only slightly by the recognition of the legal and status privileges of the Malay aristocracy and by affording special rights to land by indigenous Malay peasants. Especially in matters of potential communal and ethnic conflicts, the British tried to perform the role of impartial arbitor and guarantor of equal justice in a racially and culturally divided society.

The British administrative system also represented an institutional embodiment of the values of rational organization designed to provide certain social services for the benefit of society as a whole, As such, British administrators stressed efficiency, progress and the application of technology for the essentially instrumental goals of economic growth and material well-being. Although the colonial administrators were not dedicated to major social reconstruction, they became agents of change by imparting some of the values essential for a modern society. Similar cultural values were transmitted by the European business and managerial elites, as well as by British and American missionaries. In the postwar era, the influx of technical assistance personnel and highly trained European technicians and academics have continued to provide an important exogenous cultural, behavioral and technological input to Malaysian society.

For the most part, western values, attitudes, behavior and life styles have not been transmitted directly to the lower strata of Malaysian society. The process of cultural transmission has been indirect through native elites who have been among the first to be influenced by western values and life styles. Thus, during the colonial era, British officials

provided cultural role models for traditional Malay aristocratic elites
who were closely associated with the British in the administration of
the country. Similarly, small numbers of Chinese and Indian elites
adopted western behavior, attitudes and life styles, although for them
the role models were more likely to be the European professional or
businessman, rather than the civil servant. Today, the elites of Malaysian society have assumed the functions formerly performed by British
and European expatriates, and they are now acting as agents of change
and providing role models for the lower strata of Malaysian society.
The processes of secondary social change induced through modernizing Malaysian elites involves a dynamic process of innovation by contemporary Malaysian elites who must integrate aspects of traditional
and modern cultures into a coherent whole. What is now being transmitted to the lower strata of Malaysian society is an amalgam of many
cultures, both modern and traditional.[4]

No processes of social change affect all members of a society at the
same time nor to the same degree. In Malaysia, there are significant
(sometimes stark) differences in response to similar change factors between separate elements in the society. First, there are variations in
change responses according to social stratification. The higher the social status and economic position of various segments of society, the
more likely they are to be exposed to western culture and to be receptive to adaptation to changing social and economic conditions. By
contrast, the lower strata of Malaysian society have had less exposure
to change-inducing influences, and may also have a lesser capacity for
adaptation to fundamental change. In every society, social stratification reflects cultural differences. However, in Malaysian society, these
differences are even more pronounced than normal because of the combination of cultures and the exogenous cultural inputs which have
tended to be diffused through the upper strata of society, thus exag-
gerating elite-mass differences.

A second form of differential response to social change can be dis-
cerned according to ethnic-cultural community. Some cultures tend to
facilitate adaptation and cultural borrowing, especially along certain
dimensions, while other cultures may be more resistant to change or
accessible to change along other dimensions. Cultural variables account for the distinctive responses and adaptations to social change
and modernization exhibited by each cultural-ethnic community. For
example, the Malays have a very strong religious identification with

4. The model of social change depicted above provides a glimpse of only the
    grossest features of the processes by which Malaysian society is changing.
    There are many specific examples of social change which do not fit within
    such a generalized model.

Islam and have strenuously resisted proselytizing by members of other faiths. They retain a strong psychological and symbolic attachment to Islam, even when they acquire more secular attitudes and beliefs. Social solidarity, social esteem and status derived from involvement in community activities are more valued by most Malays than the acquisition of individual economic wealth. Consequently, Malays have been very slow to acquire a competitive work ethic and achievement norms in matters of economic life, despite the exhortation of Malay political leaders and government programs designed to make the Malays economically more competitive. Until quite recently the Malays did not place a high value on education, in part because Malay schools were of low quality and provided almost no opportunity for economic or social advancement. The average Malay valued rudamentary education primarily as a means for acquiring the skills and knowledge essential for his religious obligations, while higher secular, professional and technical education was assumed to be appropriate only for members of the raja class. Therefore, attitudes valuing educational excellence and achievement have been largely confined to aristocratic Malays, who also enjoyed privileged access to higher educational institutions, usually in the English medium. The net effect has been the differential transmission of skills, knowledge, attitudes and achievement motivations within Malay society largely according to traditional stratification patterns.

In comparison to the Malays, the Chinese have tended to be much more adaptive to modern commercial and economic practices, perhaps because a work ethic and achievement norms are more harmonious with features of traditional Chinese culture. The Chinese also prize education very highly, and have expended large sums of personal and community resources toward the education of their children. When they discovered that English education provided access to better paying jobs and proved advantageous in commercial enterprise, they sent their children in increasing numbers to English-medium schools. If, in the future, knowledge of Malay provides similar opportunities, the Chinese will very likely excel in that language too, as they are very pragmatic in matters of education. This may explain why they do well in science, professional and commercial subjects, and thus acquire a predominant position in the more highly skilled and dynamic sectors of the economy.

For the Chinese, religion has not been an essential feature of their personal or communal identity. Many Chinese have been converted to other faiths, and perhaps even more important, they have been receptive to secular norms and life styles. Although most Chinese tend to be religiously tolerant and agnostic, this does not mean that they are insincere or merely opportunistic. Rather, they appear to be receptive to new ideas, whether religious or secular, and they retain their independent views based on fairly pragmatic and practical evaluations.

Despite the generally high adaptive capacity of the Chinese, they retain some features of their traditional culture as they become more modern. Clan, family ties and kinship loyalties remain strong despite the more fragmented and atomized life styles which have tended to be a feature of industrial and urbanized society. Similarly, Chinese secret societies persist in a variety of guises despite strenuous efforts of the Malaysian and Singapore governments to eradicate such organizations. Some of these societies continue as social service organizations providing their members with insurance and supporting cultural activities. Thus, for the Chinese, some institutions of traditional society have survived and have been transformed to meet the changing demands of a modernizing society.

The Indian community has had diverse responses to exogenous cultural influences, depending largely on their rural or urban location. Urban Indians have been exposed to many cultures, and have numerous opportunities for access to diverse roles and modern life styles. As a minority community, Indians are more likely to live in ethnically mixed urban areas, although some distinctive Indian enclaves can be found in larger cities. The Indians who came to Malaysia did not retain the elaborate social structure of caste, although caste status and certain caste attitudes have tended to persist. The high esteem afforded "high caste" social functions, such as teaching, the law and white collar occupations has tended to stimulate Indians to aspire to similar economic roles and functions. Therefore, urban Indians have been over-represented in most professional and white collar positions, and they appear to acquire competitive achievement norms quite readily. Their traditional attitudes toward manual and physical labor has meant that such activities have been left to Indians of lower caste origin, frequently from families of immigrants who came to Malaya under the government-run Indian immigration scheme. However, these attitudes toward physical work appear to be changing, especially as Malaysia develops a demand for a technically trained work force. In the newer industries, a fairly high proportion of the work force is Indian.

By comparison with his urban counterpart, the rural Indian tends to be isolated in self-contained housing quarters on estates or for government public works projects. Such Indians employed as wage laborers on work gangs have much less opportunity to move into the more dynamic sectors of the economy, and they suffer from poor schooling and low wages despite their increasingly active union organizations. A combination of low caste traditional attitudes, poor education and an isolated existence has generated low aspirations and low self-esteem among rural Indians so that they have been insulated from many of the winds of change and modernization which have affected other segments of Malaysian society.

The Political Dimension

Social and Political Mobilization

The processes of social change described above in broad outline have induced various structural changes in Malaysian society. Perhaps the most significant have been the growth of voluntary and political associations dedicated to some form of social or political mobilization. Although there are a number of important exceptions, voluntary associations have tended to form along communal lines, thus providing institutional structures for communal-ethnic mobilization.

The traditional power structure of Malay society has remained largely intact, despite important social changes and the emergence of new elites. At the center of the traditional power structure is the Malay aristocracy, while at the lower levels are *penghulus* (village headmen), *ketuas* (elders) and religious functionaries. Because aristocratic Malay elites were well-represented in the colonial administration, Malays from the Malay States were slow to develop voluntary social and political associations. The Malays of Singapore, however, were not effectively served or led by these traditional Malay elites, and because they were exposed to the challenges of a dynamic, urban society and to the competitive ethos of the Chinese and Indians, they were the first to develop voluntary associations to meet their collective social and political needs.

The first Malay associations date from 1876 and were formed initially to publish newspapers and journals in Malay, with the emphasis being given to world affairs, Malay literature, and social and religious commentary. Toward the turn of the century Malay cultural and linguistic associations also began to appear, as well as societies charged with the support and operation of the Arabic *madrasah* schools which provided urban Malays with orthodox Islamic religious instruction. These early voluntary associations engaged in no open political activity, but they were instrumental in promoting among urban Malays a self-examination of their cultural and religious heritage.

By the 1920s Islamic reform movements, emanating first from Egypt and later from Indonesia, spread rapidly among the Singapore-based Malay intellectuals who engaged in a soul-searching evaluation of their identity and their cultural future. As the urban Malay community produced a new breed of intellectual elites who became agitated over questions of reform and the future of Malay society, a number of literary-political organizations were founded. From this ferment, two schools of religio-political ideology emerged. *Kaum Tau* (Old Faction) reflected the views of the traditional court-centered Malay elites who sought to preserve the political and religious institutions of Malay society by defending traditional Malay religious practices, customs and doctrines. By contrast, *Kaum Muda* (Young Faction) attracted the support of the rising urban-based Malay intelligentsia who were inspired by the new pan-Islamic revivalist ideology. Wishing to purge Malay religion and culture of its non-Islamic practices and beliefs, the latter sought to mobilize Malays to meet the challenges posed by western rulers and by the aggressive immigrant communities. To accomplish these objectives they advocated that Malays should rediscover orthodox Islam and acquire knowledge of modern scientific technology. For the Kaum Muda, the Islamic madrasah schools became the primary vehicle for social reconstruction of Malay society, with religious indoctrination receiving primacy over science and technology. Thus, Kaum Muda not only challenged the authority of traditional political and religious elites, but they also spawned associations to operate schools and to publish journals espousing the Kaum Muda cause.[5]

Although not organized as political parties, these early Malay religio-cultural societies helped to stimulate the political and social consciousness of the Malays in the inter-war era. Ultimately, a few political societies and clubs were founded, and by 1937 a number of Malay societies met together in an annual Malay Congress to facilitate cooperation and the political union of the Malays. However, the common Malay peasants remained politically inactive before the Second World War, preferring to leave political affairs as a matter for discussion and representation between their Malay Rulers and the British colonial administrators.

After the war, the political mood of the Malays underwent a drastic transformation. The close association between the Malay Rulers and the colonial authorities was difficult to restore because some Rulers had cooperated with the Japanese during the period of the occupation. Furthermore, the British, in anticipation of promised democratic reforms, began making plans to allow everyone in the country to participate in the political system. To effectuate such reforms, the Malay Rulers were to have their prerogatives curtailed, as democracy and traditional Malay monarchy seemed incompatible. Suddenly the Malays realized that they were no longer adequately represented and protected by the Malay Rulers and the Malay aristocracy. Instead of a political system based on an accord between the Malay Rulers and the British, the Malays faced the prospect of having the political system opened to

5. William R. Roff, *The Origins of Malay Nationalism* (New Haven: Yale University Press, 1967), pp. 1-125.

the full participation of the immigrant communities, who had already outdistanced the Malays economically, and who, in 1946, appeared to be better organized for popular participation in politics. Malays of various political persuasions became alarmed by the prospect of the loss of the pre-eminent Malay position in political affairs if the Malay Rulers were to be reduced to titular constitutional monarchs. In this state of anxiety and fear that they might "lose their country" to the immigrant communities, the Malays were jolted from their political lethargy.

Although a number of minor political associations which had formed in the prewar years took up the political cause of the Malays, such organizations were relatively ineffective. Instead, massive political mobilization of the Malays was accomplished under the leadership of a prominent Malay aristocrat from Johore named Dato Onn bin Ja'afar. Relying on Malay elites in the traditional power structure of Malay society, in 1946 Dato Onn organized massive Malay demonstrations against the British proposals to initiate constitutional reforms which would diminish the prerogatives of the Malay Rulers and threaten the Malay character of government by giving full democratic rights to the immigrant communities. As the movement gained momentum with massive public displays of Malay opposition, Dato Onn decided to found a more permanent and formal organization to represent Malay demands. In May 1946, the United Malays National Organization (UMNO) came into being, and it has remained ever since as the largest political party in Malaysia through its continuing ability to command the loyalty of an overwhelming majority of the Malays.[6]

The leadership positions of UMNO have been filled largely from the ranks of traditional Malay aristocratic elites, who in their new political roles have been effective in generating broadly based popular support for UMNO among the Malays. Thus, the party has been instrumental in maintaining a continuity between the traditional power structure of Malay society and the new political institutions based on democratic principles and the support of mass publics.

Most of the Malay parties which formed in the postwar years were the product of factional divisions within UMNO or the result of segments of Malay society which were never effectively recruited into the fold of the party. For example, both Party Negara and the National Convention Party were founded by UMNO dissidents who bolted from the ranks of the party after being defeated in sharp intra-party battles.

6. Ishak bin Tadin, "Dato Onn and Malay Nationalism, 1946-1951," *Journal of Southeast Asian History* 1, 1 (March 1960): 56-88; Gordon P. Means, *Malaysian Politics* (London: University of London Press, 1970), pp. 51-66, 98-102.

Party Ra'ayat and the Pan-Malayan Islamic Party were both founded by segments of Malay society that never gave full support to UMNO and its leaders. Party Ra'ayat was founded by radical urban-based, Indonesian-inspired Malays who expressed contempt or antipathy for traditional Malay elites and the Malay Rulers. Similarly, traditional Mulsim religious functionaries and those Malays who were the products of the Muslim *pondok* and *madrassah* schools were concerned that the UMNO leaders, many of whom were English educated, were too secular and did not give enough attention to religious issues in politics. In 1948, Muslim religious leaders met to found what ultimately became the Pan-Malayan Islamic Party. As it grew in strength, the PMIP attracted other Malay dissidents from UMNO, many of whom objected to the political compromises UMNO made with other communal parties. As such, the PMIP became the most outspoken proponent of Malay chauvanist politics reinforced by a militant Islamic appeal. By 1959, it had become a major opposition force in politics and the strongest competitor of UMNO for the Malay vote.

Although the Malays reached an artificially high state of mobilization in 1946 as a result of their anxiety over their political stake in the country, they have since continued to be fairly effectively mobilized for political participation at the polls. Yet, once elections are over, the Malays tend to withdraw to their daily activities and are not motivated for participation in voluntary associations seeking to influence public policy on a continuing basis. Rather, the Malay masses seem content to leave politics to political leaders who are expected to act as trustees for the interests of their Malay constituencies. Therefore, Malay political mobilization tends to be episodic, being generated at election time or during a political crisis, and the form of Malay involvement in politics has tended to produce leaders who have patronizing and manipulative attitudes toward their constituents. Such episodic Malay political mobilization has also made it more difficult for the Malaysian political system to weather disputes involving communal demands, for massive Malay political mobilization has tended to produce a political climate hardly conducive to accommodation and compromise with the other ethnic communities in the country.

Although segments of the Chinese community have been highly politicized from time to time, the Chinese have not been effectively mobilized as a community for sustained political action. Many factors contribute to this situation. The Chinese are a diverse community, with different languages, educational backgrounds and economic interests. Some commentators have suggested that the traditional Chinese attitudes toward government, which was seen as an evil institution, has influenced their attitudes toward political participation. While such attitudes may persist among some Chinese, their fairly low level of active political mobilization may be more a product of Chinese frustration over their failure to find a mode of political participation which would hold promise of producing tangible political benefits. If political mobilization holds few prospects of rewards, and involves a high cost factor, political consciousness may not lead to political involvement. Such appears to be the case with the Chinese, who have learned some bitter lessons in practical politics over the past two generations.

During the interwar period, political affairs in China held the attention of large segments of the Chinese. Within nine months of its founding in China in 1912, the Kuomintang opened its first branch in Singapore, with other branches in Malaya following shortly thereafter. The colonial authorities allowed the Kuomintang to operate legally until 1925, after which it continued as an active but illegal organization. In China, the split between the Kuomintang and the Chinese Communist Party in 1927 was duplicated in Malaya, and led to the formation of the Malayan Communist Party in 1930. Both parties concentrated their attention on politics in China and recruited almost exclusively from among the Chinese. Those Chinese who were active in either party were liable to be deported from the country if they were discovered by the police. Chinese political activity in Malaya was permitted only when it was pursued through organizations which were properly registered with the government and considered by the British to be "safe" and "legitimate," such as the Chinese Chambers of Commerce or benevolent guilds and societies. These bodies could make representations to the colonial legislative councils through the nominated members who were appointed by the British to represent Chinese interests. During this period, therefore, the Chinese were not highly mobilized nor effectively organized for participation in political affairs related to Malaya.[7]

The Japanese invasion of Southeast Asia drastically changed the political scene for the Chinese. Hostile to the Chinese, the Japanese killed and tortured many thousands and made all Chinese realize that political events had a direct bearing on their lives. During the Japanese occupation, the prewar Chinese elites were discredited because some fled to India with the retreating British, while others, under pain of death, were forced to cooperate with the Japanese. The resulting leadership vacuum in the Chinese community was filled by the Malayan Communist Party, which had years of experience in operating

7. Wilfred Blythe, *The Impact of Chinese Secret Societies in Malaya* (London: Oxford University Press, 1969), pp. 279-323; Means, *Malaysian Politics*, pp. 26-35; Victor Purcell, *The Chinese in Southeast Asia* (London: Oxford University Press, 1951), pp. 321-366.

an underground organization. The Communists entered the jungles of Malaya to form the Malayan Peoples' Anti-Japanese Army (MPAJA) and they enlisted widespread support among the Chinese. In rural areas, Chinese faced Japanese reprisals as well as forced subscriptions levied by the guerrillas, who enforced discipline by terror against those who became willing or unwilling Japanese collaborators. For most Chinese, the war years were filled with anxiety, pain and hardship.

When the British returned to Malaya at the end of the war, they found the Chinese far more politicized than before. The Malayan Communist Party emerged as a powerful political force and a founder of a conglomorate of organizations mobilized for political action. While the Communists claimed leadership of the nationalist move-ment in Malaya, in reality they enjoyed solid support of only the more militant and mobilized segment of the Chinese community. When the British initiated various measures to break the Communist control of the labor-union movement, the contest between the Communists and the government became violent. By 1948, the Communists, following the lead of Soviet strategy as enunciated by the Cominform, decided to initiate a revolutionary guerrilla war, which, while very costly for the colonial regime, was gradually contained.[8] When the Communist lead-ers left for the junges the second time, they became isolated from their power base among the urban and small-town Chinese. With their de-parture from the centers of Chinese concentration, it was easier for the pre-war Chinese elites gradually to rebuild among the Chinese sup-port which had been so badly eroded during the war years. For a de-cade the Chinese community suffered from a major cleavage between those who sympathized with the Communists' strategy of pursuing a "war of national liberation" and the more conservative Chinese elites who sought instead to cooperate with the colonial authorities to en-sure that the Chinese would gain equal access to the Malayan political system as part of the process of de-colonization and the introduction of democratic reforms. Gradually the latter group of westernized prewar Chinese leaders succeeded in winning the confidence of the majority of the Chinese, although there remained a significant minority who con-tinued to give their support to the Communists.

The appeal of the more conservative Chinese elites was based on the argument that the Chinese would secure an equitable share of political

---

8. Noel Barber, *The War of the Running Dogs, The Malayan Emergency: 1948-1960* (New York: Weybright & Talley, 1972); Justice M. van der Kroef *Communism in Malaya and Singapore* (The Hague: M. Nijhoff, 1967); Means, *Malaysian Politics*, pp. 68-80, 265-291; Lucian W. Pye, *Guerrilla Communism in Malaya* (Princeton, N.J.: Princeton University Press, 1956); Sir Richard Thompson, *Defeating Communist Insurgency* (New York: Frederick A. Praeger, 1966).

power by cooperating in the formulation of a democratic system for Malaya. In this process, the primary organization representing Chinese interests became the Malayan Chinese Association (MCA), which had been formed in 1949 during the early years of the Communist insurgency with the objective of countering Communist influence among the Chinese and persuading the Chinese of the utility of political participation through constitutional and democratic means. Since 1951 the Malayan Chinese Association has remained affiliated with the United Malays National Organization in a dominant political coalition called the Alliance. By this tactic the MCA has had access to political power derived from elections and has received major concessions on a variety of issues which are of prime concern to the Chinese.[9] However, the price of membership in the ruling government coalition has been for the MCA to acknowledge the political leadership and supremacy of the Malays in UMNO and to avoid public mobilization of the Chinese for "excessive" communal demands. In effect, the Chinese have been given a restricted access to the political system on the assumption that they avoid intense political mobilization over communal issues. When these terms have been ignored by more aggressive leaders of the Chinese community, whether in the Malayan Chinese Association or in other parties appealing for the Chinese vote, the Malayan Government has acted decisively to isolate and defeat those who pursue such tactics. In more severe crises, the government has utilized its emergency powers and the suspension of parliamentary rule to ensure that the political mobilization of the non-Malays does not jeopardize the political supremacy of the Malays as represented by the United Malays National Organization.

Over the last half century, the Chinese have learned that the price and risks of widespread political participation has always been very high. Today overt political mobilization by the Chinese is not particularly high, not so much out of apathy, as it is out of an awareness that their survival as a minority in Southeast Asia may require that they maintain a fairly low political profile.

The Indians of Malaya first became active politically in a manner similar to the Chinese: as a result of their attention to events in their land of origin. The Indian nationalist movement gained a small but dedicated following in Malaya in the thirties but no formal branches of the Congress Party were established. Instead, a number of Indian associations were founded to represent Indian trading interests, Indian laborers, or Indian cultural and welfare groups. Even though many Malayan Indians were inspired by the Congress Party's struggle against the British rule in India, Indian political activity related to Malayan affairs remained minimal before the war.

9. Means, *Malaysian Politics*, pp. 105-106, 132-147, 193-224.

When the Japanese occupied Malaya, they tried to utilize Indian nationalism to good advantage in their war effort against the Allied Powers. To that end, the Japanese sponsored the formation of the Indian Independence League (IIL) and its military wing, the Indian National Army (INA). These organizations were led by political exiles from India, first by Rash Behari Bose, and then by the famous Bengali nationalist and former president of the Congress Party, Subhas Chandra Bose. Some contingents of the Indian National Army recruited from Malaya fought in the abortive campaign which the Japanese launched to invade India in 1944. Many urban Indians associated with the IIL cooperated with the Japanese and received favored treatment as a result. However, many rural Indians suffered greatly during the war because of the disruption of the rubber industry, and tens of thousands of rural Indians were conscripted by the Japanese to work on the infamous Bangkok to Rangoon "death" railway, where large numbers of them perished.

At the end of the war, the returning British authorities initiated trials against those Indians who were believed to have collaborated with the Japanese. Although few trials were held, such action helped to spawn several organizations to represent Indian interests. Following a visit to Malaya by Jawaharlal Nehru, a number of Indian organizations met in August 1946 to form the Malayan Indian Congress (MIC). Since its founding, the MIC has been the largest, but not the only, Indian body actively speaking on behalf of Indians and seeking to mobilize them for political action. Following the introduction of elections in 1950, the MIC has followed a strategy of maximizing its political influence through coalition politics. Shortly after the United Malays National Organization and the Malayan Chinese Association joined to form the Alliance coalition in 1951, the Malayan Indian Congress successfully concluded negotiations to become the junior partner in the Alliance.[10] As with other member parties of the Alliance, admission to the ruling coalition entailed some restrictions on independent political activities. The superior political role of the Malays had to be acknowledged, and the political compromises worked out in secret among the three communal parties had to be defended in public by each party organization. Similarly, communal mobilization over communal issues had to be avoided. The Malayan Indian Congress has, therefore, faced the same dilemma as the Malayan Chinese Association: it must represent the interests of an ethnic-cultural community without mobilizing its constituents to action on the very issues which are most salient to the community as a whole. For this reason, the

10. *Ibid.*, pp. 36-41, 107-111, 207-210; Kernial Singh Sandhu, *Indians in Malaya* (Cambridge: Cambridge University Press, 1969).

Indians have not been highly mobilized by the MIC and it has been difficult to cultivate strong loyalties to the MIC except through patronage available through the party. The political ambivalence of both Indians and Chinese to their most prominent communal organization has made these two communities particularly susceptible to the appeals of opposition parties who seek to dislodge the Alliance from its position of power.

Political Institutions

Because independence was gained through peaceful means, the governmental institutions of Malaysia evolved from earlier colonial practice. The basic administrative and judicial structures survived from the colonial era with only minimal incremental changes. In the transitional period before independence elected legislative councils were added to the basic colonial administrative structure with the British parliamentary system providing the model for postwar constitutional arrangements. However, such representative bodies also had to be adapted to indigenous institutions and to the Malayan political environment.

Upon their return to Malaya at the end of the Second World War, the British decided on a policy of democratic reforms with the stated objective of transferring power gradually to popularly elected representatives as a prelude to full independence. To facilitate this policy, colonial officials in London drafted a new constitution for a Malayan Union. This draft constitution proposed to abolish the separate Malay States, to limit the powers of the Malay Rulers, and to provide equal access of all domiciled Malayans to representative institutions which were promised for the country. We have noted earlier that the Malays were quickly and effectively mobilized by their traditional elites to fight the Malayan Union proposals. Speaking on behalf of the Malays, the United Malays National Organization demanded policies to preserve the separate identity of the Malay States, to retain substantial powers for the Malay Rulers, to restrict the citizenship for the immigrant communities, and to slow the pace of democratic reforms until the Malays were better organized for politics and were ready to assume positions of power then held by British officials. By contrast, political leaders of the non-Malay communities failed to generate effective public support for the Malayan Union proposals. Therefore, the British were placed on the defensive in the implementation of their initial plans for democratic reforms based on the principle of equal access to the political system for all residents of the country.

Following the massive Malay demonstrations against the Malayan Union proposals, the British entered into extensive negotiations with the Malay Rulers and Malay political leaders for a new constitutional scheme. Instead of a unitary political system, the British agreed to establish a federal system with the Malay Rulers continuing as constitutional monarchs. Fairly stringent citizenship requirements for non-Malays were agreed upon, and a rudimentary system of legal special rights and privileges for Malays was incorporated into the constitution. The pace for the introduction of representative institutions was to be more deliberate on the expectation that special efforts would be made to train enough Malays for positions in government so that they would not be displaced in the political system by the better educated and wealthier segments of the non-Malay communities. Despite considerable objection by non-Malays to these concessions to Malay opinion, these revised British policies were ultimately incorporated into the Federation of Malaya Agreement of 1948, which document became the constitution of Malaya for the interim period prior to independence in 1957.

In the initial years of the Federation of Malaya, the Legislative Council consisted of 26 officials and 50 unofficials who were appointed by the British High Commissioner to represent various functional and ethnic interests in the country. By 1951 a form of quasi-cabinet government was inaugurated under which appointed Malayan members were given responsibility for department portfolios and were held answerable to the Legislative Council for their actions. With the introduction of local elections in the same year, political parties rapidly mobilized public support and prepared for the first federal elections which were held in 1955 for a reconstituted legislature comprised of 52 elected members, 22 appointed members, 4 ex-officio members and 11 members selected by state and settlement councils. Following the elections, a regular cabinet on the parliamentary model controlled the government, except that the British High Commissioner continued to exercise extraordinary powers if he chose to do so.[11] However, British determination to leave Malaya gracefully meant that he was circumspect in the exercise of his powers, so that for practical purposes a parliamentary system of government can be said to have begun in 1955.

Most of the political activity in the country immediately following the first federal elections of 1955 was directed to the task of drafting a new constitution for independence—more popularly referred to by the Malay word *merdeka*. Aided by a constitutional commission of foreign legal experts, the legislature ratified the new Merdeka Constitution which came into force on the date of Malayan independence, August 31, 1957. This constitution retained the basic framework of the Federa-

11. Means, *Malaysian Politics*, pp. 51-67.

tion of Malaya Agreement of 1948, but with important modifications. A bicameral federal parliament was created with the *Dewan Ra'ayat*, lower House of Representatives, composed of 104 elected members representing single-member constituencies. The *Dewan Negara*, the upper chamber or Senate, consisted of 26 members elected by the state assemblies and 32 members appointed by the government. The term of office for the lower house was set at five years or less if Parliament was dissolved earlier. Senators were assigned overlapping fixed terms of six years, so that the term of office for one-third of the senators expired every two years. A new office of Yang di-Pertuan Agong, Paramount Ruler, was created for the whole federation through the rotational election by the Council of Rulers on the basis of seniority from among the Malay Rulers of the constituent Malay States. The Paramount Ruler holds his office as reigning monarch for the country for a fixed five year non-renewable term. In most important respects, the Paramount Ruler, the Cabinet, Prime Minister and Parliament have operated much like the Westminster Parliament, at least in form if not always in ethos and basic political culture.[12]

The federal system established in 1948 provided for highly centralized legislative powers, but retained much of the decentralized colonial administrative system based on the separate states and settlements. With the Merdeka Constitution, the federal system was reformed to give each level of government administrative responsibility for subjects within its legislative competence. The constitution enumerated three lists of powers—a federal list, a state list and a concurrent list of shared powers. A "supremacy clause" assured the primacy of federal powers in matters of joint jurisdiction. All major tax powers were assigned to the federal government, but the states were guaranteed revenues through earmarked federal grants calculated largely on the basis of state population and road mileage. Because these grants have been insufficient to finance all state activities, the states have become partially dependent on the federal government. As a consequence the federal system has developed an increasingly centralist bias.[13]

The Merdeka Constitution included sections devoted to the definition of a system of Malay special rights, whereby Malays were assured of preferential treatment over other citizens. Under colonial rule, Malays had always enjoyed some special privileges, especially in matters of land rights and recruitment to the lower positions of the administra-

12. *Ibid.*, pp. 170-192; B. Simandjuntak, *Malayan Federalism, 1945-1963* (Kuala Lumpur: Oxford University Press, 1969), pp. 53-117.

13. Gordon P. Means, "Federalism in Malaya and Malaysia," in *Fédéralisme et Nations*, ed. Roman Serbyn (Montreal: Les Presses de l'Universite du Québec, 1971), pp. 215-239.

tive services. The new constitution gave constitutional status to those policies and enlarged their scope. Malay special rights extended to four main areas: Firstly, large areas of the country were designated as "Malay Reservations" where only Malays could acquire title to land. Secondly, preferential Malay quotas were established for recruitment to the civil service; for the Malayan Civil Service the recruitment ratio was set at four to one in favor of the Malays, while in the External Affairs Service, the Judicial and Legal Service and the Customs Service the ratio was set at three to one. Thirdly, preferential Malay quotas were also established for issuance of business, trading, and commercial licenses. Fourthly, public scholarships and admission to higher educational institutions were governed by similar preferential Malay quotas. In addition to the federal definition of Malay special rights, state constitutions expanded such rights by requiring that certain state administrative offices be filled only by Malay Muslims. Those Malay privileges which were protected by the federal constitution were "entrenched" by being made exempt from the normal constitutional amendment process. Therefore, such Malay rights and privileges were made more difficult to amend than the constitution itself. Presumably, these constitutionally defined Malay rights were designed to provide legal backing for the political arguments that the country was Malay and that the Malays as the indigenous people therefore deserve protection and advantages over the non-Malay communities.[14]

While Malaysia attained independence on August 31, 1957, British rule in Southeast Asia was not thereby terminated. At the tip of the Malay peninsula, Singapore remained a self-governing colony, and on the island of Borneo, the British continued to exercise control and protection over three states: North Borneo, Sarawak and Brunei. With the problem of de-colonization forcing the issue, all the British-protected states in Southeast Asia, except the tiny oil-rich Sultanate of Brunei, agreed in 1963 to join with Malaya to form the Federation of Malaysia. While space does not permit an account of the domestic and international politics involved in that decision, we can note that some constitutional changes were made to accommodate the three new states entering the federation. Because each state negotiated the terms for its entry into Malaysia, there emerged a federal system with differential distribution of powers for various states in the union. Sarawak and Sabah (formerly North Borneo) gained additional guarantees of autonomy over immigration, both domestic and foreign; the conversion to Malay as the national language was to be delayed at least until 1973; Malaysia's federal laws favoring Islam were to be slightly modified for

14. Gordon P. Means, "'Special Rights' as a Strategy for Development: The Case of Malaysia," *Comparative Politics* 5, 1 (October 1972): 29-61.

those states; "special rights" for Borneo natives were to be established similar to those for Malays in Malaya; and these two states were promised additional revenue from certain earmarked taxes.

The constitutional arrangements for Malaysia were designed to maintain approximately the same racial-communal balance in the larger federation as existed in Malaya. Therefore, the Malay and native tribal population of the Borneo states were to be balanced off against Singapore's large Chinese majority. In addition, Sarawak and Sabah were given 24 and 16 seats respectively in the lower house of Parliament which proportionately over-represented the population of these two states. To minimize its political impact, Singapore was grossly under-represented, receiving only 15 seats in the Dewan Ra'ayat, which was proportionately less than one-third of the representation by population enjoyed by the two Borneo states. To make these terms more acceptable to Singapore, the latter was given greater autonomy and larger revenue resources from its own taxing powers. Singapore gained the right to continue its free port status; it was given autonomy in education, labor and social security policies; and was permitted to retain about 75 percent of all revenues collected in the state to meet these obligations. All Singapore citizens were to be made nationals of the Federation of Malaysia, but their rights of political participation could be restricted if they moved to other states in the federation.[15]

Malaysia came into being on September 16, 1963 amid a storm of opposition from Indonesia and the Philippines. So long as Malaysia faced a campaign of harrassment and military provocations by her insular neighbors, the internal dissention in the country was somewhat muted. From the beginning, however, serious differences arose between Singapore's Peoples Action Party government led by Lee Kuan Yew, and Malaysia's Alliance government in Kuala Lumpur led by Tunku Abdul Rahman. Initially, a number of disputes arose over the terms of implementation of the Malaysia Agreement. Later, the contest widened into an ideological battle over the communal and racial policies of the federation, with Singapore arguing for application of universalistic and equalitarian norms, and Kuala Lumpur standing firm for the primacy of Malay political and legal rights over the non-Malay citizens of Malaysia. When the contest degenerated into serious electoral challenges by each party in the political strongholds of the other, racial tensions were exacerbated. By 1965, Lee Kuan Yew appeared to be making some headway in forging a coalition of opposition parties around the slogan calling for a "Malaysian Malaysia" in place of the "Malay Malaysia" which the Alliance was accused of fostering. In

15. R. S. Milne, *Government and Politics in Malaysia* (Boston: Houghton Mifflin Co., 1967), pp. 49-178.

view of the growing strength of the opposition and the heightened racial antagonisms, Tunku Abdul Rahman decided unilaterally and preemptorily to expel Singapore from the union. The decision was made secretly. Parliament and the nation were informed on July 25, 1965 only half an hour before Parliament convened and quickly passed a constitutional amendment ejecting Singapore from the federation.[16]

In the pruned union, the Alliance government was assured of continued political supremacy and the federal government thereby gained added political leverage over the state governments, thus accelerating the centralist trend in the federal system. Likewise, the pro-Malay communal policies of the federal government became more readily accepted throughout the federation as appropriate government policy, if for no other reason than that the most powerful critics of such policies were no longer in the union and the remaining critics were weakened and politically demoralized. With Singapore out of the union, Malaysia appeared to be politically stabilized, with few political leaders who were willing to openly challenge the country's constitutional arrangements or the basic institutional structures of government.

The Party System

Immediately after the war Malaya witnessed the formation of a number of small embryonic parties, frequently organized by a single aspiring political figure. However, the political controversies surrounding the drafting of a postwar constitution stimulated communal feelings and contributed to the political mobilization around communal organizations. Prior to the first elections in 1952, the three largest communal organizations agreed to form a political coalition to ensure their electoral victory and to facilitate the achievement of Malayan independence. Together the United Malays National Organization, the Malayan Chinese Association and the Malayan Indian Congress formed a political holding company called the Alliance, which has dominated the political scene and has retained control of the federal government from the date of the first federal elections in 1955 to the present. Initially, the Alliance majority of the popular vote was overwhelming, but declined gradually in subsequent elections. Nonetheless, because of the single-member constituency system and disunity among opposition parties, the Alliance has retained such commanding majorities in Parliament that it has been able to count on a two-

16. Chan Heng Chee, *Singapore: The Politics of Survival* (Singapore: Oxford University Press, 1971); Milne, *Government and Politics*, pp. 199-227; Milton Osborne, *Singapore and Malaysia* (Ithaca, N.Y.: Cornell University, Southeast Asia Program, Data Paper No. 53, 1964).

thirds majority to amend the Constitution at will, except while Singapore was in the federation and after the 1969 elections. Thus, if the Alliance is considered a single party, Malaysia's party system can be characterized as a "single party dominant" pattern.

Because of the nature of the Alliance, the basic policy processes of government have taken place within the Alliance. Important issues became the subject of secret bargaining among the three partner communal organizations who are represented on the Alliance National Council. This mechanism has been particularly successful in resolving sensitive communal issues facing the country. When the system has operated smoothly, communal political mobilization has been minimized, and public involvement in communal issues has been somewhat restricted by utilizing a political forum not subject to klieg lights of public scrutiny. With the Alliance in firm command of majorities in Parliament, the Alliance National Council and the Alliance Cabinet, headed by the Prime Minister, have become more important political arenas than Parliament.

The political success of the Alliance has depended upon its ability to preserve intact a political coalition which bridges the basic communal cleavage within the country. On the most important communal issues, the Alliance has worked out fairly moderate compromises, but with a distinct pro-Malay bias. In the elections, the Alliance has been more successful in racially balanced constituencies where no ethnic community can command a decisive majority on its own. Although the political power of the Alliance has rested with its ability to dominate the basic communal cleavage, its Achilles heal is also located along that cleavage, for serious communal differences have produced strains among Alliance parties, and communal compromises, when they are finally worked out, have not always been supported by the rank and file. In time of communal crisis, problems of party discipline are therefore endemic, and many of the more vocal proponents of communal demands, particularly at the lower ranks of the member parties, often make liaison with opposition parties, and take hard and uncompromising positions in the bargaining process conducted within the Alliance National Council. To function smoothly, the Alliance needs communal moderates in leadership positions of the constituent communal parties, and it relies upon the support of communal moderates at the polls. When these conditions have not been present, the Alliance has been rocked by internal crises, the most serious being in July 1959 and in May 1969.

Most of the opposition parties claim to be non-communal, but all of these parties find it almost impossible to recruit a balanced membership among all the major communities. Indeed, many of the opposition parties have discovered that their power at the polls has depended upon their vigorous articulation of communal grievances and demands, yet that tactic, while successful in winning a few seats, also erects formidable obstacles to the formation of an opposition coalition capable of dislodging the Alliance from its commanding position in Malaysian politics. While some observers have argued that the communal policies of the Alliance have forced the opposition parties to take communal stands, it appears far more reasonable that the cultural-ethnic divisions in the country present formidable obstacles for the formation of parties organized along non-communal lines. Indeed, when nearly all issues of politics have a communal coloration, how can parties be non-communal unless they are also non-political?

A quick survey of the opposition parties will indicate their ideological and communal attachments. The largest of the opposition parties is the Pan-Malayan Islamic Party (PMIP). It represents the point of view of those Malays who fear and resent the immigrant communities in the country, and it proposes to utilize the power of the state to ensure the political and economic supremacy of the Malays. The Islamic ideology propounded by the party has enabled it to appeal to the most basic "primordeal sentiment" permeating Malay society. Yet, despite its emphasis on religious principles, the main appeal of the PMIP has been to strident Malay chauvinist nationalism. In its political campaigning it has coined such slogans as: "Malaya belongs to the Malays," and "there must be a distinction between aliens and masters."[17] The party manifestos have called for state support for Islam; the enforcement by the state of the religious obligations of Islam; the rapid conversion to Malay as the sole national language; the reservation of top ministerial positions in government exclusively for Malays; and the extension and expansion of Malay special rights. For years, there has been a substantial faction in the PMIP which has favored some form of union with Indonesia, seeing such a redrafting of the map of Southeast Asia as a way to isolate and control the non-Malay communities, who otherwise appear politically formidable and present such an intractable social problem for those who hold to the ideal of creating a homogenous ethnic, cultural and religious nation.[18]

The PMIP can trace its origins to 1948, but it became a significant force in politics only after 1956 when the prominent Malay nationalist leader, Dr. Al-Helmy Burhanuddin became its president. In 1955, the party gained one federal seat, and had the distinction of being the only opposition facing the Alliance in the Federal Legislative Council. In the 1959 elections it won 13 federal seats; in 1964, 9 seats; and in 1969, 12 seats. Its federal percentage of the votes cast has varied between 14

17. *Straits Budget*, March 28, 1957, p. 9.
18. Means, *Malaysian Politics*, pp. 226-233.

percent and 24 percent.[19] The low point in the party's appeal was in the election immediately after the formation of the Federation of Malaysia, which the party opposed. Some PMIP officials were revealed to have had clandestine contacts with·Indonesia during the latter's intense "confrontation" campaign against Malaysia. Such revelations probably hurt the party in the 1964 elections. However, over the longer run the PMIP has been quite successful, especially since its political appeal to Malay chauvinism has been such that nearly all its policies have eventually been adopted by the Alliance, although generally in a milder or compromised form.

Apart from the PMIP, practically all other opposition parties in Malaysia claim to be non-communal. However, no party has been able to develop a racially balanced following, and few succeed in having more than token representation across the Malay/non-Malay cultural and political cleavage. In West Malaysia (Malaya), Party Ra'ayat espouses a radical nationalist and Marxian socialist ideology, but from a Malay communal perspective, and thus has attracted a small but almost exclusively Malay radical following. Similarly, the National Convention Party was founded when a left-wing faction in UMNO split away from the parent party after its leader, Abdul Aziz bin Ishak, lost his cabinet post in the government in 1963. It has attempted to reflect Malay peasant populist radicalism, and it reflected a veiled Malay communal reaction against some of the communal compromises worked out within the Alliance. Quite naturally, the party had almost exclusive Malay support, but it withered and passed from public view following the 1964 elections.

The largest non-Malay opposition party is the Democratic Action Party (DAP), which was an offshoot of Singapore's ruling Peoples Action Party (PAP). When Singapore was expelled from the federation, the PAP supporters remaining in Malaysia reorganized themselves as the Democratic Action Party and continued to espouse essentially the same program as before partition. The DAP has been a trenchant critic of the communal policies of the Alliance, campaigning on behalf of equal rights for all citizens and in opposition to Malay special rights and privileges. The party proposes to deal with the problem of Malay poverty by raising rural incomes and promoting "social and economic democracy" regardless of race. It has also favored multi-lingualism by proposing to give the Chinese, Tamil, and English languages official status, while it proposed to recognize Malay as "the common language of expression and communication among all Malaysians." Campaigning with the slogan "Towards a Malaysian Malaysia," the DAP be-

19. R. K. Vasil, *The Malaysian General Elections of 1969* (Singapore: Oxford University Press, 1972), p. 85.

came the primary protagonist of the Alliance government after 1965.[20] The leadership positions of the DAP have been filled by Chinese and Indians, but the bulk of the supporters come from the ranks of the Chinese.

In 1968, a number of moderate and English-educated political leaders from various opposition parties met to form a new broad-based party to present an alternative between the Alliance and the DAP. This new party, Gerakan Rakyat Malaysia, placed great emphasis upon forming a genuinely non-communal party, and selected an executive committee having balanced representation from all major ethnic communities. The party espoused moderate socialism and stressed the need for policies which would have the effect of promoting cultural pluralism. At the same time, the party acknowledged that the Malays and other indigenous peoples were economically weak and in need of policies which would protect them from exploitation. Gerakan proposed to give Malays special assistance for their educational and economic betterment. During its campaign, the party warned of the increasing reliance on authoritarian measures by the government and threats to democracy should the Alliance win a majority large enough to amend the Constitution at its pleasure. In the only election it has contested, Gerakan polled 8.5 percent of the votes and elected 8 Members of Parliament, 7 of whom were non-Malay. Thus, it has tended to elicit more support from the non-Malays than from the Malays, despite its brave attempt to form a non-communal party and its sincere efforts to draft proposals which would be of special benefit to the Malays.

The Peoples Progressive Party (PPP) is one of the oldest opposition parties representing non-Malay interests. It was founded by two Ceylonese brothers who utilized their law practice to good advantage in representing the demands and grievances of poor Chinese and Indians in the area of their home town of Ipoh. The party has espoused a political platform very similar to the DAP, favoring equalitarian policies and cultural pluralism. Although the PPP has made electoral agreements with other parties, it has retained its separate existence as a regional party but has failed to develop a nationwide following. It has consistently won local authority elections in Ipoh since 1961, and has polled between 20 and 25 percent of the vote in Perak state elections in 1959, 1964, and 1969, as well as capturing from 2 to 4 parliamentary seats in those years.

In East Malaysia (the Borneo states) the party system has developed

---

20. Democratic Action Party, *Who Lives if Malaysia Dies?* (Petaling Jaya, Selangor: Democratic Action Party, 1969); Vasil, *Malaysian General Elections*, pp. 16-32, 59-61.

along communal lines, with a separate party forming for each major ethnic or tribal community in each state. The pattern is too complex to describe in detail, but we may note that in Sabah, the Kadazans have been represented by the United National Kadazan Organization, the Muslim communities by the United Sabah National Organization, the Muruts by the United National Pasok Momogun Organization, and the Chinese by the Sabah Chinese Association and the Sabah Nationalist Party. In Sarawak, the Malays were recruited by two parties, the Barisan Ra'ayat Jati Sarawak and the Party Negara Sarawak. The non-Muslim tribal peoples have also divided their political allegiance between two parties: Party Pesaka Anak Sarawak, which was strong in the Rejang River basin, and the Sarawak National Party, which gained its support from Ibans and Land Dayaks in Sarawak's First, Second and Fourth Divisions. The Chinese community was politically divided among the fairly conservative Sarawak Chinese Association, the more radical and Chinese chauvinist Sarawak United Peoples Party, and the illegal Communist Party which operates through a number of clandestine front organizations. In both Sabah and Sarawak, the introduction of elections after 1962 stimulated complicated political maneuvers which produced inter-party agreements and alliances. The process of coalition-building was actively facilitated by the political intervention of the federal government and the Malayan Alliance into the politics of both states. Kuala Lumpur wished to ensure political stability and isolate the proponents of state autonomy in the belief that Malaya's communal policies and its basic political system should be extended to the Borneo states once they entered Malaysia. Thus, after several years of political turmoil and rather heavy-handed intervention from Kuala Lumpur, both Sarawak and Sabah established state Alliance coalitions of communal parties who, as a condition for their participation in behind-the-scenes political negotiations and their sharing in the rewards of office, agreed to cooperate with the federal government. By 1969, nearly all parties in Sabah and Sarawak had joined the Alliance system, with the exception of the Sarawak United Peoples Party, the Sarawak National Party and the illegal Communist Party. Two years later only the latter two parties were still outside the "Alliance system." As a consequence, public ventilation of political issues largely ceased, and the major issues of politics were a matter for secret negotiations within the Alliance structure between communal leaders of communal parties.[21]

21. Means, *Malaysian Politics*, pp. 371-390; James P. Ongkili, *The Borneo Response to Malaysia, 1961-1963* (Singapore: Donald Moore, 1967); James P. Ongkili, *Modernization in East Malaysia, 1960-1970* (Kuala Lumpur: Oxford University Press, 1972).

The Crisis of 1969

Racial and communal issues have always been central to Malaysian politics. However, the intensity of potential conflict on such issues has been muted by the Alliance system which has concealed from public view much of the politics of the country, since crucial decisions, especially on sensitive communal issues, have been worked out in secret negotiations between the member parties of the Alliance. This system was able to work quite well so long as racial-ethnic political polarization did not become so intense as to undermine the bargaining process within the Alliance or to erode the support of one or more of the communal partners in the ruling coalition. Communal-ethnic polarization has had the effect of increasing the appeal of opposition parties and of making the Alliance bargaining process much more difficult.

Although the Alliance weathered a number of crises over communal issues, the parliamentary elections of 1969 proved to be the most severe test for the survival of the Alliance system of communal bargaining. A number of factors converged to increase communal polarization and weaken the government's base of support. In 1965, Singapore's unceremonious ejection from the Malaysian Federation had strong communal overtones. The controversy over the National Language Bill of 1967, which provided for the conversion to Malay as the sole official language, inflamed communal passions among all the three major communities. Perhaps most important, the opposition parties became more effective in working out electoral agreements to maximize their electoral strength to challenge the Alliance.

While Gerakan Rakyat Malaysia attempted to cultivate a constituency which bridged communal divisions, most of the opposition parties made rather open appeals for communal support by criticizing the whole structure of communal policies which had been laboriously worked out through intra-Alliance bargaining. Thus, in the 1969 election campaign, the Alliance was attacked by the Pan-Malayan Islamic Party for giving too many concessions to non-Malays. On the other flank, the Democratic Action Party, and the Peoples Progressive Party, and to a lesser extent Gerakan Rakyat Malaysia, attacked the Alliance for its over emphasis on Malay special rights and its pro-Malay policies. Although the campaign itself was peaceful and not exceedingly militant, it had the effect of challenging many of the most important communal policies of the Alliance Government. For this reason, the outcome of the election was of great symbolic and political significance for the future course of public policy on all the most difficult issues of Malaysian politics.

After the votes were counted in West Malaysia, the Alliance had won

66 seats to assure its control in Parliament. However, the combined opposition had captured 37 seats and had polled about 51.6 percent of the vote. The Alliance had suffered a major setback by losing 22 parliamentary seats formerly held by it, and it lost control in the Legislative Assemblies of Kelantan, Penang, and Perak, while in Selangor it emerged in a deadlock with the combined opposition. The election outcome resulted from a massive defection of Chinese and Indian voters to the opposition parties and revealed the inability of the Malayan Chinese Association and the Malayan Indian Congress to deliver votes for the Alliance. This trend was magnified by a lesser defection of Malays to the Pan-Malayan Islamic Party.[22]

While the opposition parties were not victorious, the election results were psychologically distressing to many Malays who assumed that the pro-Malay policies of the government were under assault and that Malay political supremacy in the country was jeopardized. The opposition was jubilant because they had secured a sufficient number of seats to ensure that the Alliance could no longer unilaterally amend the Constitution due to its loss of a two-thirds majority in Parliament.

Malay anxieties over the election turned to paranoia when opposition parties in Kuala Lumpur staged rallies and "victory" parades to celebrate their strong showing at the polls. The following day counter demonstrations were organized by the Alliance Chief Minister of Selangor, Dato Harun bin Haji Idris. Malay youths poured into the capital to join the pro-government rallies, but very shortly the demonstrations degenerated into rioting mobs determined to "teach the Chinese a lesson." Vicious communal rioting ensued for a period of five days, leaving hundreds killed, devastating a substantial portion of the city, and making about 6,000 refugees. When the army was called to assist the police, punitive measures were directed primarily against the Chinese who were identified as the "troublemakers" and "anti-national" elements. Most of the dead were Chinese who were shot by Malay soldiers summoned to control the rioting.[23]

As a result of the riots, an emergency was proclaimed, the Constitution and Parliament were suspended, and all government authority was assumed by a National Operations Council consisting of six Malays and two non-Malays, mostly from the previous Alliance Cabinet. For 21 months this council headed by the Deputy Prime Minister Tun

22. Vasil, *Malaysian General Elections*.
23. Tunku Abdul Rahman, *May 13 Before and After* (Kuala Lumpur: Utusan Melayu Press, 1969); John Slimming, *Malaysia: Death of a Democracy* (London: John Murray, 1969); Goh Cheng Teik, *The May Thirteenth Incident and Democracy in Malaysia* (Kuala Lumpur: Oxford University Press, 1971).

Abdul Razak ruled the country by executive decree, and under its orders the more outspoken government opponents and "troublemakers" were detained, while the press and the opposition were effectively intimidated, preventing any public discussion of the government's role in the crisis and its reliance upon authoritarian measures.

Following the riots, the government gradually turned its attention to the problem of the restoration of civil rule and the lessening of racial animosities which had been so inflamed by the elections and the ensuing bloodshed. As a beginning, the government formed an advisory National Consultative Council and invited all major parties (except the outlawed Malayan Communist Party) to send representatives. However, the Democratic Action Party nominated a spokesman who had been arrested under emergency decree, and when the government refused his release, the DAP decided not to cooperate with the Consultative Council. In addition to party leaders, certain religious, professional, and minority groups were also invited to send representatives. This 65-member Consultative Council was charged with the responsibility of "finding permanent solutions to our racial problems to insure that the May 13 tragedy does not recur."[24] While the participants were encouraged to express their views with honesty and candor, the sessions of the National Consultative Council were held *in camera*, and the ultimate decisions on any recommendations rested with the National Operations Council which retained final authority under emergency decree.

Over a period of a year and a half, the National Consultative Council considered Malaysia's racial problems and drafted proposals which were submitted to the National Operations Council for approval, modification, or rejection. What finally emerged was a political strategy designed to meet Malaysia's most vexing racial and economic problems.

The Political Strategy of the Malaysian Government

By its words and actions, it was apparent that the government concluded that the basic communal issues facing the country could not be resolved by open public debate or through the free and unrestrained operation of the democratic system. Such activity tended to foster racial polarization and mobilization, thus making compromise more difficult, and creating the conditions for massive racial riots or even civil war. In particular, the government remained sensitive to the Malays' fears that they would lose their predominant position in the political system which many Malays viewed as their primary guarantee

24. *Straits Times,* January 13, 1970, p. 1.

against domination by the economically more aggressive and successful alien communities. Because of this situation, the government determined to intensify its economic programs designed to ensure the
Malays a larger share of the economy, as part of its overall program to
promote national economic growth. Thus, the government initiated a
more extensive system of Malay special rights and privileges and
turned its major economic efforts to the task of "restructuring society"
by policies designed to give the Malays a larger share of the economy
and in occupations and economic roles hitherto largely monopolized
by non-Malays. Essentially this was the strategy pursued by the Alliance before the May 1969 crisis, but now it was to be intensified and
accelerated. Implied, but unstated, in this strategy was the assumption
that when the Malays obtained a more equitable share of the country's
economy, they would be more willing to accept a greater participation
of the non-Malays in the political system.

There was one fundamental problem with this strategy: it was a very
communal answer to a problem of communalism and communal polarization. Therefore the government needed to find some way to establish a moratorium on public discussion and debate on these very communal issues, while at the same time, it tried to enlist sufficient public
support for its policies to ensure the viability of the program. It is
precisely because of this dilemma that the government resorted to the
formulation of a "national ideology," presumably on the advice of the
Consultative Council. It hoped thereby to remove certain critical matters from public politics as a prior condition for the reconstitution of
Parliament and the relaxation of rule by emergency decree. By enunciating an officially defined national consensus, the government
sought to legitimate its existing communal policies and terminate
public discussion of "communal issues." Indeed, the lack of fundamental consensus on many of these issues central to a "national ideology" made the public pronouncement of such an ideology seem more
imperative to effectuate the government's political strategy.

The National Ideology

On the anniversary of Malaysian independence, August 31, 1970, the
King issued the Rukunegara Declaration as an official statement of the
national ideology. It contained five principles and reads as follows:[25]

> Our nation, Malaysia, being dedicated to achieving a greater unity of all
> her peoples; to maintaining a democratic way of life; to creating a just

25. Government of Malaysia, *Rukunegara* (Kuala Lumpur: Di-Chetak
Di-Jabatan Chetak Kerajaan, 1970), pp. 11.

society in which the wealth of the nation shall be equitably shared; to ensuring a liberal approach to her rich and diverse cultural traditions; to building a progressive society which shall be oriented to modern science and technology; WE, her peoples, pledge our united efforts to attain these ends guided by these principles:

Belief in God (Kerperchayaan kapada Tuhan)
Loyalty to King and Country (Kesetiaan kapada Raja dan Negara)
Upholding the Constitution (Keluhoran Perlembagaan)
Rule of Law (Kedualatan Undang2)
Good Behaviour and Morality (Kesopanan dan Kesusilaan)

The following commentary accompanied the declaration to explain the meaning of these five principles:

1. Islam is the official religion of the Federation. Other religions and beliefs may be practised in peace and harmony and there shall be no discrimination against any citizen on the ground of religion.
2. The loyalty that is expected of every citizen is that he must be faithful and bear true allegiance to His Majesty the Yang di-Petuan Agong . . .
3. It is the duty of a citizen to respect and appreciate the letter, the spirit and the historical background of the Constitution. This historical background led to such provisions as those regarding the position of . . . the Rulers, the position of Islam as the official religion, the position of Malays and other Natives, the legitimate interests of the other communities, and the conferment of citizenship. It is the sacred duty of a citizen to defend and uphold the Constitution.
4. Justice is founded upon the rule of law. Every citizen is equal before the law. Fundamental liberties are guaranteed to all citizens. These include liberty of the person, equal protection of the law, freedom of religion, rights of property and protection against banishment.
The Constitution confers on a citizen the right of free speech, assembly and association and this right may be enjoyed freely subject only to limitations imposed by law.
5. Individuals and groups shall conduct their affairs in such a manner as not to violate any of the accepted canons of behaviour which is arrogant or offensive to the sensitivities of any group. No citizen should question the loyalty of another citizen on the ground that he belongs to a particular community.[26]

While the stated object of Rukunegara was to define "the fundamental principles" of the nation, it contained a number of contradictions as well as enunciating principles which did not conform to existing laws and practices. For example, in the first principle, Islam is the official religion, but other religions are promised freedom from dis-

26. *Ibid.*, pp. 17-19.

crimination. Yet, in law and practice, religious discrimination persists in a variety of ways, and substantial political and economic pressure has been applied, especially to non-Muslim natives, to convert to Islam. The third principle enunciates the major features of Alliance policy on the most contentious communal issues, including the special status of Islam, the conversion to Malay as the sole national language, the policies of special rights for Malays and the rights of other communities to acquire citizenship. Most of these policies were predicated on the assumption of a privileged legal and political position for Malays over the non-Malay communities. Yet, in the fourth principle, equality before the law is enunciated, along with various freedoms "subject only to limitations imposed by the law." The fifth principle is a general exhortation for the public not to engage in behaviour which is likely to be "offensive to the sensitivities of any group." In short, the Rukunegara ideology is a statement of support for existing Alliance policies on the communal issues, along with a general plea for moderate and civil public behavior in relations among the races. The contradictions inherent in articles three and four are also reflected in government policies, although the government has given greatest stress to article three. The Malays, obviously, have stressed the third principle, while the non-Malays have found the fourth principle to be "even more fundamental."

If there are these contradictions in Rukunegara, and the ideology neither reflected widespread public consensus nor was it harmonious with public policies and practice, we may ask: why was the ideology important, and what role did it play? The answer to those questions can be found by examining how the ideology was used by the government to further its political strategies.

As a precondition for the restitution of Parliament, the government insisted that all political parties accept Rukunegara and avoid public discussion or criticism of those sections of the constitution which were identified in the Rukunegara Declaration, including such topics as the powers and status of the Malay Rulers; citizenship; Malay special rights; and the use of Malay as the sole national language. The new Prime Minister, Tun Abdul Razak, made the acceptance of these amendments and the legislation ending public discussion on "sensitive issues" a condition for the restitution of Parliament. A constitutional amendment was drafted which removed the immunities of Members of Parliament and prohibited anyone from questioning "any matter, right, status, position, privilege, sovereignty or prerogative established or protected in the Constitution." The Prime Minister explained: "These amendments are considered very necessary to avoid the recurrence of another May 13 incident . . . It is only in this way we can guarantee the future of our democratic system of Government and the unity of our nation."[27] When Malaysia's Parliament was finally reconvened, the first order of business was to pass the "Sensitive Issues" amendment and a series of other constitutional amendments designed to "entrench" such issues in the constitution and make them impossible to amend without the consent of the Conference of Rulers. The prohibition of public discussion of these issues applied to all Malaysians, including Parliament itself. In March 1971, after several days debate, the constitutional amendments proposed by the government were approved by a vote of 125 to 17 in the Dewan Ra'ayat.[28]

Obviously, neither the government nor opposition politicians could avoid the consideration of the "sensitive issues" identified in the Rukunegara ideology. But the existence of the ideology, along with the restrictive legislation on public speech, inhibited the public ventilation of these issues. Even more important, the ideology was used to limit access to the political system and provide a partial behavior code, or "rules of the game" for politics. No politician was reported in the press as openly critical of Rukunegara. However, opposition parties which openly praise Rukunegara appeared thereby to become eligible for some access to the elaborate behind-the-scenes political negotiations which continued to characterize Malaysian politics. The selling of Rukunegara was accompanied by a political effort to reconstruct a stable political coalition crossing racial-ethnic divisions, but only among those leaders who made public obeisance to the Rukunegara ideology.

Government leverage over opposition parties was greatly enhanced by the "Sensitive Issues" amendment, by a new Sedition Act, and by legislation which empowered state governments to assume control over municipal councils if political disputes became intense. These powers only added to the formal arsenal of political and legal weapons available to the Federal Government, such as: the power to suspend state constitutions through Emergency degree; the distribution of federal patronage to opposition members who defected to or cooperated with the Federal Government; the power to allocate federal revenues to the states, which are heavily dependent on federal funds because of their feeble and insufficient taxing and revenue powers; and the power of the Federal Government to control and distribute the benefits of economic development projects to one state or another in accordance with national development plans. The opposition parties which had cultivated a power base at the state or municipal levels were thus placed in the precarious position of being deprived of the right to oppose any issue incorporated in the government's Rukunegara Declara-

27. *Malaysian Digest* (Kuala Lumpur), February 15, 1971, p. 3.
28. *Straits Times,* March 4, 1971, pp. 1 and 24.

tion, while also being threatened with diminishing government revenues and possible economic stagnation in the areas they represented. In these circumstances, the opposition parties suffered from a series of mass defections of their members to the parties in the Alliance. Consequently, under these new rules of the game, and the changed political environment, the incentives for opposition participation in the informal behind-the-scenes processes of political negotiation were greatly enhanced.

Between 1970 and 1972, Malaysia witnessed a political realignment through formal membership of opposition parties into the Alliance structure, or by means of coalition agreements whereby opposition parties retained autonomous structures, and gained limited access to informal political bargaining structures in return for accepting restrictions on their public pronouncements and mobilization activities. For example, in Sabah, all active parties dissolved into the Alliance prior to the resumption in June 1970 of the suspended 1969 parliamentary elections, thus leaving the Alliance with only token opposition in Sabah from a few independents who gained no seats. In Sarawak, the 1970 parliamentary and state elections were contested by five parties, three of which were nominally within the Alliance. In the elections the Alliance won only 9 of 24 parliamentary seats and 24 of 48 state seats but the foremost opposition party, the Sarawak United Peoples Party (SUPP) representing Chinese interests, negotiated a coalition agreement with the Alliance whereby it gained two state cabinet portfolios and access to the Federal Alliance. Only the Sarawak National Party representing tribal Ibans and led by former Chief Minister Stephen Kalong Ningkan was denied access to the councils of government and forced into the position of impotence in the opposition.

During 1972 most of the opposition parties in West Malaysia entered into negotiations for the formation of coalition governments at municipal, state and federal levels. In February, Gerakan Rakyat Malaysia agreed to a coalition with the Alliance in the State of Penang where the former controlled a majority of seats. In return it gained admission to Alliance councils at the federal level and was promised increased federal assistance for development projects in Penang.[29] In April, the Peoples Progressive Party, which was strong in Perak, negotiated a similar agreement with the Alliance.[30] By September the same year, the Pan-Malayan Islamic Party and the Alliance agreed to form a coalition government in Trengganu and Kelantan, where the former was strong, and in return PMIP leader Dato Haji Mohamed Asri was promised a cabinet position and access to the Alliance National Council where the

29. *Straits Times,* February 14, 1972, p. 1.
30. *Straits Times,* April 21, 1972, p. 1.

really significant decisions of government were worked out in secret inter-party bargaining.[31] In West Malaysia, the only significant opposition party denied access to the Alliance system was the Democratic Action Party which was stigmatized for its ties and ideological association with Singapore's ruling Peoples Action Party, and for its role in polarizing Malaysian politics in the years from 1965 to 1969 when it campaigned for a "Malaysian Malaysia" instead of what it claimed was the "Malay Malaysia" of the Alliance Government.

By the end of 1972, political stability was restored through the tactic of absorption of nearly all opposition parties and the transfer of potentially divisive political issues from public political arenas to the secret and informal processes of inter-communal bargaining between leaders of communally based political organizations. Parliamentary and elected representative institutions continued to function and to consider issues which did not arouse communal passions, as well as providing the venue for ventilation of grievances over the administration of established policies. Legally, parliamentary sovereignty was retained, but the realities of communal politics had forced parliament to surrender most of its powers and functions to extra-legal and informal political institutions.

Political Elites and Their Style of Leadership

The Malaysian political system has generated clearly defined political elites with a distinctive style of leadership. Nearly all the prominent politicians in positions of power have acquired their office by virtue of their leadership in communal organizations which rely to a large extent upon traditional institutions and the primordeal loyalties of particular ethnic-cultural communities. Thus, modern and modernizing elites have tapped traditional sentiments to build a power base within one community which is then utilized as political currency in the inter-communal bargaining processes. As a result, successful politicians have tended to be those who cultivate close ties with more traditional segments of their ethnic community, yet are mostly English-educated, have modern skills and values, and retain a high capacity for bargaining and sustaining personal relations with the political leaders of other communities.

The difference between the elites and the masses make the elites have a rather shallow attachment to democracy, in part because these English-educated modernizing elites fear that intense political mobilization and popular participation in politics may lead to severe communal conflict. Malaysian elites tend to hold ambiguous attitudes

31. *Straits Times,* September 6, 1972, p. 1.

toward the common man. On the one hand, the *ra'ayat* (peasant or commoner) is idealized in public rhetoric and ideological statements. On the other, elites tend to treat the public very patronizingly by making emotional and manipulative appeals, suggesting a rather low opinion of the ability of the public to participate rationally and sensibly in the political process. Like the colonial administrators before them, Malaysia's political elites tend to see their role as providing benevolent and paternalistic rule, with "domestic tranquility" and "law and order" receiving the highest priority.[32] Periodically, the general public is urged to participate in elections, which at the federal level are largely symbolic plebiscites to legitimize the rule of those who hold the reins of power. Yet, elections are not meaningless, because they provide confirming evidence of the power base of the political elites who engage in the continuing processes of informal political bargaining.

In the early years of the federation, the Prime Minister performed a vital role as ultimate arbiter in the political system, especially on critical communal issues. Prime Minister Tunku Abdul Rahman, as the architect of the Alliance system, tended to avoid a partisan role on behalf of the communal organization he headed, the United Malays National Organization. Instead, when issues arose within the Alliance, the other leaders of constituent parties made their demands and engaged in the process of finding a negotiated settlement. When there was a deadlock over unresolved points, Tunku Abdul Rahman would then intervene to help work out an acceptable compromise and, if necessary, make a final award. He preferred to assume the role of a "court of last resort" on political issues, and was generally acknowledged by most partisans in the Alliance to be open to reason and quite fair. However, after Singapore's entry into Malaysia, this "neutral arbiter" role was abandoned as a result of the acrimonious disputes between Singapore's Chief Minister Lee Kuan Yew and the Alliance leaders. This forced the Prime Minister to take a more partisan communal public stance, with a consequent effect of eroding the confidence of the non-Malay public in the legitimacy of the political system. The ethnic partisanship of Tunku Abdul Rahman's successor, Tun Abdul Razak, has been somewhat more pronounced, and this shift in the political role of the Prime Minister reflects the discernable shift in the political balance since the race riots of May 1969. The ideals of communal impartiality in politics and government have been formally rejected, both in the Constitution and in Malaysia's political ethos, which in turn has altered the style of leadership provided by those who hold the highest political offices in the land.

32. Some of the attitudes of Malaysia's elites are explored in: James C. Scott, *Political Ideology in Malaysia* (New Haven: Yale University Press, 1968).

The effort to rebuild a stable political system through absorbing opposition parties into the Alliance or by means of coalition agreements with opposition parties places a premium on political accommodation through the cultivation among communal elites of an understanding and empathy for the "gut feelings" of the masses of communal groups other than their own. There appears to be a heightened awareness, at least at the elite level, that communally based political organizations cannot consider only the interests and reactions of their own community. To this degree at least, at the elite level Malaysian politics is becoming somewhat less communal, and the political system retains a fairly accommodative and representative character, despite the restrictions on some political freedoms and the paralysis of some political institutions commonly assumed to be essential for the survival of democratic government.

The Economic Dimension

Economic Resources

Agriculture dominates the Malaysian economy, employing over half of the economically active population and providing from rubber alone one third of the total value of exported commodities, and in combination with forestry accounted for 31 percent of the GDP in 1970. Despite the importance of agriculture, the country is not endowed with much fertile land. Formed from eroding rock, much of the soil is heavy laterite having high acidity and low mineral content. The humus of decaying vegetation which supplements the natural soil is rapidly washed away by tropical rains when land is cleared for cultivation. Richer alluvial soils are found in low land and delta areas, but these are frequently covered with layers of peat and subject to flooding or are salinated due to tidal action. In the country as a whole only about 9.6 percent of the land is under permanent cultivation, while about 70 percent is forest land. Although this leaves a large amount of land for future agricultural development, most of the forest lands are unsuitable for food crops requiring fertile soils.

Food production in Malaysia is insufficient to meet domestic requirements. Rice is the staple food for Malaysians, and its production is left largely to Malay peasants, who cultivate wet rice, and to hill tribals, who utilize shifting swidden cultivation to grow dry rice. In the postwar years domestic production of rice accounted for only 54 to about 70 percent of domestic consumption. National self-sufficiency in rice has been proclaimed as a government goal. Programs have been launched to promote double cropping, to subsidize fertilizers, and to open new land for rice cultivation through drainage and irrigation projects. However, despite these efforts, rice production has increased only about 6 percent per annum, while population growth remains at 2.5 to 3 percent per annum. It may be a number of years before rice imports are no longer essential to meet domestic demand.

Malaysia's most important commodity is natural rubber. In 1970, almost 5 million acres of rubber were under cultivation and 1,249,302 long tons were produced. Rubber accounted for 15.5 percent of the GDP and about 34 percent of the country's exports. About half of the rubber produced comes from large commercial estates, while the remainder is grown on small holdings by private cultivators many of whom also grow other crops.

After rubber, Malaysia's next most important export commodity is tin, which accounts for about 20 percent of Malaysia's foreign earnings. Some of the richest tin deposits of Perak and Selangor have been worked for over a century and are becoming depleted. However, a vigorous government program to prospect for tin has identified new fields, and new techniques for exploiting offshore tin deposits have combined to assure that Malaysia will continue to be the world's foremost producer of tin for many years to come.

Because Malaysia produces about 44 percent of the world's natural rubber and about 40 percent of the world's tin, its economy has been closely tied to the fluctuating world market price for both commodities. When the market price falls for either product, Malaysia's economy falters and government revenues fall. The price of both products has been largely determined by the market demand of the United States and its strategic commodity stockpiling, a practice which has given the latter great leverage in setting world market prices. In an attempt to stabilize the world price for tin and improve its market bargaining position, Malaysia has taken a leading role in the International Tin Council, which, under the International Tin Agreements, established a buffer tin stock and export controls. Malaysia's share of the world total tin export is fixed at 47 percent.[33] The price of rubber has been more difficult to stabilize. However, competition from synthetic rubber places a practical upper limit on the price of natural rubber. The competitive threat from synthetic rubber is being met by government programs to promote widespread replanting of high-yield and high quality rubber. In addition, the government has as a major goal the diversification of the economy to reduce the country's reliance on rubber and tin.

The fastest growing sector of the economy is in timber and wood products, followed by palm oil. The government is also sponsoring extensive exploration for petroleum and has high hopes for positive

33. John W. Henderson et al., *Area Handbook for Malaysia* (Washington, D.C.: U.S. Government Printing Office, 1970), pp. 430-433.

Table IV.8

Volume And Value Of Exports From Malaysia

	1965		1970		Average Annual Growth Rate % 1966-70 in Value
	Volume (000 tons)	Value (M$ million)	Volume (000 tons)	Value (M$ million)	
Rubber	950	1,461	1,324	1,723	3.4
Tin	73	871	91	1,013	3.1
Timber Logs	4,114	262	7,747	642	19.6
Sawn timber	520	95	960	201	16.1
Veneer sheets	94*	4	100*	5	4.0
Plywood	20*	3	304**	45	71.9
Palm oil	140	107	393	263	19.6
Palm kernels	18	8	26	10	3.6
Petroleum (crude)	1,829	86	4,743	202	18.5
Petroleum fuel	2,505	164	2,790	155	-1.0
Iron ore	6,634	161	4,778	106	-8.0
Fish	63	41	89	95	17.9
Canned pineapples	53	40	62	43	1.6
Pepper	18	44	25	59	5.6
Copra	40	23	15	7	-21.4
Other commodities	—	387	—	533	6.6
Total Merchandise Exports	—	3,749	—	5,089	6.3
Service Exports	—	558	—	547	-0.4
Total Exports Goods and Services	—	4,307	—	5,636	5.5

*millions of square feet
Source: Malaysia, Second Malaysia Plan, 1971-1975 (Kuala Lumpur: Government Press, 1971), pp. 22-25.

results. Newly opened offshore oil wells along the Sarawak coast have already contributed to a significant increase in Malaysia's crude petroleum production. Formerly, the fishing industry was geared entirely to local consumption. It is gradually being modernized and now produces for an expanding foreign market. Sizeable deposits of iron ore have been mined in Pahang and Trengganu, with nearly all of the ore being shipped to Japan for processing into steel. A Malaysian steel mill was constructed at Prai in Province Wellesley in 1967, but the shortage of adequate local coal deposits places economic limitations on the development of a large steel industry within the country. Likewise, transportation costs for ore have been such that the production and export of iron ore has been declining since 1965.

Industrial Development

Since the war the government has actively encouraged the growth of industry. Mining, construction, public works and processing of agricultural products accounted for most of the development of industry in the immediate postwar period. However, in recent years there has been a rapid expansion of manufacturing, so that its proportion of the GDP of West Malaysia rose from 5.5 percent in 1960 to 13.7 percent in 1970 —an increase of 130 percent in a decade. Nearly all the manufacturing enterprises are in West Malaysia, with a high proportion concentrated in satellite towns and industrial estates on the outskirts of Kuala Lumpur. Apart from the processing of food, wood products, metals and rubber, most of the manufacturing industries are quite small and operate as branch plant subsidiaries of foreign corporations. Some manufacturing plants perform little more than final assembly and packaging of imports for the local market, so that the gross values of manufactured products give a distorted picture of the extent of industrial development. A more accurate indicator of industrial output is provided by comparing gross value of sales with the value added from domestic manufacturing. Such a comparison also provides some indication of the subsidiary relationship of much of Malaysian industry to foreign manufacturing enterprises.

For a developing country, Malaysia has a labor force which has a fairly high level of education, but there has nonetheless been a labor shortage for many of the technical and craft skills necessary for industrialization and economic growth. The number of Malaysians finishing secondary school and university has risen dramatically over the past decade, and enrollment in the technical and vocational courses at the secondary and post-secondary level has increased two- to three fold over the five years from 1965 to 1970. In technical and professional courses the number of students is not proportionate to the ethnic distribution of the population. Chinese and Indians have been over-

Table IV.9
Manufacturing Industries In Malaysia, 1970

Industry	Gross Value (M$,000)	Value Added (M$,000)	Value Added as % of Gross Value
Rubber processing off estates	599,702	119,769	29.9
Coconut oil processing	118,177	9,002	7.6
Tea factories	1,704	579	33.9
Food manufacturing	843,553	190,474	22.5
Beverage manufacturing	79,095	42,925	54.2
Tobacco products	274,663	84,566	30.7
Textiles	97,692	26,609	27.2
Footwear and wearing apparel	48,132	13,258	27.5
Wood products	329,949	118,219	35.8
Furniture and fixtures	28,484	8,994	31.5
Paper products	34,225	9,509	27.7
Printing and publishing	143,525	72,993	50.8
Leather and fur products	7,304	2,205	30.1
Rubber products	119,519	51,276	42.9
Chemical products	275,408	107,093	38.8
Products of petroleum and coal	173,165	41,878	24.1
Non-metallic mineral products	148,068	80,816	54.5
Basic metals	104,951	33,297	31.7
Metal products	140,464	41,690	29.6
Machinery, appliances and supplies	164,784	62,808	38.1
Shipbuilding and repair	4,395	2,562	58.2
Motor vehicles and parts	102,119	27,483	26.9
Bicycles and scooters	20,718	6,396	30.8
Miscellaneous manufacturing	67,359	26,029	38.6
Total	3,927,155	1,180,456	30.0

Source: Calculated from *Siaran Perangkaan Tahunan, Malaysia 1971* (Kuala Lumpur: Jabatan Perangkaan Malaysia, 1971) Supplementary to Table 4.2, "Annual Survey of Manufacturing Industries, 1970."

represented in such courses of study and therefore they tend to predominate in the higher paid professional, technical, and skilled vocational positions in the economy. Because Malays have had less exposure to such education and are concentrated in rural areas, they have not benefited from industrialization as much as the other communities. In 1965, only 25 percent of the wage-earning labor force was Ma-

Table IV.10

Percentage Of Enrollment To Corresponding Age Group In The Educational System Of Malaysia, 1965 And 1970

	1965	1970
Primary:		
Age group (est.)	1,394,634	1,557,918
Enrollment	1,217,309	1,421,469
Percent	87	92
Lower Secondary:		
Age group (est.)	608,068	691,570
Enrollment	231,555	378,535
Percent	38	55
Upper Secondary:		
Age group (est.)	361,748	438,755
Enrollment	41,753	89,435
Percent	12	20
Post Secondary:*		
Age group (est.)	324,831	413,823
Enrollment	14,482	18,994
Percent	4.5	4.5
University:		
Age group (est.)	792,769	1,019,565
Enrollment	2,835	8,505
Percent	0.4	0.8

*Includes Form VI, technical and agricultural colleges, and teacher training colleges.

Sources: Calculated from John W. Henderson *et al.*, *Area Handbook for Malaysia* (Washington, D.C.: U.S. Government Printing Office, 1970), pp. 177; Malaysia, *Second Malaysia Plan, 1971-1975* (Kuala Lumpur: Government Printer, 1971).

lay. Vigorous government policies designed to induce industry to employ Malays on a preferential quota system has corrected some of the imbalance, but Malays still constitute less than a third of the wage laborers.

By Asian standards, Malaysia's industrial labor force enjoys good wages and a rising standard of living. Since the war, trade unions have expanded their membership to include about 12 percent of the work force. Most large manufacturing, mining and estate operations are unionized, as are large sectors of the public services, such as teachers and railwaymen. Prior to 1948, the Malayan Communist Party had control of a large segment of the labor movement. In subsequent years, stringent government measures broke the communist grip over key unions, and since then the government has remained wary of the potential political power of a unified labor movement. Chronic unemployment of about 8 percent may inhibit the growth of the labor movement. Singapore's separation from Malaysia weakened organized labor, as has government legislation prohibiting the formation of national labor organizations. The tendency of unions to form along ethnic lines makes a unified labor movement unlikely in any case. Government oversight of union activities and its powers to "deregister" unions for illegal acts has made unions shy away from active involvement in politics. Restricted to economic functions, they enjoy the right to organize, to engage in collective bargaining and to strike. Voluntary conciliation and mediation services are provided by the government to assist in the settlement of industrial disputes. Collective agreements are considered binding on the parties, and such contracts are subject to the jurisdiction of an industrial court. In strikes seriously affecting the public interest, the government may intervene to impose a settlement. While strikes are common, the number of man-days lost as a result of strike action is not excessive.[34]

As part of its growth-oriented economic planning, Malaysia encourages foreign and domestic private investment in the economy. The Pioneer Industries Ordinance of 1958 exempted new industries from income tax and import duties on equipment for from 2 to 5 years. The Investment Incentives Act of 1968, which replaced the 1958 ordinance, continued similar investment advantages including tax credits and, in some cases, special tariff protection for products of "pioneer industries." To qualify for such benefits, companies are required to have at least 51 percent Malaysian ownership, and the company is required to maintain government-established Malay employment quotas and reserve a set percentage of stocks for public sale to Malays. Because of policies creating a favorable foreign investment climate, foreign investments per year have risen from M$244 million in 1968 to M$339 million in 1971, but because of much heavier public investment, Malaysia's reliance on foreign investment has been decreasing so that only about 5 percent of new capital formation was coming from foreign sources in 1972.[35] Despite increased capital formation within the country, foreign assets invested in some sectors of the economy remain at a very high level, particularly in the industrial and commercial sectors.

34. *Ibid.*, pp. 445-474.
35. *Straits Times,* August 31, 1973, Section II, pp. 6 and 11.

Economic Development Capabilities

In the years since independence, the Malaysian government has strengthened its capabilities in economic matters, not only in regard to industrialization and foreign trade, but also in its implementation of programs designed to penetrate into village life and the rural sector of the economy. During the colonial era, the bulk of government revenues came from export and import duties. In 1947 Malaya adopted a system of personal and business income taxes, which later in 1967 were extended uniformly throughout Malaysia. In addition, a tin profits tax and a development tax were added so that the proportion of revenue from direct taxes has steadily increased, as have government revenues from all sources. Excluding foreign grants, total federal revenues increased from M$211 million in 1948 to M$681 million in 1958, and a decade later reached M$1,872 million.[36] By 1971, federal revenues were estimated to have risen to M$2,300 million.[37] Because the federal government collects about 90 percent of all government revenues, it has utilized its superior financial resources to good advantage in pursuing fairly uniform economic and social policies through the federation despite the guarantees of state autonomy incorporated into the constitution.

The average Malaysian is hardly aware of the taxes he pays, since only a very small proportion of the public pay personal income taxes. About 90 percent of all tax revenues in Malaysia are collected from business firms, either directly through business income or profits taxes, or indirectly through export, import and excise duties.[38] Because of the dominant role of non-Malays in business activities and the emphasis given by government to programs to aid the Malays, the government has become a primary vehicle for the transfer of income, services and product from one ethnic community to another. If for no other reason, this explains why practically all economic issues facing the country are also racial-communal issues. Similarly, because of the concealed taxation, the government is faced with the prospect of continually es-

36. Henderson, *Area Handbook*, p. 516.
37. Revenues for 1971 were below expectations due to the fall in the price of rubber. Each drop of a cent in the price per kilo results in a loss of about M$30 million in government revenues over a year. Under the Second Malaysia Plan government expenditures were expected to be over M$4,000 million in 1972. To meet the deficit between revenues and expenditures the government imposed new taxes, including a 5 percent sales tax. *Straits Times*, January 4, 1972, p. 22; January 7, 1972, p. 1.
38. Direct taxes accounted for 23 percent of total revenues in 1960 and 36 percent in 1972. *Straits Times*, December 21, 1972, p. 28.

calating demands for more government programs and services from the Malays. At the same time, it must also respond to the pleas of non-Malay business interests that excessive taxes will slow or reverse economic growth by reducing incentives and drying up sources of capital investment and management skills. Government leaders realize that an economic slump produces immediate detrimental effects on government revenues, without which its social and economic programs will fail. In such a circumstance, political and economic wisdom dictates a strategy of moderation and restraint on the forms of communal mobilization which are likely to generate irreconcilable economic and political demands on government.

While the Malayan government has pursued policies to promote economic growth since the turn of the century, its involvement with economic and social planning on a broad scale dates from the 1950s. In that decade the government began by establishing several specialized agencies to concentrate on some sub-sector of the economy which appeared to need special attention and assistance. For example, in 1956 the Rural and Industrial Development Authority (RIDA) was formed to assist the rural areas, and particularly, the peasant Malays. Under the direction of the most prominent Malay politician of the day, Dato Onn bin Ja'afar, RIDA attempted to break the syndrome of rural Malay poverty by promoting community development projects, improving rural market and credit facilities, improving social services and encouraging rural peasant self-reliance. The Federal Land Development Authority (FLDA) was also established at the same time, and was charged with responsibility for assisting rural development by alleviating land shortages through projects to clear jungle or reclaim marginal land for agricultural resettlement and cultivation of cash crops. Recognizing the need for a more comprehensive planning mechanism, the government established in 1957 the Economic Planning Unit which was placed within the Office of the Prime Minister. Since that date the primary responsibility for economic and social planning has remained with the Prime Minister's Office in close liaison with the cabinet and its specialized National Development Planning Committee. By the time of the Second Malayan Five Year Plan of 1961-1965, the government had acquired the expertise and the administrative capacity for national economic and social planning on a fairly comprehensive scale.

Over the period of the first four national economic plans, public investments in economic and social development increased more than seven fold. The first plan gave highest priority to the promotion of the existing major export commodities of rubber and tin, and to agricultural development. In addition, education and housing were given fairly high priority. With the later five year plans, the emphasis shifted

Table IV.11

Public Expenditures For Five-Year Plans

Five Year Plan	Public Expenditures (Millions)	Area
First Malayan Plan, 1956-60	M$ 972	Malaya (West Malaysia)
Second Malayan Plan, 1961-65	2,150	Malaya (West Malaysia)
First Malaysia Plan, 1966-70	4,242	Malaysia
Second Malaysia Plan, 1971-75	7,250	Malaysia

Sources: Federation of Malaya Official Yearbook, 1962, pp. 152-157; Malaysia, *Second Malaysia Plan, 1971-1975* (Kuala Lumpur: Government Printing Office, 1971), pp. 68-71.

to economic diversification, to modernization of deprived and under-developed economic sectors, and to redistributive programs designed to make the benefits of economic development available to the under-privileged and more traditional segments of society. Likewise, over this period there has been a substantial shift in allocations from the private to the public sectors. Instead of placing such heavy emphasis on pro-grams designed to induce private and foreign investment, the more recent plans place increasing reliance on public corporations to ini-tiate new economic ventures and to promote national economic de-velopment in accordance with the targets set by the government.

A number of public corporations and agencies have been formed to implement the public sector segments of the economic plans. For ex-ample, the Rural Industrial Development Authority was reorganized in 1966 and renamed Majlis Amanah Ra'ayat (Council of Trust for the Indigenous People). Its powers and functions were expanded to spear-head a major effort to promote Malay participation in commerce and industry. A number of corporations were established with public funds to engage in industrial, commercial and banking activities in order to promote Malay ownership and participation in these fields. Such gov-ernment-backed corporations included Pernas, an investment holding company which has formed almost a dozen subsidiary companies to engage in insurance, foreign trade, construction, engineering, and off-shore mining and participate in joint ventures with private firms.[39] Public corporations have also been formed to promote urban renewal (Urban Development Authority), to make loans to industry (Malaysia Industrial Development Authority), and to sponsor private Malay

39. *Straits Times,* August 31, 1972, Section II, p. 3.

commercial and industrial projects (Komplex Kewangan). Similarly, State Economic and Development Corporations have been established in each state to coordinate and promote the economic development projects at the state level. Thus, the expanded role of government in the economy has been more than matched by the proliferation of agencies of government competing directly with private enterprise and engaging in economic ventures particularly in the more dynamic sectors of the economy. With government backing and protection, such ventures involve almost no risk, even when projects may not be economically feasible. The government recognizes that at times social and political objectives must take priority over purely economic calculations of profits and returns on investments.

The New Economic Policy

Following the racial rioting of May 1969, the government initiated a comprehensive reappraisal of public policies. Although the riots were linitially blamed on communist conspirators, the government eventually accepted the view that the violence erupted because of ethnic polarization and animosity heightened by the election campaign, but ultimately attributed it to an escalating sense of grievance among Malays over the failure of economic policies to overcome their relative economic deprivation in comparison to non-Malays. Derived from this assessment, the government devised political strategies to reduce ethnic polarization in politics and economic strategies to give the Malays a greater share in the country's wealth and economic growth. The political strategy became incorporated into the Rukunegara ideology and the campaign to check public political disputation through coalition agreements with opposition parties. The economic aspect of the strategy was formally enunciated as the New Economic Policy (NEP) and incorporated as an integral part of the Second Malaysia Plan.

> The plan incorporates a two-pronged New Economic Policy for development. The first prong is to reduce and eventually eradicate poverty, by raising income levels and increasing employment opportunities for all Malaysians, irrespective of race. The second program aims at accelerating the process of restructuring Malaysian society to correct economic imbalance, so as to reduce and eventually eliminate the identification of race with economic function. This process involves the modernisation of rural lives, a rapid and balanced growth of urban activities and the creation of a Malay commercial and industrial community in all categories and at all levels of operation, so that Malays and other indigenous people will become full partners in all aspects of the economic life of the nation.[40]

40. Malaysia, *Second Malaysia Plan, 1971-1975* (Kuala Lumpur: Government Printing Office, 1971), p. 1.

The first objective of the NEP was to be pursued by policies of economic growth and development which would improve the welfare of all Malaysians in all walks of life, regardless of race. The second objective was to be pursued by redistributive policies designed to increase Malay participation and ownership in the modern sectors of the economy. In short, Malay special rights and privileges were to be greatly expanded to ensure that Malays would obtain privileged access to education, to the professions, and to new jobs arising from expansion of the economy. The non-Malays were assured that the policies "of restructuring Malaysian society" by giving Malays special privileges would not involve expropriation of property or loss of jobs or rights by non-Malays. Prime Minister Tun Razak explained: "What is envisioned by the Government is that the newly created opportunities will be distributed in a just and equitable manner."[41] What was unclear at the time was how the growth-induced jobs, wealth and product were to be allocated between Malays and non-Malays.

The economic growth objectives of the NEP gave renewed emphasis to policies favoring domestic and foreign investors, including tax holidays for new industries, tariff protection for locally manufactured goods, low cost industrial sites, guarantees of remission of profits abroad, and guarantees against nationalization under treaty arrangements with some foreign states acting as guarantors for their own nationals' investments. To provide for the "restructuring of society" goals, the NEP relied heavily upon selective investments by public agencies and government corporations, and upon an extension of the system of Malay special rights from the areas of land holding, education and the public services, to the private sectors of the economy. Government plans gave high priority to industrial development in less developed and deprived areas and to labor intensive projects providing new employment opportunities in agricultural processing and forest based industries. Existing and newly established commercial and industrial ventures were required to observe quotas for employment of Malays, and were required to offer for public sale to Malays a proportion of stock shares. The quotas expected for each company were the subject of negotiations with government agencies, and were tied to licenses and tax and tariff concessions. For most industries, the Malay employment quota was set at about 40 percent, with some additional conditions imposed usually covering the training and promotion of Malays to management and executive positions.

By these measures, the government expects to achieve a fundamental alteration in the ethnic distribution of income, jobs and in the professions. In 1969, Malays owned only 1.5 percent of the total capital assets of limited companies in West Malaysia. While their share of the non-

41. *Malaysian Digest*, July 15, 1971, p. 1.

corporate capital assets was quite a bit higher, their average per capita income remained less than half that of the non-Malays. The NEP has set as its target 30 percent Malay ownership and participation in all industrial and commercial activities by 1990. To achieve this goal, Malay ownership of capital assets will have to increase at a rate of 25 percent per year if the growth rate in the corporate sector remains at the projected 10 percent per year.[42] Only by massive government investment, through government financed public corporations which are Malay managed and some of which are eventually to be turned into private Malay corporations, can such a goal be achieved. While this economic strategy may involve much waste and inefficiency, and may reduce the overall growth rate of the Malaysian economy, failure to meet the rising expectations of the Malays for a greater share in the economy could entail a much greater political cost and a high risk for the future viability of the country.

Problems and Prospects

To make an evaluation about the future development of Malaysia requires a realistic appraisal of the likely effects of the complex interlocking political and economic strategies being pursued by the government. While a thorough assessment cannot be made within the limited scope of this account, some of the more pressing and intractable problems facing the country can be identified, and some potential consequences of government policy can be mentioned.

One of the questions facing the government is: How will the Malays respond to the government's efforts to restructure society? Will they become so dependent on special privileges, quotas, and preferential income reallocation schemes that they will fail to acquire adequate achievement motivation and fail to meet the educational and economic performance standards of the non-Malays? That this is a serious problem is revealed by the extent of exhortation made by Malay leaders to Malays calling upon them to equal the performance standards of non-Malays and not expect always to be "spoon fed" by the government. The Malay absenteeism rate in industry of 6.2 percent, as compared to the Chinese rate of 2.1 percent and the Indian rate of 1.7 percent, suggests that Malay workers find it difficult to adjust to the discipline and routine of industrial production.[43] How the job quota system affects the rate is difficult to determine. Although low achievement motivation and performance may be fostered among Malays by special privileges and job quotas, it also appears that Malay elites now have a

42. *Straits Times*, July 20, 1971, p. 21.
43. *Straits Times*, March 8, 1971, p. 17.

strong sense of urgency in seeking to generate fundamental changes in Malay values and attitudes. A new highly competitive achievement oriented generation of young Malays appears to be emerging, partly in response to the preferential system of Malay special rights and the new educational, economic and professional opportunities created by government strategies.

While these policies may create short-term dislocations their longer range effects are of greater significance. It appears likely that they will produce both increased social differentiation and increased economic disparities within the Malay community. Malays who are most likely to take full advantage of special rights are those who are already urbanized, who already have a fairly good income and already have the educational background and motivation to exploit the opportunities created by the NEP. The peasant Malay in isolated rural communities may get improved social services and some marginal and indirect benefits from special rights, but it appears unlikely that his economic condition will change as rapidly as his expectations and aspirations rise, partly because the government's highly publicized promises to eradicate Malay poverty are generating a sharp rise in Malay peasant expectations. As a new class of Malays emerges with wealth, status and education, the social cleavages within Malay society will likely become more pronounced and the Malay peasantry may well acquire a more intense sense of relative deprivation and animosity toward those who acquire, at a far faster pace, the more visible economic benefits of modernization.

Malaysia's development strategy poses another critical problem: Will the non-Malay be given equal access to the political system as Malays acquire a greater share of benefits from the economic system? While the political system has been devised with a decidedly pro-Malay bias derived from citizenship requirements, under-representation of urban areas, constitutional entrenchment of Malay special rights and the reservation of key offices for Malay Muslims, these provisions are not of critical importance because the primary access to the decision-making process is controlled by the extra-legal structures of the Alliance political coalition. Although non-Malays could be effectively excluded from political influence by the Alliance, if it chose to do so, the cooperation and support of non-Malays is needed to make government strategies work. Consequently, since 1970, there has been a noticeable improvement in the access of non-Malays to the extra-legal decision-making processes. The Malayan Chinese Association has recovered from near collapse in 1969 to become a formidable power representing non-Malay interests. Opposition and non-Malay parties may not have a chance to acquire power and set a new political course or an alternative economic strategy, but they are being consulted and a consensual accommodative ethos has pervaded government circles since 1970. One non-Malay leader acknowledged that the opposition parties could not change the basic policies of the government, but was quick to add, "we most certainly can ensure a more just implementation of those policies."[44] If the government's strategy for meeting the economic needs of the Malays can be made to work, it would appear that continued political concessions will have to be made to non-Malays. Otherwise, the sense of grievance and political alienation by non-Malays could become as intense and as serious for national survival as the sense of relative economic deprivation is for the Malays. In spite of artificially rigid constitutional provisions, Malaysia will ultimately have to convert to a more equalitarian and universalistic political system, particularly as the social system undergoes transformation and modernization. At present, the regime appears to have exhibited the capacity gradually to make necessary political accommodations to meet the fundamental grievances of non-Malay interests. That the trend will likely continue will not be so much because of the parliamentary system, as it has not operated quite in accord with liberal western ideals of representative government, but rather because political realities require that the government secure widespread cooperation across communal lines.

A third problem posed by government strategies is: Will the distributive economic policies become too costly to implement, or unleash too much social upheaval for the survival of the political system? The answer to this question rests upon so many uncertainties and imponderables that trends and probabilities are most difficult to discern. It is clear that economic growth goals and redistributive goals compete with each other for attention and priority. Only with a healthy economy can either be achieved. Yet, any small nation subject to the vicissitudes of world markets and external political events faces a difficult task of maintaining a healthy and growing economy for a long enough period to pursue strategies of fundamental social restructuring and modernization. Malaysia is no exception. Instability and uncertainty in the world market for some of Malaysia's major export commodities makes it difficult to determine the country's future economic health.[45] Malaysian leaders acknowledge that the country faces an uphill effort to maintain its anticipated annual increase in GNP of 7 percent. With a population growth rate of 2.8 percent (down from 3 percent over 1952-64), the increase in per capita GNP is a modest 3 to 4

44. S. P. Seenivasagam, leader of the Peoples Progressive Party, quoted in: *Straits Times,* August 26, 1972, p. 7.
45. The price of rubber hit a 25 year low in September 1972, and six months later it reached an all time high.

percent, which leaves a rather small cushion to allocate between the incentives for growth goals and the redistributive objectives of the NEP. Malaysia's chronic unemployment of 8 to 10 percent of the labor force, with urban areas suffering much more severely, is an ominous cloud on the horizon.

In comparison with Singapore, with its 1965-72 GNP growth rate of 13 percent and its per capita GNP growth rate of over 10 percent, Malaysia has not been doing too well. Similarly, Singapore has practically no unemployment and is experiencing a labor shortage such that almost 12 percent of its labor force is immigrant, much of it recruited from Malaysia. If Singapore were to place restrictions on foreign labor, Malaysia's rate of unemployment would quickly soar to a new high and become an extremely serious political and economic liability. With Malay employment quotas vigorously enforced, the unemployment rate is particularly high among young urban non-Malays. In addition, there is concealed unemployment and underemployment among rural peasant Malays. As a consequence, any serious rise in the unemployment rate is bound to exacerbate communal tensions between rural Malays and urban non-Malays.

If Malaysia's economy remains healthy, the prospect of violent social upheaval arising from too rapid social change would not appear to be serious, especially if the government is able to meet many, if not all, of its stated objectives and goals. The likelihood of social upheaval and violence will increase in proportion to the shortfall in the government's proclaimed goals. Government propaganda on behalf of Rukunegara and the NEP is having the effect of generating sharply rising expectations, which may turn to frustration and alienation if this vision of the future proves to be merely a mirage.

If serious communal violence erupts once again, the armed forces will very likely intervene decisively. Statistics on the ethnic composition of the military are not made public, but it is no secret that the army and navy are overwhelmingly Malay from the commanding officers down to the lowest ranks, with some units, such as the Royal Malay Regiment, being all Malay. Only in the Air Force at the officer ranks do the Malays constitute a minority of about one third.[46] If the military were to intervene in force in response to communal violence, it is unlikely that they would act with equal firmness toward all ethnic communities. If violence of major proportions did erupt again, many Chinese and Indians would attempt to flee to the relative haven of Singapore, which has the capacity to maintain its independence and

46. Henderson, *Area Handbook*, pp. 557-582; *Straits Times*, August 31, 1972, Section II, p. 8. Malaysia has a military force of 50,000, including 43,000 in the army, 4,000 in the air force, and a navy of 3,000.

defend itself against threats from immediate neighbors.[47] Fortunately, most Malaysians realize that major communal violence will benefit no one and only bring terror, poverty and misery to all. The memory of 1969 and the spectre of renewed communal violence helps to sustain the ethos of accommodation and consensus which now characterizes the political mood of the country.

It is easy for foreign analysts and observers to criticize Malaysia's partially paralyzed democratic institutions, her limitations on fundamental freedoms and individual liberties, and her reliance upon ascriptive special privileges based on ethnicity, but such critics seldom attempt to devise alternative strategies which will work, and they never have to face the consequences of failure. To forge a dynamic modern and unified nation from a society seriously divided along communal linguistic and cultural lines, as well as stratified into classes and functional groupings, is no easy task, as will be apparent from reading the recent history of most former colonial states. All political and economic strategies have costs. It is Malaysians who ultimately must pay these costs, and bear the consequences of the policies devised by their leaders. We can only hope that the energies and treasure invested in their present strategies prove to be worth the sacrifices and bring them closer to the goal desired by nearly all Malaysians—a unified, harmonious, prosperous, modern and democratic country.

47. Singapore maintains a well-equipped and highly trained military force of 80,000 men.

Selected Readings

Blythe, Wilfred. *The Impact of Chinese Secret Societies in Malaya*. London: Oxford University Press, 1969.

Emerson, Rupert. *Malaysia: A Study in Direct and Indirect Rule*. New York: The Macmillan Co., 1937.

Esman, Milton J. *Administration and Development in Malaysia*. Ithaca: Cornell University Press, 1972.

Fraser, Thomas M. *Rusembilan: A Malay Fishing Village*. Ithaca: Cornell University Press, 1960.

Gullick, J.M. *Indigenous Political Systems of Western Malaya*. London: Athlone Press, 1965.

Henderson, John W. et al., *Area Handbook for Malaysia*. Washington, D.C.: U.S. Government Printing Office, 1970.

International Bank for Reconstruction and Development. *The Economic Development of Malaya*. Baltimore: John Hopkins Press, 1955.

Kennedy, J. *A History of Malaya*. London: Macmillan and Co., 1962.

Mahajani, Usha. *The Role of Indian Minorities in Burma and Malaya*. Bombay: Vora and Co., 1960.

Means, Gordon P. *Malaysian Politics*. London: University of London Press, New York: New York University Press, 1970.

Miller, Harry. *The Story of Malaysia*. London: Faber and Faber, 1965.

Milne, R.S. *Government and Politics in Malaysia*. Boston: Houghton Mifflin, 1967.

Ness, Gayl D. *Bureaucracy and Rural Development in Malaysia*. Berkeley: University of California Press, 1967.

Ongkili, James P. *Modernization in East Malaysia, 1960-1970*. Kuala Lumpur: Oxford University Press, 1972.

Osborne, Milton. *Singapore and Malaysia*. Ithaca, N.Y.: Cornell University, Southeast Asia Program, Data Paper No. 53, 1964.

Purcell, Victor. *The Chinese in Southeast Asia*. London: Oxford University Press, 1951.

Ratnam, K.J. *Communalism and the Political Process in Malaya*. Singapore: University of Malaya Press, 1965.

_____. and Milne, R.S. *The Malayan Parliamentary Election of 1964*. Singapore: University of Malaya Press, 1967.

Roff, William R. *The Origins of Malay Nationalism*. New Haven: Yale University Press, 1967.

Sandhu, Kernial Singh. *Indians in Malaya*. Cambridge: Cambridge University Press, 1969.

Scott, James C. *Political Ideology in Malaysia*. New Haven: Yale University Press, 1968.

Silcock, T.H. and Fisk, E.K. (eds.). *The Political Economy of Independent Malaya*. Berkeley: University of California Press, 1960.

Slimming, John. *Malaysia: Death of a Democracy*. London: John Murray, 1969.

Thompson, Sir Robert. *Defeating Communist Insurgency*. New York: Frederick A. Praeger, 1966.

Tregonning, K.G. *A History of Modern Sabah, 1881-1963*. Singapore: University of Malaya Press, 1965.

Vasil, R.K. *The Malaysian General Election of 1969*. Singapore: Oxford University Press, 1972.

_____. *Politics in a Plural Society: A Study of Non-Communal Political Parties in West Malaysia*. Kuala Lumpur: Oxford University Press, 1971.

Wang, Gungwu (ed.). *Malaysia—A Survey*. New York: Frederick A. Praeger, 1964.

Winstedt, Sir R.O. *The Malays: A Cultural History*. 3rd ed. rev., London: Routledge and Kegan Paul Ltd., 1953.

5   Thailand

Clark D. Neher

The kingdom of Thailand is an anomaly among the states and societies of the Third World. Despite the many similarities it shares with other Third World nations, Thailand's historical background, its distinctive cultural patterns, and the political system's remarkable capacity to cope with change are a few of the elements that make it unique and distinguish it from other states and societies with similar levels of economic development. Nevertheless, Thailand shares the salient attributes of other Third World nations: a low level of technological and economic development; psychological unity among the elites, centering on their desire to "modernize" and catch up with the economically developed societies of the world; and a geographical location that places it beyond the main centers of the contemporary international system.

The Historical Dimension

Much of the uniqueness of Thailand can be traced to its historical background. The Thai people are a synthesis of a wide array of cultures, especially Chinese and Indian, that have blended in a unique manner during various historical eras and added not only to the richness of Thai culture but also to the stability and flexibility of the nation. The Thai's ability to assimilate other cultures and at the same time to retain the main elements of their own traditional culture exemplify an extraordinary capacity to cope with continual change in a manner that has added to, rather than detracted from, the stability of the society.

The first viable kingdom of the Thais was established around 1238 at Sukhothai in present-day northern Thailand. Known as the Sukhothai

Kingdom, it was headed by paternalistic kings who were protectors of the people in wartime and the "fathers and advisors" of their subjects in peace time. After the fall of Sukhothai in the fourteenth century, a new kingdom arose at Ayuthaya, a city some 200 miles south of Sukhothai and 50 miles north of the present capital, Bangkok. The concept of the king of Ayuthaya contrasted sharply with the idea of the monarch in Sukhothai. In place of the patriarchal and earthly Sukhothai king there arose the autocratic Ayuthayan monarch. The new concept of the king grew out of the process of "indianization," a result of extensive contact with India and Ceylon during the Sukhothai era and the influx of statesmen and traders from the ancient Cambodian kingdoms, which themselves had been indianized.

The Indian impact on Thailand was manifested in new concepts of authority and man's relationship to the cosmos: kings became god-kings and their legitimacy rested on their divine nature. The autocratic king was the lord of the universe and his kingdom represented a microcosm of the universe. Under his rule, every person in the Ayuthayan kingdom was organized hierarchically in an elaborate scheme where each person was given a rank. In modified terms, this "hierarchization" of the kingdom has persisted in Thai cultural patterns to the present day.

The hierarchization of Ayuthayan society was significant for the administration of the kingdom, as well as for the social system, because interaction was determined by status differentiations. As the ranking system increasingly defined itself in terms of control over people, a system of patron-client relationships emerged that, from the Ayuthayan era to the present, has been at the heart of Thai politics.

On April 7, 1767, Ayuthaya fell to the Burmese, who so plundered the capital that its magnificent buildings were reduced to rubble, and they were never rebuilt. Thousands of Thais were slain or captured. The royal family and nobility were decimated and the administrative and social systems, which had been so brilliantly created by the Ayuthayan kings, fell into chaos. From the ruins of Ayuthaya a new dynasty emerged, whose capital was Bangkok, a city that remains to this day the center of Thai political, social, and economic activity.

The Chakri dynasty which inaugurated the new regime, has ruled Thailand for 200 years. The most famous Chakri monarch was King Chulalongkorn the Great, and under his remarkable rule (1868-1910) Thailand underwent political and social transformations of such magnitude that it is not implausible to speak of his reign as a revolution. Slavery was abolished, secular educational opportunities were expanded, and the concept of the monarchy was transformed from that of divine monarch to that of a human king. The kings also dealt effectively with western empires that coveted Thailand's markets, labor, and lure of its strategic, geographic position. The success of the Chakri kings' foreign policy is made clear by the fact that Thailand is the only nation in Southeast Asia that has remained free of western colonialism.

Much of the unique nature of Thailand can therefore be traced to its lack of a colonial past. For example, it was not faced with an "identity crisis" of the type that confronted the other Southeast Asia nations. Thais were not treated like second-class citizens in their own country, nor did they have to cope with a foreign culture that had been thrust upon them. Instead, the Thais were able to choose those aspects of westernization they could most easily and profitably assimilate into their own culture. Hence Thailand demonstrates a persistence and continuity of culture and traditions that have been adulterated in colonized nations. The remarkable stability of the kingdom and the generally conservative nature of its political system are in large part a result of the lack of colonial domination.

King Chulalongkorn was also responsible for the political reorganization that radically transformed the bureaucracy at both the central and provincial levels. Indeed, the present-day governmental structure differs very little from the structure envisioned by King Chulalongkorn in the 1880s and 1890s. His reforms introduced a differentiated government with separate responsibilities for the various ministries. In addition, he established a uniform provincial administration that eventually brought all territorial officials under the direct control of the central government, which added considerably to the power of the Bangkok administrators.

In 1932 the absolute monarchy was overthrown by a group of radical and republic-oriented students, most of whom had studied in western universities. The overthrow of the absolute monarchy, directly influenced by the severe economic problems caused by the world-wide depression was, however, intimately connected with Thai history, and especially with the political and social transformations carried out by the Chakri kings. King Chulalongkorn, for example, had in some respects undermined the power of the throne by transferring the claims of legitimacy from that of a divine monarch to that of a decision-making human. Thus the king could no longer claim god-king status to assure his legitimacy and authority.

The evolution of the monarchy from paternalism of the Sukhothai Kingdom to the autocracy of the Ayuthaya regime culminated in the 1932 revolution, when the king became a constitutional monarch. Power shifted from the royal princes to a new elite, which was generally based on the middle class, and found especially within the bureaucracy and the military forces. Thailand's form of government was henceforth transformed from an absolute monarchy to a bureaucratic

military polity in which succession was determined by coups d'etat
rather than by heredity. The 1932 coup, however, did not produce a
social revolution; the masses remained deferential toward the government, and indeed were little affected by the change in leadership. The
historical, traditional, and religious appeals of the monarchy remained, but were supplemented by nationalistic and militaristic
appeals.

The Thai polity became a bureaucratic polity, with the military in
control of the bureaucracy. Indeed, since 1932 there have been only
three years of non-military rule. The military has remained in power
by skillfully manipulating constitutions and people, by its superior
organization, and by its control over weaponry. Under the military,
the primary function of Thailand's constitutions has been the maintenance and strengthening of the regimes in power. From 1932 to the
present, Thailand has been ruled under nine constitutions and 36 cabinets, led by 12 prime ministers. From 1963 to 1973, the government
was led by Field Marshal Thanom Kittikachorn. Although his power
was legitimized with the promulgation of a constitution in 1968 and
with elections in 1969 (in which his political party won a plurality),
Prime Minister Thanom took all power for himself and his associates
in October 1971. He dissolved the parliament, abrogated the 1968 constitution, banned political parties, and declared martial law. He remained in office until October 1973 when student demonstrators forced
him to resign and go into exile. The King appointed Sanya Thammasak as his successor. The new Premier is a highly respected civilian
who has served as Supreme Court justice, Rector of Thammasat University, and member of the King's Privy Council. The military's particularly brutal attempt to put down the student protests, and the unprecedented show of power by the students may keep the military from
regaining their traditional dominance.

Geography

Thailand, located in the heart of turbulent Southeast Asia, is bordered
by Burma on the west and north, by Laos and Cambodia on the east,
and by Malaysia on the south. Its northern borders are a scant 100
miles from the People's Republic of China, while North and South
Vietnam are less than 100 miles to the east. Thailand is slightly smaller
than Texas and its shape is very much like an elephant's head in profile, with the northeast representing an ear and the southern peninsula
representing the trunk. (This imagery is especially apt since the elephant is a national symbol.)

Thailand can be divided into four distinct regions: the central plain, the north, the northeast, and the southern peninsula. The regional variances—geographic, economic, ethnic, and political—act as centrifugal forces that keep the nation from being more unified and integrated. These variances, however, are balanced by similarities that transcend the regional differences and that have made Thailand one of the most homogeneous societies of Southeast Asia.

The central plain is characterized by magnificent stretches of rich alluvial soil that grow the bulk of Thailand's rice crop. It is the heartland, the base of most of the country's agricultural wealth. The rice paddies are irrigated by the yearly flooding of the nation's greatest river, the Chao Phya. Criss-crossing the plain are natural and man-made canals, which are used for irrigation and which serve as the main routes of transportation.

There is no generally accepted delineation between the central plain and the northern region, although the north can be said to begin at the foothills that climb up from the central plain. In contrast to the central plain, the north is mountainous and is divided into major river valleys that eventually lead to the Chao Phya basin. Each river valley contains rich rice-growing areas, but most of the north is covered with forests and is unsuitable for agriculture. Several indigenous hill peoples, who are ethnically unrelated to the Thais, live in the mountains and engage in slash-and-burn swidden agriculture. For the most part, they have not been assimilated into the dominant Thai culture of the lowlands. The principal city of the north, and the second largest city in Thailand, is Chiang Mai, with a population close to 100,000.

The northeast, which comprises a third of Thailand's total land area, is the poorest region of the nation (its $80 per capita income is about half of the national average) because of its scarce rainfall and low level of soil fertility. Moreover, until very recently the northeast has been relatively isolated from the rest of the country due to the villages' subsistence economic patterns, the lack of transportation and communications networks, and the distinct Lao ethnic makeup of the Northeasterners. Largely because of fear of communist insurgency in the region in the last decade, the northeast has been a major focus of the central government's development program. Poverty, isolation, and neglect had made the area a particularly attractive target for antigovernment terrorists.

Southern Thailand, which is least like the other regions of the country in several respects, is largely rain forest due to its two monsoon seasons each year. Rice is grown in the small valleys, but not for commercial purposes; the peasants grow enough only for their own families. Fishing, tin mining, and rubber are the major economic assets of the south. Malay Muslims are dominant in the southernmost provinces, but thus far the Muslims, who number more than 1 million, have been neglected by the central government and a separatist movement threatens the stability of the area.

Thailand's capital city, Bangkok, with a population of almost 3 million, is located in the central plain some 20 miles north of the Gulf of Siam on the Chao Phya River. Bangkok dominates every aspect of Thai society and thus must be given separate attention. It is the unchallenged center of political, economic, cultural, educational, and social activity. At one time known as the Venice of the East because of its numerous canals, Bangkok has undergone urbanization and westernization and the once gracious city has become a steaming, overcrowded, concrete metropolis with only a touch of its grandeur remaining. Its canals have been filled and paved to make room for the thousands of automobiles that move more slowly than the canal boats did a few years previously. What New York, Washington, Los Angeles, Chicago, San Francisco, Detroit, and Philadelphia ensemble are to the United States, Bangkok is to Thailand.

Demographic Dimensions

In terms of the major characteristics of the population, Thailand is both homogeneous and heterogeneous but the similarities are more striking. For example, 97 percent of the population speak Thai, 93.5 percent are Buddhists, and 87 percent live in rural areas and engage in rice cultivation. However, such statistics mask a richness and diversity that complicates any attempt at gross generalization. The heterogeneous ethnic makeup of the population includes Central Thai, Lao Thai, Northern Thai, Thai-Malay, Vietnamese, Cambodian, Chinese, and various groups of Hill Peoples.

The Thai population has been growing at an average annual growth rate of 3.2 percent in the last two decades, so that the 1970 population figure for the country is near 36 million. If the current rate of growth continues, the 1970 figure will double by 1990. The extraordinarily high growth rate is due to a sharp drop in mortality and continuation in the high level of fertility. In 1937, life expectancy at birth was about 35 years, in contrast to an estimated 54 years for men and 59 for women in the period 1964-67. Much of the reason for the phenomenal decline in the mortality rate is the advance of medical technology. Until very recently, malaria, yaws, small pox, and plague ravaged the countryside, but now all of these dreaded diseases have been almost completely eradicated. For example, between 1943 and 1966 the annual death rate per 100,000 people for malaria fell from 329 to 14, and the figure for 1971 is even lower.[1]

1. *Country Profiles: Thailand* (The Population Council, Columbia University March 1972), p. 3.

The sharp decline in mortality has not been matched by a similar decline in fertility, inasmuch as birth control has not yet been introduced to most Thais and the government began to establish a national population policy only in 1970. A high rate of population growth is now seen by the Thai government as an important obstacle to the economic and social development of the country. Thai women average 6.5 births by the time they complete their reproductive cycle, although this figure may decrease significantly in the future. As a result of Thailand's family planning program, more than 400,000 women accepted the IUD, the pill, or female sterilization in 1971. At present, infant mortality is about 85 per 1,000 live births.[2]

Thailand is one of the least urbanized nations in Southeast Asia. In 1967, only 13.5 percent lived in urban areas that had populations of at least 10,000. Fully 73 percent of the urban dwellers lived in the central plain region while 59.8 percent of the total number of urbanites lived in the combined metropolitan area of Bangkok-Thonburi.[3] And as in other modernizing societies, the urban population is growing at a higher rate than the rural population.

The Bangkok-Thonburi megalopolis has retained its status as the primary urban area by growing at the rate of 7.5 percent per year. Indeed, by 1967 the population of Bangkok-Thonburi was 32 times that of the next largest city, Chiang Mai, which numbered only 81,600.[4]

Despite the dominance of Bangkok, in the last decade urbanization has occurred in every region and has become an important factor in the economic and political development of the nation. The growing number and size of towns throughout the kingdom affect not only the people within the urban areas but also rural people who live outside the towns but make use of the latter's marketing, employment, and entertainment opportunities.

The Economic Dimension

Agriculture, and especially rice agriculture, is at the heart of the Thai economy, and over 80 percent of the economically active people are directly involved in farming. Of this group, 82 percent own their own farms, and the average farm is about 10 acres. Farmers who own 10 or fewer acres are subsistence farmers, that is, their families consume all that is produced. Those who farm more than 10 acres sell their surplus rice to a middleman (often a Chinese), who in turn sells the rice to a mill owner, and the rice is eventually sold to Thai consumers or is exported abroad.

2. Ibid., p. 3.

3. Sidney Goldstein, "Urbanization in Thailand," *Demography* 8, 2 (May 1971): 221-222.

4. Ibid., p. 218.

The growing of rice is an arduous, time-consuming task inasmuch as most rice paddies are irrigated and drained by manual laborers. As soon as the fields are properly irrigated, they are plowed with steel plows, which are drawn by water buffaloes. Every seedling is sown one at a time by hand and machines are rarely used at any phase of the planting-to-threshing cycle.

Most Thai farmers, however, do much more than grow rice for a few months of the year. Subsistence farmers, who have no capital, must engage in a variety of activities, including manual labor for wealthier farmers or for government-sponsored construction projects. Also, a family may work together as carpenters, making furniture and farm tools, or may engage in the weaving and selling of clothing and blankets. Chickens are raised for eggs, and vegetable gardens are often planted during the off season.

In the last two decades, Thailand has undergone a virtual revolution in the diversification of the agricultural sector. New crops have been introduced throughout the nation, so that rice now accounts for less than half of the agricultural income. Some of the new crops, including maize and kenaf, are grown almost exclusively for export, whereas cotton, tobacco, fruits, vegetables, coconuts, and sugar cane are grown for home consumption. From 1950 to 1952, some 2 million acres were planted with crops other than rice. By 1965-67, that figure had quadrupled to 8 million acres.[5]

Because subsistence farmers cannot take the risks involved in experimenting with new crops, rice assures security since the farmer knows he can feed his family by continuing to grow that crop. On the other hand, farmers who have been able to take risks have reaped tremendous financial benefits. In contrast to rice which brings the least cash return to the farmer, other crops have consistently produced much greater profits. Farmers who can afford to do so are enthusiastic about diversifying their crops, thereby supporting the notion that the Thai response is in accord with a model of rational economic behavior.[6] The implications for the rural society, in which a few wealthy farmers get richer and most farmers remain at the subsistence level are ominous.

Despite the overwhelming importance of the agricultural sector, it has been declining each year relative to the industrial and services sectors of the total economy. Indeed, since 1951 the Thai economy has undergone fundamental changes, as can be seen in Table 5.1.

The agricultural sector has continued to grow in the last decades,

5. James C. Ingram, *Economic Change in Thailand, 1850-1970* (Stanford: Stanford University Press, 1971), p. 260.
6. Ibid., p. 263.

Table V.1[7]

Gross Domestic Product

Sector	1951	1968	Change
Agriculture	50.1%	31.5%	-18.6%
Industry	18.3	31.1	+12.8
Services	31.6	37.4	+ 5.8

but at a slower rate than the industrial and services sectors. The agricultural growth rate has averaged about 4.5 percent per year versus about 10 percent for industry and services. The regional percentages of the GDP of the various sectors show that the central plain—and mainly Bangkok—accounts for the lion's share of the total value of the industrial and services sectors. In 1963, for example, 65 percent of the new construction was erected in the central plain, versus 13, 11, and 10 percent in the north, northeast, and south. More than half of the factories (excluding rice mills) are located in the Bangkok-Thonburi municipality.

The Thai economy has been growing at an average rate of more than 7 percent per year, so that by 1970 the GNP (in constant 1962 prices) exceeded $6 billion. In 1969 and 1970 the GNP had a phenomenal growth rate of 9.5 percent. When the population growth rate is subtracted, the per capita GNP is seen to have risen at more than 4 percent per year. In the decade 1960 to 1970, per capita income increased from $100 to $160, with most of the growth in the last half of the decade. Although the growth rate is exceptionally high relative to most of the nations of the Third World, its low base keeps Thailand in the ranks of the economically underdeveloped.

The Thai government has played an active role in the nation's economy, and state enterprises have been established in several major industries: tobacco, paper, sugar, gunny sacks, and others. Originally set up to counter the growing dominance of the economic sector by the Chinese, the enterprises gradually came under the control of the regimes in power. Although their management has been inefficient and unprofitable, they have been used as sources of income and patronage by the political leaders. These enterprises have assumed less importance, however, as private business opportunities become increasingly available to the leaders.

In 1961 the Thai government promulgated the First National Economic and Social Development Plan (1961-66), which was followed by a Second Plan (1967-71) and also by a Third Plan (1972-76). It is almost impossible to measure their impact on economic development, but cer-

7. Ibid., p. 235.

tainly the most important outcome has been an economic infrastructure and a centralized administration that coordinates economic planning, so that coordination and long-range planning far surpass that of any previous era. However, the impact of United States investments and military involvement in Southeast Asia probably have had more impact on Thailand than the plans. The Thai economy is still very much affected by outside influences.

The Third Plan has as a basic policy the acceleration of agriculture production for export. This is partly to improve the economic and social conditions of the farmers and partly to solve the immediate economic problem of a large deficit in the balance of trade. The Second Plan failed to solve the very fundamental problems of inequitable distribution of income and agricultural development. The Thai villager still farmed without adequate irrigation and machines, and without suitable markets for his crops. In addition to solving these problems, the Third Plan will attempt to reverse the decline in the growth rate of the GNP that began in 1970. The decline stemmed from the reduction in United States investment in Thailand and from the reduction of American troops stationed in bases throughout the country. The Plan envisions a seven percent average annual GNP growth rate and predicts that the decline in the population growth rate due to a newly launched family planning program will result in an annual growth rate of some 4.5 percent in per capita income.

The Social Dimension

For most Thais, the family is the most important unit of identity. Their nuclear family, usually consisting of parents and children, and sometimes grandparents, is in many respects similar to the typical American family. The nuclear family, however, often becomes an extended family when relatives move into the household. For example, when children marry, the daughter or son and spouse may choose to live with one set of parents for a short time, usually until a baby is born, when the new family sets up its own household. When the parents are too old to work, one of the daughters or sons and the spouse will move into the family compound to take care of the parents. Rural children who want to continue their education or be closer to their places of employment move in with their kindred and are accepted into the family. Children are taught to obey their parents, to take care of them when they are old, and to keep the good name of the family. The rural education system reinforces the cultural patterns learned within the family.

Ninety-two percent of Thai children receive four years of education, but less than 30 percent continue past the fourth year, and only 5 percent are enrolled in grades eight through ten. For most Thais, then, the early years are the most important for learning cultural values. The emphasis of the primary schools on *riabroi* (behaving in a desirable, orderly manner) and the deference demanded by the teachers suggest that the primary schools have the function of maintaining traditional attitudes.

Although conventional wisdom indicates that education encourages social mobility from lower to higher class levels, there is almost no correlation in Thailand between intergeneration social mobility and level of education. Instead, an individual's level of education is correlated with his/her father's occupation. The children of manual laborers are provided little education, and also become manual laborers, whereas high-level bureaucrats' children have the opportunity to attend more years of school and consequently become high-ranking officials themselves. Thus, education connotes the inheritance of the father's social status rather than the creation of intergenerational mobility.[8]

Thais also identify with their village community, although the relationship is somewhat tenuous and depends on the particular region and village structure. However, Thai villages conform to certain patterns, so that they are distinguished more by their similarities than by their differences. A self-sufficient subsistence economy, irrigated rice farming, a central-village Buddhist temple, several influential kinship groupings, and common religious ceremonies (including the worship of spirits) are the most important elements in almost every Thai village. Yet Thai villages also exhibit varying patterns. In addition to regional differences, the principal factors influencing village structure and behavior are a village's resources, its proximity to main roads and urban centers, kinship patterns, internal cohesion, government programs, and local leadership. As these factors combine into various patterns, a village takes on an identity that distinguishes it from other Thai villages.

Only a few village groups demand the involvement of the villager. The Buddhist temple and the school are symbols of the community but they do not necessarily symbolize, or demand, a special esprit. This is not to say that there is no "community" in the Thai villages; there is much evidence of group activity that is based on a loose quid pro quo relationship but does not demand conformity or special allegiance. For example, the farmer rarely works alone in his fields. In addition to the children, who work along with him, neighbors and kin work to-

8. Ken'ichi Tominaga et al., "Thai Modernization and Industrialization of Thai Society: A Sociological Analysis," *East Asian Cultural Studies* 8, 1-4(March 1969): 15.

gether on an informal basis of mutual aid. Although no formal record is kept of who worked for whom and for how long, each farmer is expected to return all services rendered to him by others.

Class Structure

Social classes have not evolved in rural Thai society, at least partly because most relationships are based on vertical ties that crosscut socio-economic classes. Generally, Thais relate to persons of higher or lower status as individuals rather than as members of a group or class. Yet, despite the lack of a rigid class system, there is little evidence of an exceptionally high rate of social or economic mobility in Thailand. Children of peasant farmers are likely to become farmers while children of merchants or officials also are likely to follow the vocations of their parents.

Among the more privileged groups in Thailand, and in the capital city of Bangkok, there is a class hierarchy that is headed by the traditional elites and noble families. A new elite, which has emerged since the 1932 revolution, consists of high-level government officials, military officers, and wealthy business leaders. Under these traditional and modern elite classes are two middle-class groups: Chinese entrepreneurs, who represent about 10 percent of the total Thai population and about 45 percent of Bangkok's population, and lower-level government officials, including bureaucrats, teachers, and technicians. None of these classes are formalized or rigid, except that of the Chinese merchants, who form a separate class outside the Thai status system. However, recent studies have concluded that Thai society may be moving toward a more restricted class system and a decline in social mobility as the high socio-economic classes develop a subculture that only those with wealth and a Western education may enter.[9]

The Individual and Society

Thai society is generally characterized by a lack of rigid role conformity, and high value is placed on individualism in the sense of spontaneity and absence of binding involvements. Spontaneity is shown in the ease with which interpersonal relationships are initiated and terminated and in the frequency with which a villager moves from one place to another when he feels he can improve his standard of living.[10]

9. See Hans Dieter Evers, "The Formation of a Social Class Structure: Urbanization, Bureaucratization, and Social Mobility in Thailand," *American Sociological Review* 31,(1966): 480-488.
10. See Steven Piker, "The Relationship of Belief Systems to Behavior in Rural Thai Society," *Asian Survey* 8,5 (1968): 384-399.

Thais are not joiners; and one of the striking elements of their social system is the lack of structured groups that demand personal commitment. But this is not to say that interpersonal relationships play no role in Thai society. On the contrary, Thai society can be accurately analyzed in terms of the various interpersonal relationships that have pervaded the society both historically and at present.

The lack of rigid role conformity has led many scholars to refer to Thailand as a "loosely structured society" that is characterized by excessive leeway for individuality and idiosyncrasy.[11] And although the model of the "loosely structured social system" has had significant impact on many of the subsequent studies of Thailand, it has also given rise to considerable debate. This debate centers on the "loosely structured" notion versus the findings of many scholars that village life tends toward a norm of behavior that emphasizes conformity. Thus if an individual joins several local groups, or is a teacher, or is relatively wealthy, he automatically becomes one of a few people who stand out from everybody else.

This apparent contradiction can be explained in several ways. Firstly, the diverse regions of Thailand have given rise to varied cultural patterns. Secondly, Thais deal with each other in at least two fundamentally different ways. In face-to-face situations, the relationship between two persons is tightly controlled; Thais know instinctively how to relate to persons, depending on the respective statuses. A person's language, facial expressions, and general demeanor immediately and vividly clarify the interaction. Yet once face-to-face contact is terminated, Thais show a remarkable independence; no longer is there the tightly patterned behavior one sees in the face-to-face relationship. Rather, their forms of behavior are much more in tune with the notion of loose structure as they "follow their own heart."[12]

Superior-subordinate Relationships

The key element in the structure of Thai society has been superior-subordinate relationships. When two or more persons interact there is an automatic feeling out of relative status that ascertains who is superior and who is subordinate. In most cases there is little if any ambiguity, since one person will clearly be older, wealthier, better educated, and

11. John F. Embree, "Thailand—A Loosely Structured Social System," *American Anthropologist* 52,(April 1950), 181-193.
12. See Herbert Phillips, "The Scope and Limits of the Loose Structure Concept" in Hans Dieter Evers, *Loosely Structured Social Systems: Thailand in Comparative Perspective* (Cultural Report Series No. 17, Yale University, Southeast Asia Studies, 1969), pp. 28-29.

the holder of a higher position. Once the superior-subordinate relationship is established, "proper" behavior patterns emerge.

The ideal superior acts as a patron and is expected to protect, aid, complement, and give generously to those whose status is inferior. In return, the subordinate, or client, is expected to act deferentially to the superior, who is his patron. He is expected to perform tasks efficiently and with the least amount of trouble for his superior. The subordinate maintains his inferior position by not challenging the superior or undermining the latter's position. Initially, patron-client bonds stem from such personal relationships as kinship groupings, official ties within the bureaucracy, school ties, or common village origins and are based largely on personal loyalty. Over time, however, the personal element declines in significance as the tie becomes instrumental.

The patron-client relationships that pervade Thai society help to shape the society into a national whole; patron-client groupings are not separate and isolated entities but related parts of an overall system of groupings. The patron of one grouping is a client to a group higher in the hierarchy. Theoretically, it is possible to graph a hierarchical chain of patron-client bonds that extends from the peasant farmer to the highest reaches of the power elite in Bangkok. Information and resources flow through this network of overlapping and interrelated groups. At every level, patron-client groupings carry out the political functions of disseminating information, allocating resources, and organizing people. Thus the groupings play a key role in the integration of Thai society; the "web" of the society, they consist of an infinite number of dyadic groupings that act as links in a network of reciprocities that extends throughout Thai society and cuts across bureaucracies and extra-bureaucratic structures. In some cases a patron-client grouping is complete in and of itself, whereas in other cases such ties run through the entire governmental hierarchy.

The Psycho-Cultural Dimension

All political activity occurs in the context of a general societal culture. The role of the citizenry in the political process, the authority of political decision-makers, the kinds and range of policies put forth are all affected by the attitudes, feelings, and beliefs of the people.

An overriding theme of Thai culture is the expectation of pleasant, "cool," and correct interpersonal relationships. The "cool heart" (chai yen), a highly regarded trait of the Thais, ensures that overt confrontations and violence will be kept to a minimum. A person who keeps a cool heart when interacting with others is held to be in the right no matter what the objective issues may be. The manner in which alternative claims are expressed is as important as their validity.

Although confrontation and violence are unacceptable behavior, they occur throughout Thai society, as a reading of the daily press will make abundantly clear. Armed bandits roam the countryside and extort the citizenry. Murder, rape, and mayhem occur daily. Within every organization and family unit there are arguments and infighting. Indeed, the superficially pleasant smile can mask resentment, frustration, and anger, which must be sublimated in order to meet societal role expectations. Sublimation can take such forms as calumnious gossip *(nintha)*, sarcasm, avoidance and withdrawal, superficial cooperation, intermediaries, and the indirect expression of one's feelings.

Prachot (indirect expression) is a social procedure in which "the individual who has been antagonized, insulted or hurt in some way does not express his displeasure directly but turns it toward another object."[13] This is done quite consciously, and with the express purpose of having the other person know that one is annoyed, angry, or disgusted with him. For example, a parent who is angry with his spouse might express his anger by reprimanding a child or by hitting the dog, but the facade of amicable relations remains. Although prachot is an acceptable means of expressing discontent and conflict, most conflict is internalized in order to convey an impression of coolness and equanimity. It is difficult to predict if or when conflict will reach the explosive point since the appearance of harmony almost always precedes an outburst.

The individuality and spontaneity of the Thai should not be thought of as irrational behavior. Indeed, the essential rationality of the Thai is part of his inherent cultural pattern and has been noted in much of the literature. The patron-client relationship, however, is only one example of Thai rationality in that the relationship is based on maximizing reciprocal benefits without submitting to enduring personal bonds. The profit motive, an example of economic rationality, is another important determinant of behavior in Thailand, as farmers' response to the diversification of crops so strikingly indicates. If an action will bring profit, it will be done. Conversely, if the Thai sees no immediate return to his investment of time, labor, or money, they will not be invested.

Perhaps somewhat inconsistent with the putative instrumentality and rationality of the Thais are the notions of *sanuk* (fun) and *sabai* (pleasure). The most important element of any occasion, whether in the rice fields, at school, or at a political or board of directors meeting, is the fun and pleasure enjoyed by the participants. At harvest time, the

13. William Klausner, "The 'Cool Heart' : Social Relationships in a Northeastern Thai Village," *The Journal of Social Sciences,*Chulalongkorn University), 4 (May 1966): 120.

feeling of accomplishment is less important to the farmer than enjoyment of the communal experience. Although few observers of the Thai scene deny the importance of fun in Thai social patterns, there is far less agreement on whether this attitude interferes with hard work, but the evidence suggests that Thais will work as hard as persons in other cultures to improve their chances in life. However, the mood of the Thai work situation differs significantly from cultures in which personal relationships are a less salient part of the political and social system.

Religion

The Thai versions of Buddhism and spirit worship are important elements of the cultural framework vis-à-vis political activity. Buddhism, however, is not a religion in the commonly used sense of the word, for it is not a system of faith and worship. In Buddhism, no belief must be taken on faith, such as belief in a Supreme Being; rather, all faith must be believable in light of one's experience and reason. Buddha guides his followers by pointing out the path on which they can proceed, but each person must tread the path himself.

The most distinctive doctrine of Buddhism is *kharma* which pertains to the sum of one's good and bad actions. Moreover, all change is determined by kharma. Good actions in this life will lead to a better spiritual and material existence in the next life. The operating principle in the kharmic process is merit *(bun)*, which can be accumulated by performing meritorious deeds. Good and bad actions affect one's next existence but not the state of one's present life—just as the present is the consequence of the sum of actions in previous existences.

In order to achieve *Nirvana,* the absence of suffering, one must be freed from the cycle of kharmic rebirth and must live by the Four Noble Truths. The first Noble Truth holds that all existence is suffering; the second teaches that suffering is caused by desire and greed; the third teaches that suffering will cease when desire and greed cease; and the fourth truth indicates the Noble (eightfold) Path that one must follow to bring suffering to an end. The Noble Path connotes right understanding, right thought, right speech, right action, right livelihood, right effort, rightmindfulness, and right concentration. But following the eightfold path is impossible for the layman, who must cope with the daily vicissitudes of life. Thus Buddhism emphasizes the need to withdraw from society in order to meditate and perfect the discipline that is necessary for achieving Nirvana. Buddhist monks have chosen to follow this path.

In addition to their Buddhist observances, the Thais propitiate spirits, practice magic and divination, and live in fear of ghosts and sorcerers. In Thailand, the first name given to a baby is often an ugly one (e.g., Little Rat), so that the evil spirits will be fooled into thinking the newborn is unloved and therefore will not covet the baby and take him away. Astrologers are consulted for auspicious times from when to begin feeding rice to a baby to promulgating new constitutions. Miniature spirit houses are found next to houses and are used to propitiate the house spirits. Thais also wear amulets for protection against malicious and evil spirits. In the rural areas, spirit doctors are utilized to exorcise disease and evil from afflicted persons.

Spirit worship is an important alternative to the Buddhist explanation for suffering. In contrast to the Buddhist teaching of individual responsibility, spirit worship provides a more satisfying explanation by placing the blame for suffering on malicious spirits rather than on the person himself.

There is a widespread tendency to explain Thai political behavior in terms of the religious beliefs of the people on the assumption that their religious norms are an internalized part of the motivational system. The Thais' deference to authority, for example, is sometimes explained by noting that people of high status (superiors) are those who in their previous existences performed virtuous deeds. Subordinates, on the other hand—by the same rationale—have less virtuous backgrounds and hence are duty bound to respect their superiors. Similarly, the Thais' political passivity, the low level of economic development, and the lack of materialistic values have been explained in terms of the Buddhist idea that desire and greed cause suffering. Finally, the Thais' spontaneity and individualism have been seen as the product of the Buddhist stress on the individual's responsibility for attaining Nirvana.

Such explanations, however, are at best tenuous because religious beliefs are not usually an important element of one's motivational system and because these beliefs contain contradictions. Deference to authority may be congruent with Buddhism's notion of merit, but deferential behavior was an operative force in Thailand even before Buddhism was firmly established. Non-Buddhist Thais, as well as non-Buddhists in most of Asia, behave deferentially. Nor is deference necessarily consistent with the Buddhist idea of personal accountability for moral perfection—an idea that could conceivably promote egalitarianism rather than elitism. Most importantly, there is little evidence that the Buddhist idea of kharma affects behavior patterns. Deference to superiors, for example, can be explained by the instrumental rationality of the Thais. Superiors have resources that subordinates need—money, land, jobs, shelter—for which the latter offer deference in return.

The relationship between the Buddhist norms of desire and the low

level of economic development is also tenuous. Although, normative-
ly, Buddhism eschews desire, it teaches that a more comfortable existence awaits the person who does good deeds. The desire for a more
comfortable existence—for a higher standard of living—is therefore an
important determinant of behavior. Furthermore, the Buddhist who
builds a temple in order to gain merit may be more "materialistic"
than the person who spends his money on material goods, as the former seeks to guarantee a more comfortable life for himself in his next
existence. To stress the point again, it is the desire for a better life,
rather than belief in kharmic rebirth that motivates behavior.

Many studies have indicated that the villagers' religious beliefs do
not limit their level of production or consumption, nor do they lessen
the Thais' strong interest in money, security, and comfort. Herbert
Phillips, in his study of the peasant personality in central Thailand,
found an overriding concern with such practical matters as money,
earning a living, achieving status, and having sufficient food. These
Thais gave some attention—but relatively little—to religious concerns
and to satisfactions of an interpersonal nature, including those of
one's family. The overwhelming majority of informants in Phillip's
study expressed desire for only one thing: money.[14]

The foregoing should not lead one to the conclusion that Buddhism
and spirit worship have no impact on political activity. On the contrary, Buddhism's inherent tolerance, flexibility, and lack of dogma
have encouraged the principle of compromise in Thai politics and
discouraged narrow ideological dogmatism. Moreover, the Buddhist
emphasis on serenity and virtue has mitigated the violence of the rulers
toward the ruled. Also, Buddhism provides a sense of national unity
and identification that is partially responsible for the high degree of
social stability. The Thai king, as the spiritual leader of Buddhism,
symbolizes the Thai nation, and rarely is any political activity undertaken without the blessings of the Buddhist monks.

Approximately half of all Thai males enter the monkhood for at
least three weeks sometime during their lives. However, this high percentage is not the most important factor, since, as John de Young suggests, "whether a male goes through the temple service or not, the
experience is important for all of them, for it represents the ideal that
every male should follow, and even those who do not go through the
experience find they are affected by the ideal."[15] Many Thais, moreover, see a virtual identity between their religion and their society.

14. Herbert Phillips, *Thai Peasant Personality: The Patterning of Interper-
    sonal Behavior in the Village of Bang Chan* (Berkeley, California, Univer-
    sity of California Press, 1966), pp. 196-199.
15. John E. de Young, *Village Life in Modern Thailand* (Berkeley, California:
    University of California Press), 1955, p. 57.

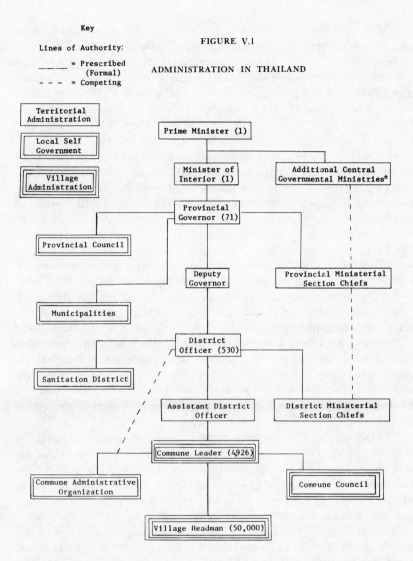

Key

Lines of Authority:

_____ = Prescribed (Formal)

- - - = Competing

FIGURE V.1

ADMINISTRATION IN THAILAND

*Includes the Ministries of Industries, Public Health, Justice, Finance, Agriculture, National Development, Education, Communications, Economic Affairs, Defense, and Foreign Affairs.

The Political Dimension

Local Administration

Local government in Thailand operates in several contexts of separate but interrelated patterns of authority (Figure V.1 sets forth the three patterns of authority and the basic administrative hierarchy). The first line of local authority emanates from the central government in Bangkok and is referred to as territorial or provincial administration.

The Province.   The province *(changwat)*, of which there are 71 in Thailand, is the primary unit of territorial administration. Each province is administered by a governor, who is the highest official of a territorial administration. The provinces are subdivided into *amphur,* districts, which are administered by *nai amphur,* district officers. Thailand has 530 districts, or about eight districts in each province.

The role of the governor is in part determined by Thailand's administrative history, particularly the Sukhothai and Ayuthaya traditions when the governor was almost absolute. At present, the governors are not royal family members, as they were in the past, but much of their legitimacy and influence is derived from their connections with the ruling elite in Bangkok. Their functions are to act as (1) chief representative of the central government in the provinces; (2) chief coordinator of the services of various central government ministries; (3) chief supervisor of local self-government units in the provinces; (4) agent of provincial citizens in representations to the central government; and (5) chief administrator of provincial affairs. Carrying out these functions has given the governors a great deal of power.

Despite his exalted position within his province, a governor does not exercise complete power. The Ministry of Interior in Bangkok supervises the governors through a staff of inspectors, and all major decisions are first referred to the Ministry of Interior. In addition, the Ministry of Interior has the power to appoint, transfer, or remove governors.

The District Office.   Although the district office is the lowest administrative unit of the central government, it is one of the most important links in the central government's control of the nation. The programs that are planned in Bangkok ultimately meet their test in the ability of the districts to put them into effect. Each district is under the control of the district officer, who is appointed by the Ministry of Interior and is directly responsible both to the governor of the province in which the district is located and to the Department of Local Administration in the Ministry of Interior. District officers have jurisdiction over 86 percent of the Thai population and 99.6 percent of the country's total area.

Having administrative and supervisory responsibility for the district, the district officer must manage the activities of 20 to 50 staff members, depending on the size of the district, and look after the welfare of 5,000 to 150,000 inhabitants. He directly supervises all Ministry of Interior personnel and has general supervisory power over the district section chiefs, who are representatives of central government ministries. In addition, the district officer spends considerable time working on the reports, forms, routine correspondence, and memos that come to his desk. The local administration section alone, for which the district officer is the section chief, must send more than 290 forms to the provincial or central government every month. These reports include such diverse items as elephant registration, gun licenses, gambling permits, and census records of births, marriages, divorces, and deaths.

As the central government's highest-ranking representative in the district, the district officer officiates at the opening of new schools, health stations, canals, and the like. He must also plan locally initiated and funded projects, as well as the yearly budget, which is submitted to the provincial governor for approval. He also must supervise the self-government units within the district, including the sanitation district committee, which he chairs, and the commune councils.

The formal duties of the district officer are performed within the framework of laws and regulations promulgated by the central government. However, this framework is not so rigid as to preclude great administrative diversity among the districts. The district officer's style of leadership as well as the available manpower and budgetary resources determine the administrative performance in every district.

The Village and the Commune.   The second pattern of authority is shaped by the traditional village leaders. Thailand has some 50,000 *muban*, villages, each of which elects a *puyaiban*, village headman. These villages are combined into 4,926 *tambon*, communes, each with a *kamnan*, commune leader, who is chosen by the village headmen of the particular commune. There are about ten villages in the average-size commune, which in Thailand is a political or territorial combination of villages rather than an economic unit, as are the Chinese cooperative communes.

Village leadership patterns vary enormously throughout the kingdom. In the central plain region, for example, there is very little correlation between the villages' political and social systems, on the one hand, and their administrative system on the other hand. The integrated, self-governing village has largely disappeared, mainly because the commercialization of agriculture and the rapid increase in population has resulted in large farms that are part of more then one village.[16] In the northeast and north, however, the peasants' social and economic communities seem to blend with the administrative structure, and in these areas the headman is a much more powerful political figure.

The lack of clear differentiation between the social and political spheres makes it difficult to analyze the power structure of Thai villages. Potentially, the village headman is very influential because he holds a position of authority and is often a relatively wealthy and edu-

16. Ibid., p. 148.

cated member of the community. The headman is usually elected by the villagers. Any male between the ages of 21 and 60, who is neither a priest nor civil servant and has lived in the village for at least six months, is eligible. The election of the headman appears to differ from village to village. In some areas villagers do not seek the position, and in fact attempt not to be chosen, whereas in other villages they campaign for the position.

The headman plays a middleman role between his village and the district officials. Sometimes, unfortunately, his position as representative of the village before the district authorities conflicts with his position as representative of the officials to his village constituency. As a middleman, the headman is constantly subjected to conflicting pressures and is therefore in a most unenviable position.

In addition to his middleman role, the headman performs a multitude of functions. He attends monthly meetings at the district office, and for many headmen in isolated areas a trip to the district office is a full day's journey. The headman has authority to make arrests in such cases as illegal gambling, buffalo theft, and homicide, and is often called on to arbitrate civil disputes. He must keep records on everything from the slaughter of animals to births. He plans festivals and acts as patron in weddings. He is responsible for reporting calamities, such as floods, and for obtaining the government's help in emergencies. He receives a monthly remuneration of $3.75 to $7.75, depending on his length of service.

The village headmen choose one of themselves to be the commune leader, whose role, like that of the village headmen, varies according to region and circumstances. In the central region he generally plays an insignificant role in the social-political structure, while in the north he is most influential. In addition to his headman duties, the commune leader performs a wide array of functions. He submits periodic reports to the district officials on births, deaths, movements of persons in and out of the commune, land surveys, diseases, taxation, military conscription, and marriages and divorces. He is also responsible for deciding how to spend the tax funds allocated to the commune.

The commune leader, though not a civil servant, is entitled to wear a uniform, receive various official benefits, and be paid an honorarium for his services. His monthly remuneration ranges from $7.50 to $10.00. In addition, he receives special allowances for delivering mail, attending sanitation district meetings, and collecting taxes.

Local Self-Government.   The third form of authority in local government—and the one that has least power—is referred to as local self-government. These governmental units operate at four levels of administration.

Theoretically, the *sapa changwat,* provincial councils, were established as the legislative organ of the provinces, and the members are elected by the citizens of each province on the basis of district constituencies. The members serve five-year terms. The first elections for provincial councilmen in over ten years—and because of the coup d'etat in 1971 probably the last such elections for some time—were held in January 1968. The councils, which were meant to be a forum for debating matters of general interest to the provinces, had the power to pass the bylaws of the provinces and approve the provincial budgets. However, since the central government maintains close control over the procedural and law-making functions of local government, the councils are of limited effectiveness.

Similarly, municipal government units also have been overshadowed by the authority of the central government. *Tesaban,* municipalities which, on the basis of population size, are divided into three categories, were established in the urban areas of the kingdom. The purpose behind municipal self-government was to promote more active citizen involvement in local government, but the practice has not measured up to the lofty goals. Although the 120 municipalities are becoming more important centers of political power as they become more important economically, municipal government is at present the creature of the central government—not the expression of civic spirit in the towns.

Sukapiban, sanitation committees have been established at the district level where there are concentrations of population and an expectation of revenue that will support limited governmental activities—in areas that are not large enough to be municipalities. Every district in Thailand has at least one sanitation district, and there are 585 sanitation districts throughout the country that serve the 3 million people who live within their boundaries.

The services of a sanitation district include garbage collection, street paving, electricity, slaughterhouse regulation, street and house lighting, water and sewage facilities, recreational facilities, and health centers. At present, the sanitation district is not an efficient organ of government; it neither operates its services nor extracts revenues in an effective manner.

The *ongkan borihan suan tambon,* commune administrative organization, was established in 1956 to advance the progress of local self-government in Thailand. Only 53 of the 4,926 communes in the country were selected for this status, and during the subsequent thirteen years no additional commune administrative organization has ben established. The functions of this moribund unit of administration are similar to those of the sanitation district.

National Politics

National politics in Thailand has always involved very few people. Kings, royalty, and nobility ruled supreme during the Sukhothai, Ayuthaya, and Bangkok eras, and the 1932 coup d'etat which overthrew the absolute monarchy did not bring any fundamental changes; a small, bureaucratic elite replaced the monarchical elite.

Since a relative scarcity of resources in terms of wealth, prestige, and power is available to the elite, the tendency in Thailand is to eliminate as many of the elite as possible, thereby preserving its exclusive nature and maximizing the benefits of the ruling class. Those who constitute the elite are willing to share the perquisites of power with others only if the act of sharing will result in a favorable quid pro quo. Elite domination of Thailand's politics also results from the passivity of the citizenry vis-à-vis politics, from the socialization process, which has fostered specialized political skills and the desire of a few to use these skills, and from the traditional attitude that those in power have the right to rule while those who are not in power have the duty to obey.

In spite of the personal and elite nature of Thai politics, there has been an institutional context for the study of Thai politics throughout the kingdom's recent political history. These institutions have included constitutions, elections, parliaments, and separation of powers, but substantial changes have been made in these elements as they were adopted from the west and integrated into the national culture. These structures, although superficially western in form, are distinctly Thai and can be only partially understood in a western framework of analysis.

Since the 1932 revolution and overthrow of the absolute monarchy, Thailand has been governed under eight constitutions, of which three were provisional and five were "permanent." Indeed, the Thais' propensity for changing constitutions has been referred to as "faction constitutionalism,"[17] whereby each successive constitution has reflected, legitimized, and strengthened major shifts in factional dominance. Thai constitutions have not been considered the fundamental law of the land; rather, they have functioned to facilitate the rule of the regime in power.

Since the 1932 revolution the major political institutions have been organized on the principle of an unequal separation of powers. Although the central government has been composed of separate executive, judicial, and legislative branches, the major source of power has been the executive branch.

17. David A. Wilson, *Politics in Thailand* (Ithaca, N.Y.: Cornell University Press, 1962), p. 262.

The Monarchy.   Above these three branches, and theoretically and legally above politics, is the monarchy. Indeed, it is difficult to conceive of Thai politics without the magnificent pageantry that surrounds His Majesty, the Lord of Life, the King of Thailand, who is revered by his subjects as are few other modern monarchs. Even today, the king is the national symbol, the Supreme Patron who reigns over all, and the leader of the Buddhist religion.

The prestige and influence of the monarchy, moreover, has increased since 1950 with the coronation of King Phumipon Adunyadet, who, with his wife, Queen Sirikit, has traveled throughout Thailand and abroad on goodwill trips. Prime Ministers Sarit and Thanom have encouraged the king's endeavors to be closer to his subjects as both a means to increase the legitimacy of the regime in power and to decrease the potential for insurgency by providing the people with a symbol of Thai unity. Nevertheless, the direct impact of the monarchy on politics has been slight, as was shown by the king's inability to prevent coups d'etat and by his silence on issues before the government. His indirect influence is difficult to assess, although the various governments have hesitated to set forth any program that would contravene the values of the king. Thai leaders have not been willing to precipitate a confrontation between themselves and the monarchy, and in that sense the king acts as a moderating influence.

The Executive Branch.   The executive branch of government, as has been said, dominates the political scene. Since 1932 the prime minister has wielded great authority as the leader of both the cabinet and the military, which in turn has provided the executive for thirty-seven of the forty years of constitutional government. During most of this time the executive branch has consisted of the prime minister and the other cabinet level ministers. Next to the prime minister, the ministers of interior and defense have the greatest power. The Ministry of Interior controls local-level administration, as well as the Department of Police, while the Defense Ministry is responsible for all military matters. Traditionally, however, these positions have been retained by the prime minister or entrusted to one or two of his closest confidants. The other cabinet level ministers are often experts in their field, as well as politically influential individuals.

Serving under the various cabinet ministers are some 260,000 regular (non-military) civil servants, who comprise the official bureaucracy. The top civil service employee in each ministry is the undersecretary. In keeping with the 1971 reorganization of prime minister Thanom, the undersecretaries function both as non-political leaders of the ministry (as in the past) and as political leaders with significantly increased powers. Below the undersecretaries are the various departments, which are headed by directors general and divided into divisions and sections.

The Thai bureaucracy, like Thai politics in general, cannot be adequately analyzed in terms of the western model of an impersonal or legal administrative system. In his standard work on the subject, William Siffin has noted that the Thai bureaucracy should be viewed as a social system—a collection of basic rules and relationships that set the standards for the behavior of those within the system.[18] Hierarchy, personalism, and security are the dominant values of this social-bureaucratic system, and the actions of bureaucrats must be judged in the context of these values rather than on the basis of productivity or efficiency, which are secondary rather than primary values. The bureaucracy's primary objective is not to produce services for the general public; rather—according to Siffin—the function of the bureaucracy is to provide personal security, to secure personal status, and to establish the guidelines for reciprocal patron-client arrangements. Thus the system is concerned primarily with its own officials, but in fulfilling its self-serving functions it necessarily relates to the general populace. The secondary functions of resource procurement, allocation, and utilization make sense only when they are seen in light of the values of the Thai social system.

Legislative Branch   The legislature has never been a politically powerful branch of the national government. On the contrary, the legislative branch has regularly been used to enhance the power of the executive. The resources available to the legislative branch have been minimal, and hence legislators have had to rely on the executive branch for favors. The executive's control of the legislature has come about partially through the government's power to appoint half of the legislative body and partially because of the fact that the representatives hold office only by the sufferance of the army. Also, the ever present threat of a coup has prevented legislators from performing their constitutional duties. When the legislature has attempted to perform its proper functions, as in 1971, it has been disbanded by the army.

Elections and Political Parties.   In a western framework of analysis, elections provide the populace with both the opportunity to make their views known to the decision-makers and to change the government if this is deemed desirable. Parties aggregate the demands of the people by synthesizing diverse desires into issues that are presented to the government. Also, representatives in most Western political systems provide an integral link between the rulers and the ruled as they process the citizenry's demands and provide their constituents with information, services, and resources. But the Thai notion of elections is

18. William J. Siffin, *The Thai Bureaucracy: Institutional Change and Development* (Honolulu, Hawaii: East-West Center Press, 1966), p. 160.

in sharp contrast to, say, the American idea that elections are held essentially for providing the opportunity to make changes in the government. In Thailand, elections are held when the ruling groups become convinced that elections will enhance their power.

Although elections are not held for the purpose of expressing —or finding out—the views of the citizenry and then acting on the information, national elections have played an important integrating role. During the 1969 National Assembly elections, for example, many villagers were told about an environment far different from that of their self-contained villages. District officials, National Assembly candidates, commune leaders, village headmen, village elites, school teachers, and ordinary citizens interacted in a common election-time phenomenon. If only for a brief moment in the election booth, almost 50 percent of the adult Thai villagers made a positive act that transcended their daily and routine activities. The Thai villager has had few such opportunities.

Thai political parties have had the most rudimentary organization, almost devoid of programs or issues. Party lines are not based on ideologies but, rather, on the personalities and aspirations of political leaders. The parties' lack of revelancy in Thai politics is suggested by the fact that since the 1932 coup d'etat political parties have been banned for a longer period compared to the years they were permitted to exist. Even when political parties have been allowed, they have acted essentially as a vehicle for a particular leader and his close associates. A further indication of party impotence is the fact that legislators of one party easily shift to other parties when their interests are better served. In 1969, after the elections for the National Assembly, the government party coopted a large group of independent and opposition party legislators.

The governing United Thai People's Party, has traditionally had considerable advantage over opposition parties in recruiting members because the ruling group has had control of the state machinery and patronage appointménts. Supporters of the party could be promised hundreds of bureaucratic and political positions. In addition, the government has controlled the distribution of a wide array of resources to various groups. Because of extensive ties with the business community, government leaders have been able to provide opportunities to party members for corporation directorships, or merely for useful contacts, and the government party has generally been able to give its candidates considerable financial help during campaigns. Depending on its candidates' personal affluence, the government party gave each candidate $250 to $5,000 for campaign expenses in the 1969 elections.

Pro-government candidates have also enjoyed the support of village and district officials. Indeed, in 1969 prime minister Thanom urged all civil servants to support the government party. And although the election law stipulated that all government officials must remain neutral during the election, many attempted to wield their influence for certain candidates. Thus, with 49 percent of Thailand's 14,280,180 eligible voters casting ballots for representatives in the National Assembly, and with a plurality choosing the government party, the 1969 election exemplified the Thai view that the primary purpose of an election is the perpetuation of the regime in power.

Because the elections were relatively honest, prime minister Thanom's government was able to undercut much of the criticism of opposition forces. It would be a mistake, however, to view the election as an indication of public support for either the party or governmental policies. Political ideologies were not significant in determining party affiliation or campaign practices. In general, the personality of candidates was much more important than their party affiliation.

The Political Elite

The elite in Thailand's national politics are top-level bureaucrats, high-ranking military officers, the royalty, distinguished journalists, directors of large business corporations, intellectuals, and politicians with mass constituencies. Indeed, the formally installed government elite comprises a very high percentage of the available elite.

In the Thai political system, the arena of politics is within the government itself, with little or no competition for political power emanating from outside the bureaucratic institutions. Even national-level politics is confined to groups within the administrative structure. The effect of this form of oligarchy is to reduce the number of persons engaged in politics and to narrow the range or scope of political activity. Yet top-level politics in Thailand, as in more diffused systems, is characterized by competition and conflict, cleavage and manipulation. Power struggles are at the heart of national-level politics as groups compete for what there is to get: power, wealth, position, and perquisites.

To maximize the chances of achieving these ends, patron-client groupings amalgamate into what are usually referred to as cliques, and the workings of these factional groups are probably best understood in the context of patron-client relationships. The society's sharp status differentiations and lack of more institutionalized groups are reflected within the cliques, which—like their smaller subunits, the patron-client groupings—are held together by bonds of personal loyalty and reciprocity, so that the alliances are mutually advantageous.

National-level politics is primarily concerned with the cliques' competition for additional power and for all that accompanies the possession of power. Invariably, the leader (patron) of a clique is a person who has power, or access to power, or potential power. The members (clients) of a clique represent constituencies (the army, Chinese business interests, the police, etc.) that are sufficiently strong and well organized to ensure perpetuation of their leaders' and their own positions. Each member of a clique is a patron to his subordinates, so that reciprocity works both upward and downward.

Once in power, and therefore concerned with maintaining its power, a clique must dispense the prerogatives of office in a judicious manner, and since the clique's leaders are also the highest governmental officials, the political and the administrative elites are one and the same. Thus personal loyalty and other ascriptive criteria are more highly rewarded than administrative know-how. As a minister of state, a clique leader uses the resources of his ministry to strengthen his clique and to ensure the perpetuation of his position and power. One way to judge the power of a top official who is a member of the ruling clique is to measure, over time, the budget allocations for his ministry or department. The more money he receives, the more he is able to distribute to his clients.

Thus, the seizure of power in 1971 by prime minister Thanom and his clique resulted largely from the refusal of parliament to meet the budgetary requests of the ruling group. This refusal, or limitation, was perceived as an intolerable restriction on the power holders, and so the dominant clique, led by the prime minister, disbanded parliament and approved its own budget. The clique's outrage was caused not only by the budgetary restrictions but also by the fact that the restrictions were imposed by an extra-bureaucratic body.

The cabinet represents the highest level of political activity because its ministers have greatest access to the government's resources and are closely affiliated with the prime minister. Generally, therefore, cabinet members include members of the dominant clique. Those who are closest to the prime minister usually head the ministries of Interior and Defense. Ministers who are not members of the ruling clique may be formerly high officials who gave indirect support to the ruling group.

Cabinet members must cater to major constituencies to retain their position. They must support their patrons, who are usually the prime minister and his associates; they must serve the interests of their particular ministry; and they must provide their clientele with sufficient favors so as to retain their loyalty. The overlapping and at times conflicting claims of these constituencies require great adroitness on the part of cabinet ministers.

The Military

In the struggle for power, wealth, and status the military has been particularly successful. Indeed, since the overthrow of the absolute monarchy the military has dominated the office of prime minister for all but three years. This is not to say, however, that the Thai army has militarized the political system but, rather, that the military has held the key political positions and thus has been "bureaucratized" by the political system.

The military leaders, like the would-be kings in Thai history, have seized power in the absence of institutionalized norms of succession. And even during the constitutional period, military leaders have used the coup d'état to seize power from both civilian and military regimes. The coup, which is the ideal mechanism for politically ambitious military groups, has become the standard means by which Thai governments change. Indeed, several constitutions have deemed the coup d'etat a legitimate and sanctioned means for establishing new governments.

Thailand is a superb example of a nation with the proper preconditions for a coup d'état. Since high political posts are held by only a very few people and since governmental participation is concentrated in the bureaucracy, it is possible to dominate the entire political system merely by controlling the bureaucratic structure. And, since extra-bureaucratic institutions have been inconsequential, they are easily bypassed. In addition, the fact that Bangkok is the nation's only major city considerably eases the logistical problems in carrying out a coup. Finally, Thailand has been independent of foreign influence that opposes the means or the results of coups d'état. Since World War II, the United States has had pervasive influence in Thailand but has not opposed the leaders of coups, principally because the latter have consistently proclaimed anti-communist and pro-American sentiments.

The military is the best organized group in the kingdom, and in terms of discipline and hierarchy has no rival. Thus, the national emphasis on hierarchy, deference, and status is congruent with the military's organization, which is based on superior-subordinate relationships. In addition, the army can count on the loyalty and obedience of its followers to a much greater extent than can ad hoc groups of politicians. The record of civilian rule during the constitutional period has been neither lengthy nor illustrious. By decrying civilian ineptness, corruption, and malfeasance, and by proclaiming the threat of communist-led insurgency and the inability of civilian regimes to cope with the threat, the military leaders have been able to persuade the bureaucratic polity that they can do a better job of governing the nation. Accordingly, the coups have been remarkably free of violence.

Although they have involved the movement of troops and the strategic placement of weaponry, and thus the threat of force, the coups have been almost totally bloodless.

The success of the military has also been due to its capacity to meet the demands of the elite. Since 1932 the military regimes have allocated the nation's meager resources—which have recently been supplemented by massive United States aid—in such a way as not to alienate any potential opposition group. In some instances, however, the military has been forced to rely on heavy-handed tactics to stay in power, and the fact that the military controls the weaponry of the nation has ensured its monopoly of the use of force. The discrimination against the Chinese minority, the southern Muslims, and the northern hill people are examples of such heavy-handedness.

Contemporary Politics

The promulgation of Thailand's eighth constitution, in 1968, and the national elections in February 1969 for the House of Representatives did not substantially change the bureaucratic-elitist system of government. As in the past, the new constitution served the regime in power by strengthening its position. Indeed, the political scene after the elections provides abundant material for viewing Thai politics as a struggle among various factions for power, wealth, and status. The politics of factionalism was manifested within the cabinet, within the pro-government United Thai People's Party (UTPP), within the opposition parties, led by the Democrats, and within the National Assembly. From the time of the elections to the military seizure of power in 1971, a series of controversial issues provided the focus for factional splits, although substance was less at issue than the opportunity they provided for enhancing the political position of the various competing groups.

The factional infighting among members of the UTPP centered on a struggle for the scarce resources of money and position. A group of Government Party members who had been elected to the lower house of the bicameral National Assembly demanded that large sums of money be spent in their provincial constituencies in return for their support of government policies. The clientele of prime minister Thanom, which fell into disarray as he came closer to retirement age, began moving toward leaders who appeared to be in the ascendancy. Cabinet members vied among themselves for a larger share of the budget. In 1971 factionalism continued to be the dominant trend of Thai politics, until the ruling elite was threatened by the possibility of losing its power to competing groups. To prevent this, Generals Thanom and Prapat, in a coup against their own government, seized complete control.

Although factionalism was the dominant variable in the 1971 crisis, there were substantive issues that provided additional impetus for the military's seizure of power. In 1970 and 1971, the National Assembly had delayed approving the government's budget requests. Since 1969, the government had felt hampered by national assemblymen who demanded personal and material gains for themselves at the expense of the military budget. The government also claimed that its economic development program, as well as national security, was endangered by the delays of the recalcitrant legislature. Prime minister Thanom said that if the country was to pursue the constitutional process, the government must be able to act swiftly to cope with internal and external problems, and the delays were felt to exacerbate the precarious economic situation, which featured a negative balance of payments and a growing trade deficit. As the American military investment continued to decrease with the United States' withdrawing its troops from Thailand, thereby adversely affecting Thailand's balance of payments, members of the government warned that the economic problems could be exploited by insurgents.

Another factor that the government claimed was important in the decision to overthrow the constitutional order was the admission of the People's Republic of China to the United Nations. The government's fear of Thailand's indigenous Chinese was expressed by Thanom after he seized power, when he voiced concern about the loyalty of the Chinese. Moreover, the new prominence of China increased Thailand's dismay at the withdrawal of United States troops from Southeast Asia. Thanom argued that the new foreign policy considerations would precipitate uncertainties that only a strong, centralized government could cope with.

The seizure of power by Thanom, against his own constitutional government, was bloodless, swift, and without apparent opposition, although the King, instead of issuing a legal royal pardon to the coup leaders as he had in previous coups, simply issued a proclamation requesting support for the new regime. The 1972 fiscal budget was immediately promulgated with the military's share larger than that agreed to by the House budget committee. In an action intended to deter would-be-criminals, summary executions of criminals by a government execution squad were carried out. Thai newspapers reported on the rapid decrease in crime throughout the nation following the overthrow.

The new leaders decided to merge the twin cities of Bangkok and Thonburi into the "Greater Bangkok Municipality" and began to focus attention on urban rather than rural problems. During the legislative period from 1969-1971, the rural areas had become of paramount interest, but after the coup the government's attention shifted to problems of urban pollution, slums, foreign investment, crime in the streets, and urban planning. The new regime did not, however, move swiftly to legitimize its status through constitutional means. An "interim" constitution was not promulgated until December, 1972, more than a year after the coup.

The Revolutionary Party transformed itself into the National Executive Council (NEC), with Field Marshall Thanom as the chairman. Thanom, like most prime ministers before him, had his major base of power in the military. His networks of clientele arose out of the military bureaucracy. Thanom, who was born on August 11, 1911, in northern Thailand, received his higher education at the Military Academy and the National Defense College. After graduating from the academy in 1930, he rose quickly through the military ranks, first as a teacher at the Academy and then as a field officer. By the time of his first elevation to the premiership, Marshall Thanom was commander of the key First Army Corps, a position of great power, with control of the vital areas around Bangkok.

Following Marshall Sarit's seizure of power in 1958, Thanom served for nine months as prime minister and minister of defense while Sarit was in the United States receiving medical treatment, and later that year was promoted to full general. When Sarit seized power in October 1958, Thanom assumed his old position of deputy prime minister, and succeeded Sarit as prime minister in 1963, when Sarit died. He was then, concurrently, supreme commander of the Thai armed forces.

In the official chain of command, army general Prapat Charusathiara ranked second but was regarded as the strong man of the regime. Prapat was considered by many officials in Thailand to be a corrupt and ruthless leader, and consequently his elevation to the position of prime minister would have been met with much dismay. A number of factors probably contributed to General Prapat's reluctance to bid for the top position, but most important was that he was able to excercise almost unlimited power in his number-two position. In fact, General Prapat appeared to make the crucial decisions, while Thanom, whose son is married to Prapat's daughter, presented the image of a capable and honest leader to the Thais and to the world.

Under the 1972 constitution, Marshall Thanom retained his positions as Prime Minister and Minister of Defense. In addition, he assumed the foreign affairs portfolio. Deputy Prime Minister and Interior Minister Prapat enhanced his already dominant position by assuming the directorship of the centralized police department. In an extraordinary grant of power, the prime minister could take any steps "appropriate for the purpose of preventing, repressing or suppressing actions which jeopardize the national security, or the Throne, or the economy of the country, or the national administration, or which subvert or threaten law and order or the good public morals or which damage the health of the society."[19] Moreover, the legislature's functions were closely circumscribed to insure executive dominance in all matters. The new "legislative body" of 299 National Assembly members was handpicked by the regime in power. Thanom appointed 200 military officers and 99 civilians.

The fall of the Thanom-Prapat government in October 1973 followed massive street demonstrations by students demanding an end to repression, corruption, and military rule. The demonstrations were unprecedented in scope and intensity and resulted in the deaths of about sixty-five persons when the police and soldiers fired into the crowds. The new Premier, Sanya Thammasak, promised a return to constitutional rule and civilian dominance.

The Politics of Change

Thailand is at present undergoing dramatic and far-reaching changes, such as universal and secular education and an increase in the number of university graduates, which is causing the new generation to have higher expectations than their parents. To meet these expectations, the government must develop the necessary institutions and amenities. Thus far, however, the Thai elite has not created the extra-bureaucratic institutions that can absorb the new, educated generation; instead, it has relied on the expansion of the lower levels of the bureaucracy to meet this need. Thus the lack of adequate long-term planning has resulted in a potentially volatile group of frustrated and unemployed citizens.

The spread of communication media into even the most remote areas of the nation has introduced a whole new world to people whose horizons at one time stopped at their village boundaries. As roads are built, transportation to and from a village suddenly becomes easy instead of difficult. Commerce follows quickly thereafter, and new market centers are built. However, the new opportunities can be frustrating for farmers who have no surplus crops to transport or sell. Thus far, only a small percentage of Thai villagers can afford to diversify their crops and join the central government-sponsored irrigation associations and farmers' groups that supply the fertilizer and capital that, in turn, make surplus crops possible. At present, the immediate gains of group action have gone to the small numbers of already well-situated rural elites.

Another challenge to the political system is rapid urbanization. Even provincial towns are experiencing a high rate of population

19. Constitution of the Kingdom of Thailand, December 15, 1972, Article 17. Translated in the Bangkok Post, December 17, 1972.

growth, but the most extraordinary growth rate is in Bangkok, which, like many other big cities around the globe, has been virtually ungovernable and a center of administrative corruption and chaos.

Among the northern hill peoples, the Muslims in the southern provinces, and the poverty-stricken Northeasterners, terrorist activity and insurgency has increased steadily since the early 1960s. Yet the number of persons who are either directly or indirectly involved in insurrection is only several thousand at most—a miniscule percentage of the Thai people. Thus far, the attempts to turn Thai citizens against their government and have them espouse the ideology of wars of "national liberation" have failed. There are many reasons for this failure, but the most important reason is the fundamental satisfaction—at all levels of society—with the status quo. However, as modernization is thrust upon the kingdom and expectations rise faster than the government's ability to meet them, Thailand's traditional stability may be jeopardized. If this should happen, insurrection may no longer be confined to the minorities; it may become a challenge to the larger society.

Thailand must also cope with a grave foreign-policy problem—her relationship with the United States. Since the end of World War II the United States and Thailand have been closely allied, and the Thai-American alliance has been continually strengthened by a series of mutual commitments: the Economic and Technical Cooperation Agreement and Military Assistance Treaty in 1950, the Southeast Asia Collective Defense Treaty in 1954, the Rusk-Thanat Bilateral Assistance Agreement in 1962, and the secret Military Contingency Plan in 1965. President Johnson's decision for large-scale intervention in Vietnam and his subsequent decisions to station 48,000 American troops and to build air force bases in Thailand were regarded by the Thai government as tangible proof that the United States' commitment was unconditional.

Later, however, because of the disengagement of the United States from Southeast Asia, the Nixon Doctrine that Asian wars are to be fought by Asians, and the rapprochement between the People's Republic of China and the United States, Thailand's leaders have begun to reshape their foreign policy and to encourage a revival of nationalism, which has taken the form of non-militant anti-Americanism. Although the United States has extended well over $1 billion in economic and military aid to Thailand since 1951, the Thais are now compelled to reassess the reliability of their Western ally both in terms of national security and economic support. In the past, the Thais have shown great flexibility in their foreign relations, and there is every reason to believe that they will adapt themselves to the new foreign-policy imperatives. Nevertheless, the adaptation may require fundamental changes in the national government's basic assumptions and policies, and these changes represent still another challenge to the political system.

Thailand's political system must also cope with the continual struggle of the elite to gain or to perpetuate themselves in positions of power. Although the pattern of clique politics is inherently instable, it is deeply rooted in Thai history. Governments will continue to change by means of coups d'état as long as personalities have more political importance than parties, ideologies, and institutions. The military will always face challenges from their fellow soldiers, who will want to install themselves in the seats of power. And the new class of young, westernized, highly educated civilians—some unemployed and some in the bureaucracy—will continue to challenge military rule.

As long as extra-bureaucratic institutions do not flourish and power remains in the hands of a small military elite, political stability will be tenuous. Political instability, in turn, may severely shake the bureaucratic foundation that has provided continuity to the Thai political system for so many years.

In the past, when it has been confronted with major strains, Thailand's political system has managed to cope by resorting to judicious adaptations, compromise, and generally conservative policies that have been directed by adroit leaders. Such flexibility may no longer be possible as the forces of change bear inexorably upon the kingdom.

Selected Readings

Chakrabongse, Prince Chula. *Lords of Life: The Paternal Monarchy of Bangkok, 1782-1932*. New York: Taplinger, 1960.

Coast, John. *Some Aspects of Siamese Politics*. New York: Institute of Pacific Relations, 1953.

Darling, Frank C. *Thailand and the United States*. Washington: Public Affairs Press, 1965.

deYoung, John E. *Village Life in Modern Thailand*. Berkeley and Los Angeles: University of California Press, 1958.

Hanks, Lucien M., Jr. "Merit and Power in the Thai Social Order," *American Anthropologist* (December 1962): 1247-1261.

Ingram, James C. *Economic Change in Thailand since 1850* (rev. ed.). Stanford: Stanford University Press, 1971.

Kaufman, Howard K. *Bangkhuad: A Community Study in Thailand*. New York: J.J. Augustin, for the Association of Asian Studies, 1960.

Keyes, Charles F. *Isan: Regionalism in Northern Thailand*. Ithaca: Cornell University, Southeast Asia Program, Data Paper No. 65, 1967.

Landon, Kenneth Perry. *Siam in Transition*. Shanghai: Kelly and Walsh, 1939.

Moerman, Michael. *Agricultural Change and Peasant Choice in a Thai Village*. Berkeley: University of California Press, 1968.

Neher, Clark D. *Rural Thai Government: The Politics of the Budgetary Process*. DeKalb: Center for Southeast Asian Studies, Northern Illinois University, 1970.

Noranitipandungkarn, Chakrit. *Elites, Power Structure and Politics in Thai Communities*. Bangkok: Research Center, National Institute of Development Administration, 1970.

Phillips, Herbert P. *Thai Peasant Personality: The Patterning of Interpersonal Behavior in the Village of Bang Chan*. Berkeley and Los Angeles: University of California, 1965.

Rabibhadana, Akin. *The Organization of Thai Society in the Early Bangkok Period, 1782-1783*. Ithaca: Cornell University, Southeast Asia Program, Data Paper No. 74, 1969.

Riggs, Fred W. *Thailand: The Modernization of a Bureaucratic Polity*. Honolulu: East-West Center Press, 1966.

Siffin, William J. *The Thai Bureaucracy: Institutional Change and Development*. Honolulu: East-West Center Press, 1966.

Silcock, T. H. *The Economic Development of Thai Agriculture*. Ithaca: Cornell University Press, 1970.

_____.*Thailand: Social and Economic Studies in Development.* Canberra: Australian National University, in association with Duke University Press, Durham, North Carolina, 1967.

Skinner, William G. *Chinese Society in Thailand: An Analytical History.* Ithaca: Cornell University Press, 1957.

_____. *Leadership and Power in the Chinese Community in Thailand.* Ithaca: Cornell University Press, 1958.

Thompson, Virginia. *Thailand, the New Siam.* New York: Macmillan, 1941.

Vella, Walter F. *The Impact of the West on Government in Thailand.* Berkeley and Los Angeles: University of California Press, 1955.

Wales, H. G. Quaritch. *Ancient Siamese Government and Administration.* London: Bernard Quaritch, 1934. Reissued, New York: Paragon Book Reprint, 1956.

Wilson, David A. "The Military in Thai Politics." In *The Role of the Military in Underdeveloped Countries,* edited by John J. Johnson, Princeton: Princeton University Press, 1962, pp. 253-75.

_____. *Politics in Thailand.* Ithaca: Cornell University Press, 1962.

_____. *The United States and the Future of Thailand.* New York: Praeger, 1970.

Wit, Daniel. *Thailand Another Vietnam?* New York: Charles Scribner's Sons, 1968.

Wyatt, David K. *The Politics or Reform in Thailand: Education in the Reign of King Chulalongkorn.* New Haven and London: Yale University Press, 1969.

6   Indonesia

Allan A. Samson*

The cultural and geographical diversity of Indonesia have been important factors in determining its pattern of political and economic development. An area comprised of 3,000 widely-dispersed islands containing numerous languages, ethnic groups, and diverse religious traditions, Indonesia has been independent since 1945. While centuries of inter-island communication, cultural contact, and long-distance trade have established patterns of commonality not otherwise indicated by the area's diversity, it was the colonial experience which created the mortar of national consciousness. Indonesian nationalism was, in a very basic sense, the product of opposition to Dutch colonial rule. The development of a common sense of national unity was a response to colonial domination rather than a logical outcome of inter-island trade and cultural contacts.

The rise of the nationalist movement in Indonesia was channeled through varied political, religious, and social forces. Western-educated intellectuals opposed colonialism for its exploitative quality, its implied denial of the dignity of all men. Muslims opposed the domination of a Christian colonial elite over an Islamic population. Indigenous small businessmen opposed the advantages given to European and Chinese entrepreneurs in commerce and manufacturing. With the winning of independence, however, disparate local, regional, and religious sentiments reasserted their sway and competed with na-

*This article is based upon two previous articles I have written: "Indonesia 1972: The Solidification of Military Control," *Asian Survey* 14, 2 (February 1973): 127-139; "Indonesia 1973: A Climate of Concern," *Asian Survey* 14, 2 (February 1974): 157-165.

tionalism as prime foci of indentification and commitment. In this sense, the national motto of Indonesia, *Bhinneka Tunggal Ika* (Unity in Diversity), is an appropriate term to characterize the reality of diverse linguistic, cultural and religious groups in search of an overarching national identity.

Dutch colonial rule was abruptly ended in 1942 by the decisive victory of Japanese forces. Their victory demonstrated to many Indonesians that Asians were capable of defeating the European powers and, were thus, also able to govern themselves. The Japanese occupying administration, though harsh, encouraged nationalist sentiment on the part of Indonesians, going so far as to promise independence within the framework of a Japanese-sponsored "Greater East Asia Co-Prosperity Sphere." It was widely recognized that Japanese intentions were to train Indonesians for numerous administrative positions in order to free Japanese forces for work deemed more vital to the war effort. Nonetheless, thousands of Indonesians were given positions of responsibility to which they could never have aspired under colonial rule. By the end of the war a corps of administrative and military talent existed which turned out to be instrumental for success in the revolutionary struggle.

On August 17, 1945, three days after Japan officially surrendered, Indonesian independence was proclaimed by Sukarno, soon-to-become the first President of the Republic of Indonesia. Dutch forces returned in the wake of the Allied victory and the revolutionary period, which was to last until December 1949, commenced. Intermittant military struggle and negotiations characterized this period. It was a time of remarkable bravery and achievement and continues to evoke a sense of idealism among all Indonesians.[1]

Politics in Indonesia does not lend itself easily to categorization. To speak of the existence of a developmental pattern may confuse rather than elucidate. In recent years, Indonesian politics has ranged from the revolutionary romanticism characteristic of the Sukarno era to the military predominance of the Suharto administration. During the former period, it was contended that the creation of a sense of national unity through the utilization of emotional appeals was synonymous with political development. It is currently maintained with equal assurance by proponents of the Suharto government that the essence of political development is found in a model of a pragmatic military and a sober bureaucracy jointly striving for socio-economic modernization.

1. In a certain sense it is ironic to hear one-time revolutionaries who have become prosperous and conservative with success continue to reaffirm their revolutionary credentials. As will be noted later in this article, urban students, more than most other groups in Indonesian society, retain the idealism of the *Revolusi* as a guide to action.

In order to consider public policy and the developmental process in contemporary Indonesia, it may be advisable to note briefly the political character of the Sukarno era. From 1950 to 1965, Indonesian politics was dominated by the volatile style and charismatic personality of President Sukarno, whose conceptions, fervor, and revolutionary zeal established the emotional and ideological tenor of the times. He affirmed that national unity could only be achieved through revolutionary momentum. "Come brothers, come sisters," he once exhorted, "Let us become logs to feed the flames of revolution!" Sukarno dominated the field of symbolic activity, envisioning himself as the unifier of all Indonesia, synthesizing the diverse socio-religious traditions by his actions.[2] Gestures and ritual abounded in profusion. First stores were laid and first seeds planted. Medals were conferred and monuments constructed. Numerous symbols were used to evoke patriotic pride, inspire indignation, and create a feeling of national oneness. Sukarno's singular emphasis on symbolic activity and revolutionary zeal resulted in lowered economic and administrative efficiency, as economic tasks were viewed as being of secondary importance to ideological "truth" and political enthusiasm.

The Sukarno era may be divided into two distinct periods, Liberal Democracy (1950-1959) and Guided Democracy (1959-1965). The former period was characterized by the existence of an active parliamentary system composed of numerous, ideologically-based, political parties. Indonesia's first election, held in 1955, reflected an inconclusive division of national political influence in which no single party received as much as one-quarter of the total votes cast. The parliamentary system was hopelessly paralyzed between secular, Islamic and communist parties—all seeking their divergent political interests. Succeeding administrations floundered over issues of religion, ideology, regionalism, centralized governmental control and economic policy. By 1959, in the wake of an anti-government regional revolt and acrimonious ideological debates in the Constituent Assembly, the parliamentary system was thoroughly discredited. One year later, with the support of the army, Sukarno dissolved Parliament and established an appointed Parliament with members drawn from several of the existing parties and functional groups thus beginning the period of Guided Democracy.

With the establishment of Guided Democracy, Indonesia's parliamentary system was thoroughly emasculated. All the political parties, with the exception of the PKI (Indonesian Communist Party), were essentially circumscribed and came to depend directly on Sukarno for

2. See Hubert Feith, "Dynamics of Guided Democracy," in *Indonesia*, edited by Ruth McVey (New Haven, Conn.: HRAFP) 1964, pp. 309-409.

maintenance of the bureaucratic positions and economic sinecures to which they had grown accustomed. Their actual influence, however, was drastically curtailed. Only the PKI, which by the end of the 1950s had become the third largest communist party in the world, maintained its autonomy and expanded its influence.

The PKI was one of the two major institutional components of the Guided Democracy period. The other was the Indonesian military, which was strongly anti-communist, but opposed to the return of a parliamentary system, whose ineffectuality, it contended, was responsible for Indonesia's economic and political instability. A very large portion of the military regarded Sukarno with wariness. It was acknowledged, however, that only Sukarno could inspire broad popular support throughout Indonesia. Both the military and the PKI hated and feared each other, but preferred Sukarno to the outbreak of premature strife. This political situation has been characterized as triangular in nature, with the military and the PKI occupying the bases of the triangle, and Sukarno at the apex occupying the center of balance. It was, however, not so much a tripolar balance of a power situation as it was a duumvirate, with Sukarno and the military possessing authority in separate governmental and administrative spheres. The PKI, while continually expanding its base of popular support, possessed neither effective force nor official authority, but depended instead upon Sukarno for "protection" against the military. Sukarno himself possessed no institutional power base, but utilized his strategic position vis-à-vis the military and PKI to maintain his influence.

The situation was at best unstable. By 1964 it had become apparent to many observers that Sukarno clearly favored the PKI, which he probably considered the appropriate heir to his revolutionary aspirations.[3] His options were limited, however, as the military maintained an effective preponderence of force. Throughout 1964 and much of 1965, rumors of Sukarno's ill-health fueled fears of violence. The PKI suspected that the military would move to crush it at the first sign of Sukarno's incapacity, while the military feared the continued expansion of the PKI could only result in civil war. The stage was thus set for the unsuccessful coup of October 1, 1965, led by elements of the PKI, and the military-civilian anti-communist alliance that followed it, resulting in the decimation of the PKI and the slaughter of several hundred thousand persons.

Indonesia's "New Order," existent since the decimation of the PKI in 1966 and the consolidation of President Suharto's power, has been characterized by military-civilian alliances of varying compositions.

3. Herbert Feith, "President Soekarno, the Army and the Communists: the Triangle Changes Shape," *Asian Survey* 4,8 (August 1964):969-980.)

Students, religious groups, civil servants and intellectuals have all, at one time or another during this period, supported the paramount political role of the Armed Forces of the Republic of Indonesia also known as ABRI. The alliance was initially predicated upon a commonly held antipathy to the PKI; later, it came to be based upon ABRI's monopoly of force and the estimation that no other force in society was capable of maintaining security and providing economic stability. ABRI's political preeminence was aided by its self-perceived role as guardian of national unity—above the squabble for petty political advantage, regional aggrandizement and religious bickering. ABRI's legitimacy was also buttressed by its image as a modernizing force, capable of bringing Indonesia back from the nadir of chaos and inflationary excesses to the threshold of self-sustaining economic growth. This received expression in an "army-administrator-economist" managing elite, with the army clearly occupying the position of senior partner. By 1971, inflation had been brought under control, agricultural productivity showed significant improvement, and the confidence of foreign investors and aid-givers was apparent. Public policy was determined by the military power-holders of the New Order and their economist advisors. It was essentially an elitist administrative configuration, entailing only a peripheral level of popular participation. The governing elite perceived the appropriate role of political participation to be that of passive approval or legitimization through controlled symbolic acts.

Table VI.1

Indonesian Parliamentary Election Of 1971

	Number of votes won	Percent of votes won	Seats won
Golkar	34,348,673	62.80	227
Nahdatul Ulama	10,213,650	18.67	58
PNI	3,793,266	6.94	20
Parmusi	2,930,746	5.36	24
PSII	1,308,237	2.39	10
Parkindo	733,359	1.34	7
Partai Katolik	603,740	1.10	3
PERTI	381,309	0.70	2
IPKI	338,403	0.62	—
Murba	48,126	0.09	—

The General Election of July 3, 1971 (shown in Table 1), was intended to be just such an act of symbolic legitimization. A decisive victory was achieved by *Sekber Golkar* (Joint Secretariat of Functional

Groups)—the government sponsored "non-party"—which received 62.8 percent of the votes cast. Golkar's message emphasized *modernisasi* and *pembangunan* (development), while its candidates contrasted its pragmatism with what they termed the ideological bankruptcy of the political parties. The Golkar campaign was aided by a military and civilian bureaucratic effort from the national to the village level—a process which opened it to charges of coercion and "steamroller" tactics. Whatever the admixture of coercion and voluntary support, the proportion of Golkar's victory was unarguable and was interpreted as providing electoral legitimacy to the physical fact of military predominance. Conversely, the already small influence of the political parties was even further limited.

What was not known was the post-electoral character of Golkar and, by extension, the dimensions of future military involvement in Indonesian politics. Would Golkar be an autonomous political institution or would it merely be an electoral vehicle for ABRI's interests? Would it be a loose assembly of factions and cliques or a unitary mobilizing party on the order of the Mexican and Turkish models? The events of the early 1970s have given some indication of Golkar's character and military intentions.

The Dimensions of Political Power

The year 1972 began a direct confrontation between students and the government over the plans of a government-supported private foundation, *Yayasan Harapan Kita* (Institute of Our Hope), to construct a "Miniature Indonesia" complex, a project envisaged as an Indonesian Disneyland, Its supporters maintained it would spur tourism and bring in foreign exchange. Opponents, many of whom were students, contended that it was extravagant, kept funds from critical economic projects, and was inappropriately headed by the President's wife. The admixture of a private project headed by the President's wife and receiving governmental support was opposed by many who felt such a situation to be of questionable probity. Opposition to the "Mini Project" was expressed through demonstrations and student-sponsored discussion groups. In a stern speech Suharto warned the demonstrators that they were disturbing public order and that he would have no hesitation to invoke emergency powers to ban the demonstrations and dissolve the groups involved. Shortly thereafter, *Kopkamtib* (The Operational Command for the Restoration of Security and Order), did ban public demonstrations and detained and interrogated several outspoken critics of the "Mini Project."

Lieutenant General Sumitro, deputy head of Kopkamtib, stated that opposition to governmental policies was allowable, but should be carried out through appropriate channels, such as the press, the DPR (Parliament), and the university community. This underscored the rather ambiguous capacity of ABRI to tolerate criticism. Limited criticism of policies was allowable so long as it was not sustained and did not focus on prominent ABRI or governmental figures. The problem of corruption, for example, could be criticized in a general manner by the press, but those newspapers which zealously attempted to focus public scrutiny on the acquisitive activities of influential military figures were tacitly warned to desist. The pro-governmental composition of Parliament made it a rather unlikely source of criticism, given the fact that the government controlled 336 out of 460 seats. It was clear that ABRI did not relish being the recipient of public scrutiny. Such scrutiny, it was feared, could lead to a reopening of the issue of military corruption and to public discussion of the appropriateness of ABRI's *dwi-funksi* (dual function—military and civilian functions). It was evident that Suharto and ABRI would countenance no untoward criticism of military predominance or allow a level of popular participation that was perceived as threatening to the established distribution of power. What was desired was a perpetuation of the army-economist-managing elite model, free from broad external accountability.

The early 1970s has seen a further diminution of the already limited influence of Indonesia's political party system. Before the 1971 election, ABRI's policy had been to circumscribe party autonomy by manipulation and obstruction. In this manner, the modernist Islamic *Partai Muslimin Indonesia (Parmusi)* and the nationalist PNI (Indonesian Nationalist Party) were "purified" of obstructive leadership by the withholding of "clearance" from Parmusi's Executive Board and *de facto* military intervention at PNI's 1970 Congress. Only the traditionalist Islamic party, *Nahdatul Ulama* (NU) was considered by ABRI to be a "constant factor," content to hold minor cabinet seats in exchange for its acquiescence to secular control of government.

After the election the parties could no longer be considered obstacles, let alone potential rivals, of ABRI. Parmusi, which at one time hoped to identify itself as the successor to the Islamic modernist party, *Masjumi* (dissolved by Sukarno in 1960 and not allowed to reorganize by Suharto), received 5.4 percent of the vote. Since its establishment in 1968, Parmusi's internal affairs were obstructed and manipulated by ABRI to such an extent that its autonomy remained in serious question. Parmusi's poor electoral showing was a reflection of this fact.[4] Many of the party's potential supporters severely disapproved of the party's government-appointed leadership and, rather than support

4. See my "Army and Islam in Indonesia," *Pacific Affairs* 14,4 (Winter, 1971-72): 545-565.

what they perceived as shabby opportunism, voted instead for NU—or even Golkar, which at least could not be accused of religious hypocrisy.

The biggest loser in the election was PNI. It was generally perceived as representing the interests of the *pamong praja*, the Javanese civil service. From its showing of 22.3 percent of the votes in the 1955 election, PNI was reduced to 6.9 percent in the 1971 election. The pamong praja was dragooned into the service of Golkar, and PNI was overwhelmed. It was a badly divided party. PNI's problem was serious; it had always been "protected" by authority—from association with Sukarno to its control of the pamong praja. With the establishment of Golkar its primary base of support was cut away and it was floundering.

The only party to maintain its base of support was NU, which received 18.7 percent of the vote. NU's strength lay among the traditionalist Muslim villagers of East and Central Java, for whom Islam was a total way of life. Religious faith was transformed into political support through the efforts of rural *kiyais* (religious teachers) who legitimized NU's political activities in terms of religious imperatives. Such support, based as it was upon the fervor of religious belief, was less amenable to dissipation through governmental actions. Golkar made an effort to appeal to wavering NU adherents through *Guppi* (Union for the Improvement of Islamic Education), but NU was less affected by "Golkar-ization" than any of the other parties. NU's mass support is overwhelmingly rural, but this has been modified somewhat in recent years by a gradual increase of support in urban areas and among younger members.

The proportion of their electoral defeat fully indicated that the political parties were a negligible force. The newspaper, *Kami*, noted that they had become government-owned "services," adjusting and reacting to the initiatives of ABRI and Golkar.[5] Several Golkar figures felt it incumbent to state that it was not the intention of *Golkar* or ABRI to destroy the political parties. What was desired was a party system neither too large nor too small—large enough to provide a channel for alternate opinions on specific issues, but not large enough to challenge effectively ABRI or Golkar. The irony of this situation was humorously put by Major General Ali Murtopo, who stated that political parties should not be eliminated because Golkar "needed a political party as a sparring partner in the ring."[6]

Throughout 1972 the government encouraged the parties to fuse or federate into two basic parties: one consisting of the nationalist and

5. *Kami,* January 28, 1972.
6. *Pedoman*, September 21, 1972.

Christian parties, the other of the existing Islamic parties. In the face of governmental pressure, but with some reluctance, the Islamic parties announced their intention to federate. While the Islamic parties were united by a common religious affirmation, they were divided by years of theological disputation and divergent political styles. Fusion or federation, many feared, would mean the loss of party identity and personal influence. The nationalist and Christian parties were quicker to establish a framework for federation, though each possessed a separate ideology.

It was Suharto's intention to establish "three flags" to compete in the scheduled 1976 national election. One would consist of Golkar as the party of the government, with the two opposition parties arrayed against it. It was envisioned that neither would present a threat to the preeminence of ABRI and Golkar, but would serve constructively as an issue-oriented loyal opposition, replacing the short-sighted, parochial sentiments which the government felt had characterized the party system.

Pursuant to its intention of reducing the influence of political intermediaries between it and the masses, the government introduced the concept of "floating mass" in which the political parties would not be allowed to operate at the village level except during election campaigns. This proposal was introduced by Golkar spokesmen, who argued that in view of the low educational level of the peasantry it was improper to involve them in national politics at the expense of their immediate concerns. Such a program would create a "floating mass" of politically quiescent villagers, as political organizations would not be allowed to function below the *kabupaten* (district) level. While Golkar officials claimed that the regulations would circumscribe their own freedom of action to the same extent as that of the parties, Golkar's functional groups would continue to operate at the village level and Golkar-supporting local military and civilian authorities would be unrestricted in their own activities. The effect of the concept's implementation would be to further increase the government's power at the expense of the parties.

That Golkar was the vehicle of the government was doubted by no one. What remained less clearly known were the contours of the political forces which comprised Golkar and a consideration of the relationship between Golkar and ABRI. Was Golkar an autonomous, modernizing political institution, or was it little more than a vehicle designed to provide electoral legitimacy to military predominance? Further, was it likely to sustain its concern for modernization, or would it do little more than reflect factional competition within the army? Golkar was initially established in 1964 as a military-dominated conglomerate of functional organizations designed to match the strength of the PKI in the political arena. It continued to exist under the New Order, but was of minor importance until the government decided to utilize it in the scheduled 1971 election. Golkar's 269 components were reorganized into seven KINO (Basic Organizational Units) but real power was divided among three sources: *Hankam* (The Ministry of Defense and Security, strongly influenced by Lt. General Sumitro, acting head of Kopkamtib); the Ministry of Home Affairs, headed by Major General Amir Machmud; and *Opsus* (The Special Operations Agency, headed by Major General Ali Murtopo, a close advisor of President Suharto).[7]

The three exercised different functions in Golkar's electoral effort. Hankam utilized its widespread hierarchy and power from the national to the local level to ensure (and in many instances, coerce) support for Golkar. The Ministry of Home Affairs utilized its administrative network in a similar manner, relying upon patterns of deference which often typified relations between the peasantry and officialdom. Opsus, located in Jakarta, formulated national strategy and Golkar's development and ideological goals. Many Jakarta intellectuals were active in this effort and joined in campaign swings to the Outer Islands and rural areas which quickly became termed the "Golkar safari."

Post-election events brought competition among the three factions, a pattern which already indicates the likely contours of Golkar influence and its relationship with ABRI. Only *Hankam* could be said to possess an autonomous and institutionalized power base. Suharto could, of course, eliminate it or promote individual officers, but Hankam represents institutionalized army interests and priorities. Suharto's power base is in ABRI, and to create a divergence of interests would weaken his own actual influence. The Ministry of Home Affairs is also an institution, but its authority is ultimately dependent upon the President; while it controls the important civil bureaucracy, it cannot compete with Hankam in mobilization of resources of physical power. The Golkar intellectuals possess no institutionalized base of support and also are no match for Hankam. Most of them are dependent upon Ali Murtopo, whose own influence is dependent upon his personal relationship with Suharto.

Early in 1972, public attention focused on what was interpreted as rivalry between Lt. General Sumitro and Major General Murtopo, given semi-public expression in the "Mini Affair."[8] To the extent that

7. R. William Liddle, "Evolution from Above: National Leadership and Local Development in Indonesia," *Journal of Asian Studies* 32,2 (February 1973):287-309.

8. It was said that Lieutenant General Sumitro was sympathetic to the critics of the project, though Kopkamtib ultimately banned demonstrations and arrested leading critics, while Major General Murtopo pressed for the project throughout.

personal rivalry existed, it appeared to be attributable to clashing group interests over influence in Golkar. This was more fully corroborated when the newly-appointed Golkar chairman, Major General Amir Murtono, castigated intellectuals who criticized military influence in Golkar. Murtono's blunt statement left no doubt about ABRI's primacy:

> Assuming *Golkar* is in disarray, there are still government employees and ABRI. If the government employees. . . are in disarray we still have ABRI. Can you imagine ABRI to be in disarray?[9]

Murtono's remarks were interpreted as being directed primarily against the intellectuals in Golkar, for whom Golkar represented a modernizing organization. It is probable that Hankam considered Golkar little more than a vehicle for mass organization and electoral victory. The continued participation of civilian intellectuals in Golkar was desired, but clear primacy was to be held by Hankam.

Another pole of influence in Golkar is KORPRI(Corps of Civil Servants), which was established by General Amir Machmud as the organization to represent all government employees. KORPRI replaced an organization which had been limited to civil servants in the Ministry of Home Affairs. It was stipulated that all government employees must join KORPRI and within the framework of *monoloyalitas* (single loyalty) resign from all other political organizations. This process was described as striving for the *"Panca Sila-*ization" of government employees.[10] This, combined with the implementation of the proposed concept of "floating mass," would have meant that all political-administrative activities in the villages would be monopolized by ABRI and Golkar.

It was a source of speculation throughout 1972 as to whether KORPRI was an independent organization or part of Golkar, and if a part of Golkar, what its relationship with ABRI would be. In this regard the interrelationship between Hankam, KORPRI and Golkar's "intellectuals," as well as so-called "rivalries" among Generals Sumitro, Machmud, and Murtopo—were much discussed. Certainly

---

9. *Kami,* June 2, 1972. Murtono, Assistant for Socio-Political Development in Hankam, had recently been appointed Chairman of Golkar by President Suharto. Brig. General Supardjo of Hankam was appointed Golkar's Secretary General.

10. *Suara Karya,* April 18, 1972. Panca Sila, or Five Principles, is the Indonesian state ideology. It draws upon Indian and Javanese motifs to provide an ideology which can appeal to all. Its five points are "Belief in one God," "Nationalism," "Humanitarianism," "Democracy," and "Social Welfare."

the more independent KORPRI was, the greater its political influence would be within or without Golkar. To control the several million government employees in KORPRI would be to control an important base of influence. Such control, however, was far exceeded by Hankam's authority over the military bureaucracy and its control of physical power. It was the preponderence of this power which clearly relegated Golkar's "intellectuals" and KORPRI'S bureaucrats to junior partner status.

The government's plan to "simplify" Indonesia's political party system was completed in 1973. In the face of sustained governmental pressure throughout 1972, the four Islamic parties (Nahdatul Ulama, Parmusi, PSII, and Perti) fused to form the United Development Party (PPP), on January 5, 1973. The religiously traditionalistic Nahdatul Ulama was the largest of the Islamic parties and received the bulk of leadership positions in the PPP. Idham Chalid, Nahdatul Ulama's Chairman, became head of PPP while H. M. Mintaredja of Partai Muslimin became Vice-Chairman. The four Islamic "component-parties" were then instructed to divest themselves of their political identity and revert back to a more basic socio-religious orientation. Government-sponsored fusion was not popular among the Islamic rank and file. While Islam was established as the raison d'etre of the PPP, long-held differences in theological orientations and political styles placed limitations on the unifying elements of a commonly-held religion. It was conjectured that fusion might also result in a loss of party identity and personal influence. Given the government's determination to fuse the party system, however, opposition would have been ineffectual and perhaps foolhardy. On all matters save those which concerned religion, PPP's central leadership uncritically accepted the government's policies and initiatives. Much of its membership, however, remained critical of the government for its economic and religious policies. Two months after PPP's establishment three of its members who sat in the DPR (Parliament) and were openly critical of governmental policies were recalled by the party's Executive Board —an act which was said to reflect the government's wishes. The recall was criticized as being of questionable legality by many, including former Vice-President Muhammad Hatta, who described the political climate as undergoing a "period of adjustment" in which "democracy has not yet grown."[11]

On January 10, 1973, the Indonesian Democratic Party (PDI) was formed through the fusion of five nationalist parties (PNI, IPKI, *Partai Katolik, Parkindo*, and *Murba).* Stressing its programmatic rather than ideological character, thereby hoping to curry governmental fa-

11. *Kompas*, March 1, 1973.

vor, the PDI nonetheless possessed a weaker base of support than the PPP. For all its internal factionalism and political timidity, the PPP was generally perceived as the political spokesman for millions of Muslims. Neither the PDI nor any of its components could claim to articulate the interests of so large a group. The PDI was in this sense a more artifical entity than the PPP. Many viewed it as "an alliance of minorities," possessing slight cohesion or influence.

Golkar was clearly intended to be the political vehicle through which broad popular support for the government was to be mobilized. What Golkar was, however, remained a question that was continually asked throughout 1973. While there was union, there was no unity. No cohesive bond existed among Golkar's variegated functional organizations that could bring into being an overarching organizational identity. Indeed, this situation was humorously noted by military strongman, Lt. General Sumitro, who referred to Golkar as *blendrang,* leftovers which are rewarmed and served as breakfast the next morning.

To what extent, it was asked, would the military remain the dominant factor within Golkar? Would ABRI eventually be willing to support an independent Golkar? Intellectuals within Golkar maintained influence would indeed gravitate to the intellectual and bureaucratic components of the Golkar coalition. They pointed to the 1973 federation of farmers', laborers', and students' organizations under the Golkar umbrella, in which intellectuals were performing major organizational roles.

The FBSI (Federation of All-Indonesian Workers) was formed on February 20, 1973 and was followed within six months by the establishment of the HKTI (Indonesian Farmers' Association) and the KNPI (National Committee of Indonesian Youth). Their formation was preceeded by a concerted effort to incorporate and subsume most existing labor unions, farmers' associations, and student groups within the new Golkar-supported organizations. If sucessful, its effect would be to clear the field of Indonesia's numerous autonomous functional groups, replacing them with the equivalent of several Golkar-sponsored "company unions." That such federations would provide outlet for the energies of Golkar's "intellectuals" was not doubted; whether they would represent the interests of their constituencies or ABRI was another matter. Noting the first meeting between leaders of the HKTI and President Suharto, one observer ironically commented: "Our farmers have made tremendous progress. All of them were properly dressed, complete with coats and neckties."[12] By the fall of 1973, HKTI and FBSI were successfully consolidated while the KNPI had achieved only partial success in consolidating existing student orga-

12. *Sinar Harapan,* May 21, 1973.

nizations, many of which looked back to recent traditions of independence, idealism, and political activism. This was to be amply demonstrated by the events of late 1973 and early 1974.

The second MPR *(Majlis Perwakilan Rakyat*—Peoples' Deliberative Assembly) met in march, 1973. Held every five years, the MPR was empowered to select Indonesia's president and vicepresident and establish the broad outlines of national direction. It was an important symbolic event. The MPR was composed of 920 members. The government maintained an overwhelming majority with 392 seats allocated to Golkar, 230 to ABRI, 130 to government-supporting regional representatives, 126 to PPP, and 42 to PDI. Extreme caution was exercised by Kopkamtib as the date of the session approached. A "month of quiet" was called for, the dangers of communist subversion were stressed, the gathering of groups was prohibited, theaters were instructed to show no films which depicted violence and cruelty, and (most grievous of indignities) several of Jakarta's red-light districts were forced to close at 6:00 p.m.

The MPR session renominated Suharto as president and supported his personal choice, Sultan Hamengku Buwono IX, for the vice presidency. There was talk among several delegates about the advisability of selecting a non-Javanese as vice-president, but the Sultan was widely respected as a sober, "safe" symbolic figure.

Deliberations in the MPR over the broad outlines of state policy generally proceeded smoothly but encountered some snags over religious issues. Islamic groups had become increasingly apprehensive of governmental support given to *kebatinan,* or Javanese mystical, organizations, while proponents of the major mystical organizations have long urged that kebatinan be officially recognized by the government, along with Islam, Christianity, Buddhism, and Hinduism. The MPR essentially satisfied them by acknowledging the existence of *kepercayaan* (belief) as an appropriate spiritual category. At the insistence of the Islamic faction in the MPR, a clause stressing the importance of religious education was included, but far greater emphasis was placed upon "education which is based upon the philosophy of the Panca Sila State."[13]

13. Islam and Panca Sila have long been considered to be the ideological expressions of dichotomous world views. It was generally maintained that the ascendency of one implied at least partial decline for the other. The Islamic faction in the MPR could have easily been voted down on the clause pertaining to religious education. However, ABRI desired that decisions in the MPR session be reached through consensus, utilizing the traditional concepts of *musyawarah* (mutual discussion) and *mufakat* (unanimous agreement reached through a "sense of the meeting"). It agreed to the

The MPR took no decision pertaining to the concept of "floating mass." This concept, first introduced by Golkar in 1972, was intended as mentioned earlier, to limit the operation of political parties at the village level except during election campaigns, without disturbing the activities of Golkar-affiliated functional organizations. The decision not to act upon it was not a reflection of Golkar's failure; rather it was a realization that the "floating mass" was a redundant issue. Golkar had become so imposing that the unrestrained activities of PPP and PDI at all levels would make little difference.

The formation on April 1, 1973 of Indonesia's second "Development Cabinet" produced few substantive changes from the technological and administrative character of its predecessor. Greatest comment pertained to the transfer of Sumitro Joyohadikusumo from the Ministry of Trade to the Ministry of Research, a change interpreted as a "kick upstairs." Wijoyo Nitisastro, head of Indonesia's planning agency, *Bappenas,* maintained his position as leading economic advisor, being made Minister for Economic, Financial, and Industrial Affairs. Military influence remained predominant. The ABRI Chief of Staff, Gen. Panggabean, became Minister of Defence, replacing President Suharto, while Lt. Gen. Sumitro, considered by many to be second only to Suharto in influence, moved up from acting to full head of Kopkamtib and was chosen as Deputy Commander of ABRI.

The first Golkar National Congress was held in Surabaya in September 1973. Preceeding the Congress, the political activities of the seven KINOs *(Kesatuan Induk Organisasi*—Basic Organizational Units) which comprised Golkar were halted and were integrated directly into the Golkar structure. This, along with the formation of the Golkar-affiliated HKTI, FBSI, and KNPI, was interpreted as an attempt to unify and strengthen Golkar's central leadership structure. Since its substantial victory in the 1972 election, Golkar has been beset by factional rivalries even within the overall context of military primacy. The Surabaya Congress represented an effort at consolidation and unification. Major Gen. Amir Murtono retained his position as Golkar's chairman, while influential positions were also gained by certain civilian figures in the functional groups.

In the wake of the Golkar Congress, a two-tiered question appeared: Was Golkar in the process of becoming an autonomous political in-

clause after the Islamic faction made clear its intention to call for an open and recorded vote. In general, however, Islamic spokesmen were disappointed. Reviewing the proceedings, one cynically commented, "Thanks be to God that religion was still mentioned." See *Tempo,* March 31, 1973, p.9.

stitution, less dependent upon ABRI? If not, then to what extent was ABRI prepared to utilize Golkar in a concerted modernizing effort rather than merely using it as an "umbrella" to mobilize popular support? The latter was somewhat more difficult to come to grips with, for the dwi-funksi (dual function) of ABRI provides conceptual justification for an active military role in developmental programs. However, the roots of solipsism and personal interests in the New Order run deep. At present, politics still remains an intra-bureaucratic affair played out within ABRI, Golkar, and the bureaucracy with the poltical public serving as little more than passive spectators.

Rice and the Economy

The economy of Indonesia is essentially agrarian. Table 2 indicates that while in recent years the contribution of agriculture to the overall economy has been slowly declining, it nontheless continues to constitute the major economic sector. The cultivation of rice has been the primary economic activity throughout the densely populated areas of the Indonesian archipelago for more than two millenia. It has been, and continues to be, an important determinant of social and political organization, at both the village and national levels. Wet-rice cultivation, based upon the necessity of an integrated irrigation network, has called forth an intricate pattern of social organization resulting, as in

Table VI.2

**Gross Domestic Product By Major
Economic Sector
1960-1970 (percent, at 1960 prices)**

	1960	1970
Agriculture	53.9	47.4
Manufacturing	3.7	5.6
Construction	2.0	2.7
Electricity and Gas	0.3	0.5
Transport and Communic.	3.7	3.0
Wholesale/Retail Trade	14.3	17.6
Banking	1.0	1.5
Ownership of Dwellings	2.0	2.0
Public Admin. and Defense	4.5	5.3
Services	6.2	5.4
	100.0	100.0

Sources: Statistical Pocketbook of Indonesia 1970/71 and Economic Indicator, April 1973 (Central Bureau of Statistics) in Dwight King, "Social Development in Indonesia," *Asian Survey* (forthcoming).

Java, in a high degree of centralized governmental control. Wet-rice, or *sawah,* cultivation is most prevalent in Java, where 25 percent of the land is occupied by *sawah* fields. In contrast, only 1 percent of the land in the Outer Islands (e.g., Sumatra, Kalimantan, Sulawesi, etc.) is devoted to sawah culture. Outside Java, swidden, or slash-and-burn, agriculture is the most common form of cultivation.

Overpopulation and a consequent shortage of land is Indonesia's most serious economic problem. The problem is most acute in overpopulated Java, as may be inferred from the data in Table 3.

Table VI.3

Population Of Indonesia By Province and Density, 1971

	Population	Percentage of Indonesian population	Area (square kilometers)	Density per square kilometer
Java + Madura	76,102,486	63.83%	134,703	565
Sumatra	20,812,682	17.45	541,174	38
Kalimantan	5,152,166	4.32	550,848	9
Sulawesi	8,535,164	7.16	227,654	37
Other Islands	8,630,001	7.24	572,708	15

Source: Statistik Indonesia, 1970 & 1971, Biro Pusat Statistik, Djakarta, pp. 24-25.

This situation has resulted in a considerable degree of rural underemployment and extremely low living standards. Millions of impoverished farmers have migrated to Java's large cities, where they hope to better their economic condition but in fact merely add to Indonesia's already vast body of urban unemployed. While migration to one of the relatively underpopulated Outer Islands can relieve much of the population pressure, an effective transmigration program, relocating millions of Javanese migrants, remains prohibitively expensive. Observers have noted that such a situation presents a potentially serious threat to future political stability.

Indonesia's economic potential is great. Oil, tin, sulphur, bauxite, lumber, copper, rubber, and nickel are in abundant supply and remain to be exploited. For the present, however, rice production continues to be the linchpin of sustained economic growth. Ultimate self-sufficiency in rice production is considered to be a sine qua non of industrial expansion and continues to be given priority by the government. Since 1966, sustained efforts have been made to increase rice production, but with only partial success. As Table 4 indicates, Indonesia's rate of agricultural production has done little more than keep pace with its increasing population; Indonesia is already the fifth most populous nation in the world, with a population currently approaching 125 million. The hyper-inflation of the Sukarno era has been controlled and a measure of economic stability has been achieved, but rural poverty remains endemic and urban unemployment is taking on serious proportions.

Table VI.4

Population Growth and Agricultural Production

	Population (millions)	Index of Agricultural Production (1963=100)
1960	97.0	101
1961	97.4	97
1962	99.3	104
1963	101.2	100
1964	103.3	105
1965	105.4	105
1966	107.6	110
1967	110.0	104
1968	112.4	113
1969	114.9	114
1970	117.5	123
1971	120.1	—

Sources: United Nations *Statistical Yearbook for Asia and the Far East*, p. 135; *Statistik Indonesia,* 1970 & 1971, Biro Pusat Statistik, Djakarta, p. 20.

During the first three years of Indonesia's first Five Year Plan (1968-1973) agricultural production increased according to plan. A catastrophic rice crisis occurred in the fall of 1972, however, and threw all plans and projections into disarray. The severe shortage occurred suddenly and little preparation had been made to diminish its intensity or prepare the population. As late as mid-August, 1972, President Suharto stated that rice production was progressing favorably and recommended a reduction from 15.4 million tons to 14.8 million tons in the coming year. The shortage began in September, and by December rice prices had doubled in several areas.

The rice shortage was partially caused by a prolonged dry season, but it was mainly attributed to distribution bottlenecks and governmental lack of preparedness. In particular, *Bulog* (Bureau of Logistics—the governmental agency responsible for the stabilization of the rice market), was singled out for the major share of blame. Indonesia's first harvest of 1972 had been above average. Under such circumstances it would have been the function of Bulog to purchase rice from the producer in order to protect him from falling prices as well as to stockpile rice for future contingencies. Bulog's purchases were limited, however, and farmers were forced to sell their rice to private rice brokers at reduced prices. Consequently, because its stockpiles were low, Bulog was unable to supply sufficient rice to the market during the dry season in order to stabilize prices.[14] Both producers and consumers suffered, while the rice brokers profited.

It was asked whether the crisis was entirely a result of well-meaning mismanagement or an unintended consequence of Bulog's relations with the army and wealthy rice brokers. Headed by an army general and responsible directly to the President rather than to the Minister of Agriculture, Bulog was to provide funds for the army as one of its functions. In this regard, it was said to cooperate with Chinese businessmen in matters of mutual economic interest. The businessmen provided economic expertise, while army support assured ease of access in the bureaucracy.[15] The term *cukong*-ism was widely used to describe the situation, implying governmental "protection" of Chinese business ventures in restraint of competition, and consequent division of profits between the cukongs and their governmental "protectors." The ability of Chinese entrepreneurs to provide capital was much greater than that of indigenous businessmen. Suharto's statement, made early in 1972, that non-indigenous companies would be obliged to sell 50 percent of their shares to the government, which would then sell them to indigenous businessmen, met with widespread approval but received no further clarification.

The rice shortage has continued to be Indonesia's most serious economic problem.[16] As the extent of the international rice crisis became evident and it was realized that large-scale imports might not be available, the government raised the domestic procurement targets for all provinces. This had the effect of raising procurement targets down to the sub-district and village levels, as well. In many areas the targets were set unrealistically high, failing to take into account local crop failures and the unwillingness of many peasants to sell rice to the government at prices lower than they would otherwise receive on the open market.

The government's procurement effort was channelled through BUUD *(Badan Usaha Unit Desa*—Village Business Unit), initially in-

14. *Mahasiswa Indonesia*, 3rd week of September, 1972, p.1.
15. Harold Crouch, "Military Politics Under Indonesia's New Order," *Pacific Affairs* 45, 2 (Summer 1972): 217.
16. Much of the following section on Indonesia's rice difficulties is based upon Peter McCawley's "The Indonesian Economy: Survey of Recent Developments," *Bulletin of Indonesian Economic Studies* 9, 3 (November 1973): 1-27.

tended as a series of autonomous rural cooperatives, but which came to be regulated by local government officials who received their orders and specified targets from higher levels in the national bureaucracy. It was the function of BUUD to regulate agricultural production and administer procurement targets. The unwillingness of many farmers to meet the onerous production targets established by BUUD (especially at the lower-than-market prices which the government offered) produced an uncomfortable level of governmental coercion. Theoretically 10 percent of the farmers' crops were to be sold to BUUD. In many areas, however, overzealous officials demanded 20 to 30 percent. In early June 1973, as it became apparent that sufficient rice was not being stockpiled, the government banned the inter-provincial shipment of rice in an attempt to force farmers to sell to local BUUD. Many district heads even forbade inter-district trade. What resulted was an intensification of smuggling and corruption and the creation of numerous black markets. Prices fell sharply for producers, while rising for consumers. One West Javanese rice trader described the consequent debilitating situation:

> After I have bought rice from the farmers I must act like a thief, concealing the rice in several places. This requires expenses. Having loaded it in a truck, I must pay the Sub-District Military Command Rp.2,000 for every truck to leave the village. On the highway I will come across some Regional Logistic officials who are going to and fro by jeep and I must pay Rp.5,000 to them. Reaching the border at the Kedung Gede post, I must pay at least Rp.10,000. And the Land Communications Service at Pulo Gadung must also have their share. At present, besides truck rentals and other expenses, I must set aside between Rp.20,000 and Rp.25,000 per truck.[17]

By mid-1973 it was officially acknowledged that the government's procurement and stockpiling program had failed. On July 3, 1973 it revised the procurement system by withdrawing most of the restrictions on the domestic movement of rice and abolishing the national domestic procurement target for 1973. By that time it was evident that the government had failed to accomplish its objectives of increasing rice production and farm incomes, acquiring a national rice stockpile, and establishing price stability.

The developments of the years 1972-1973 placed a special hardship on the Indonesian economy, which was striving for self-sufficiency in rice production. During the first three years of *Repelita I* (Indonesia's first Five Year Plan) rice production experienced steady growth, leading planners to expect that self-sufficiency might be achieved at the end

17. *Pedoman,* June 8, 1973.

of 1973. Perpetuation of the current crisis would certainly appear to dispel such hopes until well into *Repelita II*.

Inflation reached serious proportions in 1973, continuing the spiral begun with the rice crisis of 1972. Using 1971 as base year, the price index for rice in Jakarta rose to 168 by December 1972 and to 210 by August 1973. Prices of other foodstuffs, clothing and housing increased to a lesser extent, but the inflationary situation was more severe than at any time since the early days of the Suharto government.

Oil has continued to be Indonesia's economic success story, with both production and prices rising sharply. Already the eighth largest oil exporting nation in the world with a daily production of 1.5 million barrels, Indonesia expected to double its oil output in a few years. In early 1974, the price per barrel was $10.80, up from $3.75 in mid-1973. Production value reached $1.95 billion in 1973 and with the new price it was expected to exceed $5 billion in 1974.

The government's policy of encouraging large-scale investment (both foreign and domestic) while giving low priority to small and traditional industries has been a continuing source of resentment toward the government on the part of Indonesia's numerous small businessmen. The government's policy is presumably predicated upon an assessment that large-scale economies can make greater developmental contributions than can relatively inefficient small firms. This policy, however, has opened the government to charges of favoring foreign investors and wealthy Chinese entrepreneurs at the expense of indigenous businessmen. To partially meet such criticism two organizations, P.T. Bahana and P.T. Askrindo, were set-up in mid-1973 to provide credit and advice to small-scale producers. Organizational funds, however, are extremely limited and it seems unlikely that the government can simultaneously implement dual economic policies of "betting on the strong" while aiding the weak.

Foreign investment continues to play an important role in the Indonesian economy, but is regarded with some suspicion on both sides. Many potential foreign investors have become dissatisfied because of the uncertainties created by bottlenecks, corruption, and inefficient bureaucracy, and often arbitrary assignment of tax rates. Conversely, an increasing number of Indonesians are becoming disillusioned with the dependence of the Indonesian economy upon foreign investment and what is felt to be the control of the nation's resources by foreign capital. Most critics admit the necessity of foreign investment for Indonesia's development but urge that such investment be directed into the economic sectors where it can contribute to economic development in coordination with the national plan and where its effect upon technological and employment patterns can be shaped by national priorities.

Of the foreign investing nations, the role of the U.S. is largest, but it is concentrated in oil and mining. Japanese investment is next and is highly diversified and visible, leading many Indonesians to criticize what they term the "Honda-ization" of the Indonesian economy. Japanese investors are often perceived as rigid and arrogant in their business dealings, frequently unwilling to provide Indonesian partners or employees with meaningful decision-making responsibility.

Foreign investment and foreign aid has recently attracted strong criticism, with the international aid consortium to Indonesia, IGGI (Inter-Governmental Group on Indonesia), becoming a prime target. The nations which constituted the IGGI were accused of providing aid to Indonesia with their own investment interests primarily in mind by tying credit to goods purchased and to the entry of private capital from the IGGI countries.[18] Critics also maintained that large amounts of foreign aid and investment had a restrictive effect on domestic capital and savings. Expressions of dissatisfaction with investment policy were closely related to rising dissatisfaction against high-level corruption and arbitrary governmental practices.

A Climate of Concern

During 1973, public dissatisfaction with political and economic conditions reached its highest level in the seven-year history of Indonesia's New Order. It received its most vocal expression in late 1973 and early 1974 through the proliferation of student demonstrations against corruption, an inequitable distribution of income, rising prices, unemployment, governmental abuse of power, and harmful side-effects of foreign aid. Student protests and petitions expressed critical sentiments which many shared but felt constrained not to articulate. In 1966 students had been the driving force in launching an anti-communist and anti-Sukarno coalition which brought the Suharto administration into power. Their influence had gradually diminished over time until they came to be considered (even within their own ranks) as a negligible political force. The events of late 1973 and early 1974, however, once again tapped the well-spring of student idealism and brought forth a determination to return the movement to a more active role.

Much of the students' criticism was initially directed against foreign aid, an oblique way of criticizing corrupt military figures without running the risk of proscription. Such criticism noted that high levels of foreign aid solidified the existing system and fostered corruption, waste, ostentatious consumption, and unresponsive government.[19]

18. *Merdeka*, February 16, 1973; *Kompas*, November 23, 1973.
19. In this manner a group of Yogyakarta students issued a statement rejecting foreign aid until there was a certainty "that the aid is handled by a truly clean government."

Many people felt that elections, the existence of political parties, and the perpetuation of a "rhetoric of modernization" masked a basic insensitivity to civil liberties and the democratic process on the part of the military. ABRI's interests, while conducive to some degree of socio-economic change, have basically revolved around the perpetuation of power and wealth.

To what extent ABRI can satisfy student demands is conjectural. ABRI's central command will brook no debate on its dual military and civilian functions. This *dwi-funksi*, critics maintain, is little more than a euphemism for the perpetuation of military power and privilege. As initially formulated, it connoted ABRI's potential as a modernizing force, and through much of the "New Order," military predominance was viewed as a necessary, if transitional, stage. *Golkar's* substantial victory was interpreted in this light. As the economy worsened, high-level corruption intensified, and the gap between the wealthy and poor widened, the dimensions of military control and interests have come under broad critical scrutiny. Criticism of economic policy, inflation, foreign investment, advantages given to Chinese rather than indigenous entrepreneurs, etc., are widely recognized as being directed against ABRI.

These developments, although not presenting an immediate threat to the Suharto government, cannot help but call its legitimacy into question. Such legitimacy is in part predicated upon the government's own assertion that the military is the force best capable of providing economic stability and promoting modernization. There has been little recent indication of confidence that these goals were being satisfactorily implemented. What has resulted, rather, has been a noticeable climate of concern, a fear that somehow private interests were taking precedence over public aspirations.

The events of the early 1970s appear to indicate that Golkar is not likely to sustain its stated concern for modernization, but rather is likely to reflect the dimensions of ABRI's interests. Such interests may be conducive to a moderate degree of socio-economic change in specific circumstances, as is borne out by managerial capacity of the army-economist alliance, but they are as likely to revolve around the retention of the perquisites of power and wealth where developmental programs are supported so long as they do not reduce military power and privilege. Politics in Suharto's Indonesia remains an intra-bureaucratic affair. The events of the last few years indicate that what the Indonesian military desires is a mobilizable but non-participant public. Such a model may be conducive to the maintenance of order and result in some economic advance, but is unlikely to promote a committed pattern of modernization.

Selected Readings

Anderson, Benedict R. O'G. *Java in a Time of Revolution: Occupation and Resistance, 1944-1946*. Ithaca: Cornell University Press, 1972.

Brenda, Harry J. *The Crescent and the Rising Sun: Indonesian Islam Under the Japanese Occupation, 1942-1945*. The Hague: W. van Hoeve, Ltd., 1958.

Dahm, Bernhard. *Sukarno and the Struggle for Indonesian Independence*. Translated by Mary F. Somers Heidhues. Ithaca: Cornell University Press, 1969.

Feith, Herbert. *The Decline of Constitutional Democracy in Indonesia*. Ithaca: Cornell University Press, 1962.

Geertz, Clifford. *Agricultural Involution: The Process of Ecological Change in Indonesia*. Berkeley: University of California Press, 1966.

———. *Peddlers and Princes: Social Change and Economic Modernization in Two Indonesian Towns*. Chicago: University of Chicago Press, 1963.

———. *The Religion of Java*. New York: The Free Press, 1960.

Geertz, Clifford, *Social History of an Indonesian Town*. Cambridge, Mass.: M.I.T. Press, 1965.

Hindley, Donald, *The Communist Party of Indonesia, 1951-1963*. Berkeley: University of California Press, 1964.

Holt, Claire. ed. (with the assistance of Benedict R. O'G. Anderson and James Siegel), *Culture and Politics in Indonesia*. Ithaca: Cornell University Press, 1972.

Hughes, John. *Indonesian Upheaval*. New York: David McKay and Co., 1967.

Jay, Robert R. *Religion and Politics in rural Central Java*. Cultural Report Series Monograph, No 12, Southeast Asian Studies, Yale University, 1963.

Kahin, George M. *Nationalism and Revolution in Indonesia*. Ithaca: Cornell University Press, 1952.

Legge, J. D. *Sukarno: A Political Biography*. New York: Praeger Publishers, 1972.

Lev, Daniel S. *Islamic Courts in Indonesia: A Study in the Political Bases of Legal Institutions*. Berkeley: University of California Press, 1972.

Liddle, R. William. ed. *Political Participation in Modern Indonesia*. Cultural Report Series Monograph, No. 19, Southeast Asian Studies, Yale University, 1973.

Palmier, Leslie. *Communists in Indonesia: Power Pursued in Vain*. Garden City, New Jersey: Anchor Books, Anchor/Doubleday, 1973.

Roeder, O.G. *The Smiling General: Sukarno of Indonesia*. Djakarta: Gunung Agung, 1969.

Selosoemard, Jan. *Social Changes in Jogjakarta*. Ithaca: Cornell University Press, 1962.

Sukarno, *Sukarno: An Autobiography* (as told to Cindy Adams). Indianapolis: The Bobbs-Merrill Co., Inc., 1965.

Van der Kroef, Justus M. *Indonesia After Sukarno.* Vancouver: University of British Columbia Press, 1971.